HEROES OR ZEROS?

THE MEDIA'S PERCEPTIONS OF PARALYMPIC SPORT

EDITED BY:
OTTO J. SCHANTZ & KEITH GILBERT

HEROES OR ZEROS?

THE MEDIA'S PERCEPTIONS OF PARALYMPIC SPORT

EDITED BY:
OTTO J. SCHANTZ & KEITH GILBERT

Common Ground

First published in Champaign, Illinois in 2012
by Common Ground Publishing LLC
as part of the Sport and Society series

Selections and editorial matter copyright © Otto J. Schantz & Keith Gilbert 2012;
Individual chapters copyright © individual contributors 2012

All rights reserved. Apart from fair dealing for the purposes of study, research, criticism or review as permitted under the applicable copyright legislation, no part of this book may be reproduced by any process without written permission from the publisher.

Library of Congress Cataloging-in-Publication Data

Heroes or zeros? : the media's perceptions of paralympic sport / edited by Otto J. Schantz & Keith Gilbert.
   p. cm.
Includes bibliographical references and index.
ISBN 978-1-61229-057-7 (pbk : alk. paper) -- ISBN 978-1-61229-058-4 (pdf : alk. paper)
1. Paralympics. 2. Sports for people with disabilities. 3. Mass media and sports. 4. Mass media and sports--Social aspects. I. Schantz, Otto. II. Gilbert, Keith, 1950-

GV722.5.P37H47 2012
796.087'4--dc23

2012006047

Table of Contents

Acknowledgements x

Contributors xi

Chapter 1: The Media, Sport and Disabilities Debate 1
Otto J. Schantz & Keith Gilbert

Part I : National Narratives and Paralympic Sport

Chapter 2: Media Coverage of the Paralympic Games from 1960 to 2004 by the Sport Newspaper 'L'Equipe' 25
Change in Event and Participation Representation
Fréderic Reichhart & Aggée C. Lomo Myazhiom

Chapter 3: An International Comparison of the Role of Public Service Broadcasters when Reporting on Disability Sports 37
Natascha Rother, Inga Oelrichs & Nina Geske

Chapter 4: Disability Sport in the German Media 55
Christoph Bertling

Chapter 5: Disability Sport in the Swiss Media 65
Sue Bertschy & Jan D. Reinhardt

Chapter 6: The Austrian Press 77
Media Coverage during the 2008 Beijing Paralympic Games
Julia Lebersorg & Maria Dinold

Chapter 7: Coverage of the Beijing Paralympic Games on German Television 85
Nicole Raab & Simone Janda

Chapter 8: French Perspectives on the Media and Paralympics 95
Anne Marcellini

Chapter 9: British Media Portrayals of Paralympic and Disability Sport 105
Ian Brittain

Chapter 10: USA vs. Canada 113
An Analysis of Media Coverage of Paralympic Athletes
Anna Fong & Sid Katz

Chapter 11: A Way Forward 121
Researching International Perspectives on Media and the Paralympics
Eric de Léséleuc

Part II : Visibility of Disability

Chapter 12: Analyzing Disabled Athletes' Photographs 137
The Case of the 2008 Beijing Paralympic Games
Capucine Germain & Julie Grall

Chapter 13: Disabled Heroes in the Media 147
Louise Charbonnier & Cristina Popescu

Chapter 14: Media Coverage of Pistorius 157
What are the Angles? What is Missing?
Gregor Wolbring

Chapter 15: Post-modern Perspectives of the Media and Disability 165
Emily Coutant

Chapter 16: Rehabilitating Heteromasculinity 171
The Sexual Politics of Murderball
Cynthia Barounis

Part III : Reconceptualizing Paralympic Sport, Disability and the Media

Chapter 17: Paralympic Athletes' Perspectives of Media Coverage . 181
Whose Story is it?
Donna de Haan

Chapter 18: Paralympic Sport, British Media and the Absence of Black Faces 193
Brenda-Kammel Atuona

Chapter 19: Debunking Disability 209
Media Discourse and the Paralympic Games
Maxine Newlands

Chapter 20: An Implosion of Discontent 225
   Reconceptualising the Rapport between the Media and the Paralympic Movement
   Keith Gilbert & Otto J. Schantz

Chapter 21: Researching the Future 237
   Otto J. Schantz and Keith Gilbert

Index 241

Acknowledgements

We believe that the development of this book provides a much needed addition to the research literature surrounding the media and Paralympics and we hope that it is used as an initial baseline text to further stimulate research into the relationship between various forms of the media and Paralympic sport. However, there is no doubt that without the support of the authors in this text that it would not have come to fruition. In this respect we would like to take this opportunity to thank each individual author as we know that many interrupted their own work schedules in order to be able to provide the chapters for us. We understand the current problematics placed on academics and writers who labour in higher education across the world and realise that for some the development of a chapter for this book was a herculean effort as many pressures had been placed on them in their own university environments. Again we thank the authors for their efforts and hopefully we have set the seed for them to join us and be involved in writing for a further text in five years' time to review the research on the media and Paralympics.

There have been others who have kindly spent time and effort supporting the development of this book. One such person is Kathryn Otte our enthusiastic editor from Common Ground Publishing who has been supportive and with us every step of the long and often arduous process of translation, from French and German, to English. We also thank Common Ground Publishing for providing an opportunity for us to work together and supporting our emergent ideas for 'Heroes or Zeros'. Also our thanks go to the authors who we called upon later in the piece who happily assisted us with chapters which have strengthened and allowed us to broaden the scope of the text and give it a truly international flavour.

Our thanks go to our respective universities – the University of Koblenz and the University of East London – and the individuals, to many to mention within them who have provided library, statistical and financial research support for the fine tuning of the book. Without this constant backup and support from our own institutions research work of this kind would not be possible. We thank the academic staff and also the many postgraduate students who have influenced our thinking and caused us to redirect our thoughts and ideas. They have challenged us as we have challenged them in the past.

Finally, it would be remise of us not to thank our respective partners Eva and Yuen Ching who provided us with moral, psychological and academic support and advice through the development of this book and more importantly in our lives together.

Otto J. Schantz and Keith Gilbert

Contributors

Brenda-Kammel Atuona is a PhD student in the Centre for Sport Studies at the University of Kent, United Kingdom.

Cynthia Barounis is a PhD candidate in English at the University of Illinois at Chicago, USA.

Dr. Christoph Bertling is a Lecturer at the Institute of Communication and Media Research at the German Sport University, Cologne.

Sue Bertschy is a Paralympic athlete and a PhD student at the University of Lucerne and also with the Swiss Paralympic Federation, Nottwil, Switzerland.

Dr. Ian Brittain is a Senior Research Assistant at Coventry University, United Kingdom.

Dr. Louise Charbonnier is a Lecturer in the *Institut National des Sciences Appliquées* (National Institut of Applied Sciences), Lyon, France.

Dr. Emilie Coutant is responsible of a study group on fashion, the GEMODE/Cea at the Sorbonne University in Paris, France.

Dr. Maria Dinold is a Senior Lecturer in the Sports Faculty at the University of Vienna, Austria.

Anna Fong is with the Faculty of Pharmaceutical Sciences, University of British Columbia Vancouver, British Columbia, Canada.

Capucine Germain is a postgraduate student at *Ecole Normale Supérieure de Cachan (ENS)*, Sport Sciences and Physical Education Department, Paris, France.

Nina Geske is a PhD student and works as a research assistant at the Institute of Communication and Media Research at the German Sport University, Cologne.

Dr. Keith Gilbert is a Professor in the School of Health, Sport and Bioscience at the University of East London, United Kingdom.

Julie Grall, postgraduate student, *Ecole Normale Supérieure de Cachan (ENS)*, Sport Sciences and Physical Education Department, Paris, France.

Donna de Haan is a Lecturer in International Sports, Management and Business at the *Hogeschool van Amsterdam*, Netherlands and is currently studying for a Doctor of Philosophy degree at Loughborough University, United Kingdom.

Dr. Simone Janda is a Lecturer in the Institute of Sport Sciences at the University of Koblenz-Landau, Germany.

Dr. Sidney Katz is a Professor at the Faculty of Pharmaceutical Sciences, University of British Columbia Vancouver, British Columbia, Canada.

Julia Lebersorg is a postgraduate student at the University of Vienna, Austria.

Dr. Eric de Léséleuc is an Associate Professor in the Research Unit "Health, Education and Situations of Disability" at the University of Montpellier 1, France.

Dr. Aggée C. Lomo Myazhiom is an Associate Professor in the Sports Faculty at the University of Strasbourg, France.

Dr. Anne Marcellini is a Professor in the Research Unit "Health, Education, and Situations of Disability". The University of Montpellier 1, France.

Dr. Maxine Newlands is a Senior Lecturer in Journalism in the School of Arts and Digital Industries at the University of East London, United Kingdom.

Inga Oelrichs is a course coordinator and Ph.D. student at the Institute of Media and Communication Research at the German Sport University Cologne.

Cristina Popescu is lecturer at the University Pierre Mendès France, Grenoble, France, and PhD student in Communication Studies at the University Jean Moulin, Lyon, Fance, and at the University of Bucarest, Rumania.

Nicole Raab is a postgraduate student in the Institute of Sport Sciences at the University of Koblenz-Landau, Germany.

Dr. Fréderic Reichhart is director of the Ecole Supérieure en Travail Educatif et Social (University of Social and Educational work), Strasbourg, France

Dr. Jan D. Reinhardt is an academic in the Department of Health Sciences and Health Policy, University of Lucerne and also with the Swiss Paralympic Federation, Nottwil, Switzerland.

Natascha Rother is a PhD student and works as a research assistant at the Institute of Communication and Media Research at the German Sport University, Cologne.

Dr. Otto J. Schantz is Professor and Dean of the Institute of Sport Sciences at the University of Koblenz-Landau, Germany.

Dr. Gregor Wolbring is an Assistant Professor at the University of Calgary, Department of Community Health Sciences, Program Community Rehabilitation and Disability Studies.

Chapter 1
The Media, Sport and Disabilities Debate

Otto J. Schantz & Keith Gilbert

Introduction

Mass media plays an important role in all societies and according to a broadly shared view by experts in mass communication they have the potential to influence, to control and to innovate, and within the disability context they offer "a major source of definitions and images of social reality"; indeed, they provide "the primary key to fame and celebrity", and impart a "source of an ordered and public meaning system which provides a benchmark for what is normal, empirical and evaluative" (McQuail, 1993, p.1). These aspects are of great relevance in the field of sports which is often characterized by the athletes struggle for fame and celebrity and where the normal criteria are to disregard people with disabilities.

The overall aim of this book is twofold: Firstly, we want to present original research results and stimulate future research on media representations of sportswomen and men with disabilities. We consider that this kind of research is of great importance, as the media coverage of Paralympic sports is not only an indicator of public representations of, and attitudes towards these activities but also an analyser of societies' attitudes towards people with disabilities in general (Noelle-Neumann, 1994). Secondly, we want to contribute to the disability debate and assist in changing people's opinions and thereby promote more adequate media coverage of sportswomen and men with disabilities. The way mass media cover Paralympic sports still seems to be characterized by two extremes: either they do glamorous hagiography by transforming the athletes into tragic heroes who have overcome their terrible fate or they just ignore disability sports and reduce the Paralympic athletes into the "zeros" category. In completing this task we feel that this critical analysis of the media discourse and presentation should contribute to lasting change.

Media Effects

The Media construct almost all of our knowledge beyond direct experience and they play a key role in shaping our representations of the world (cf. Früh, 1994; Luhmann, 1996; McCombs, 1994)[1]. Their influence on our daily lives is so pervasive that often our thoughts, behaviors, styles and opinions are based on the mass media's actual construction of knowledge (cf. Kellner, 1995, pp. 151-152). Early studies of the media effects on society have claimed that one of the major influences of the mass media is to reinforce existing norms and attitudes (Lazarsfeld & Merton, 1948). Even though it is uncertain if and in how far the media discourse reflects and influences the opinions and attitudes of the public (cf. Schönbach, 1992) some research indicates, that under certain conditions the media might serve to change public opinion (cf. Berelson, 1960; Kellner, 1995; Noelle-Neumann, 1994). Transactional theories regarding media impact indicate the interdependence between news selection/construction by the media and consumers' attention. Indeed, there is also substantial research stating that the family's and peer group's influence is more pertinent than the media's, but mass media have the power to inform or not to inform about an event or to construct reality from a particular perspective (Berghaus, 1999). They thus have power to influence our perspectives of the so-called "disabled sports" and in particular the Paralympic Games. In this regard the agenda-setting approach of mass media (Dearing & Rogers, 1996; Erbring et al., 1980) suggests that media continually create subject matter which interests and influences people to talk about and discuss issues further. In fact, different studies indicate, that the public's knowledge about and attitudes towards individuals with disabilities are mostly constructed indirectly, often by the mass media (Hackforth, 1988; Stautner, 1989; cf. Farnall & Smith, 1999). This is significant because news and entertainment media seem to have played a significant role on the manner in which society stereotypes people with a disability (Farnall & Smith, 1999; Greenberg & Brand, 1994; Oakes et al., 1994).

---

1. Jean Baudrillard (1991) takes an extreme position and completely separates the real events and the reality constructed by the media. Paraphrasing the title of a novel from Jean Giraudoux he states in a provocative way: "La guerre du Golfe n'a pas eu lieu" - (The Gulf War never happened).

Although, the most influential mass medium is television, many chapters of this book concentrate on printed material. The print media appears to offer marginal sports, sports for all and sport for people with disabilities a chance to become better known by the public, while TV coverage focuses mainly on show and spectacle (cf. Hackforth, 1994). However, even sport spectators who watch television still seem to consult newspapers regularly in order to get further information about sport (Oehmichen, 1991). This is interesting in particular for information regarding athletes and some other groups who are marginalized within society.

Marginalization of Athletes with a Disability

Over the past twenty years the media coverage of sport has undergone a process of spectacularization and sport has gradually become a commodity; whose media value is "determined by the size and composition of audience and how it can deliver to potential advertisers and sponsors" (Maguire, 1993, pp. 38-39). However, generally the whole range of media doesn't seem to have a great opinion regarding the value of sport for persons with disabilities. Indeed, sport media coverage still marginalizes the Paralympic athletes as they do not meet the socially constructed ideals of physicality, masculinity and sexuality which according to Karin DePauw represent three key aspects of sport (DePauw, 1997). This concept defines physicality as the "socially accepted view of able bodied physical ability" (p. 421), masculinity includes "aggression, independence, strength, courage" (p. 421) and sexuality is defined as the "socially expected and accepted view of sexual behavior" (p. 421). Concerning the key aspects sexuality and physicality it is widely believed that, even more than the sexual behavior or the physical ability, appearance in form of stereotyped erotic attractiveness of the sporting body, especially the female body, plays an important role in the media coverage of sports (cf. e.g. Bette, 1999; Guttmann, 1996; Pfister, 1989; Rowe, 1999). A striking example is beach volleyball where the sexual attractiveness is emphasized by specific official rules and regulations limiting the covered surface of the female body. It could be argued therefore that, female athletes with a disability are exposed to a form of 'threefold discrimination', as in general they do not fit the social constructs of able-bodied athletes, including those of masculinity and sexual attractiveness. Recently Dame Tanni Gray Thompson, the ex British Paralympian, was being interviewed on the BBC television programme 'Hard Talk' but mid interview the program was unceremoniously cut and the BBC switched to the boring live trial of ex Egyptian president Mubarack. The BBC was thus forced to show a topical event [like all the other channels] but in doing so not only succeeded in marginalizing the Dame but also in promoting the concept that coverage of disability is worthless. If this occurs to the top level members of society then we can only imagine what the television producers think of disabled athletes and disabled individuals in local communities.

Sport Specific Newsworthiness

We can draw conclusions about the consumers' attentions and attitudes towards the Paralympics and the athletes with disabilities by analyzing how the print media construct the reality of these Games or disabled athletes in order to interest the recipients. This can be achieved principally by examining information that media consider to be newsworthy.

According to the theoretical concept of news factors (Bell, 1991; Eilders, 1997; Galtung & Ruge, 1965), sport specific coverage of the Paralympic sport should focus on similar topics, which are considered to be newsworthy on the usual sports pages. When representing sports, the mass media in general emphasize action, records, elite performances, aggressive behavior, heroic actions, drama, emotions and celebrities (sport stars). However, the newspapers also focus on performances, results, statistics, and behind the scene stories. Photos capture celebrities, actions and emotions (cf. e.g. Becker, 1983; Coakely, 1994; Hackfort, 1988; Krüger, 1993). Along with this, newspaper sport reporting emphasises a number of important general news values, for example the frequency criterion as a continuing activity, or simplicity due to the nature of winning or losing. Sports then are "consonant with expectations, their script follows a familiar pattern" (Bell, 1991, p.160) and at the same time the unexpected outcome creates excitement (cf. Elias & Dunning, 1970).

Another inherent condition of sport coverage involves play and competition between nations, which allows the newsworthy reporting of ethnocentric issues. Sport personalities are depicted as celebrities and as such are often cast to the forefront of public interest. Sport is organized conflict with losers and winners all of which can be highlighted in the press. Negativity, which is another important news value, can thus be represented by "bad guys" who take drugs or individuals who abuse the referee (cf. Becker, 1983; Bell, 1991; Hackfort 1988; Krueger, 1993).

Reporting Disability in the Print Media

Studies in the 1990s indicated that the quality and quantity of print media coverage of people with disabilities were of a low standard and the media often portrayed these people unrealistically and stereotypically (e.g. Keller et al., 1990; Lachal, 1990a; 1990b; Nelson, 1994; Shapiro, 1993; Yoshida et al., 1990). Riley II (2005, p. ix), the co-founder of WeMedia, the first multimedia company devoted to people with disabilities, ascertains that we still can find a "patronizing, trivializing, and marginalizing ur-narrative of disability in the media today". Recently, in his qualitative and quantitative analysis of German newspapers, Scholz found that these papers still use a cliché-ridden style, focus on medical perspectives or mention disabilities even if they add no information of interest to the reported topics (Scholz, 2010). Longmore (1985) explained these stereotypical media portrayals as a reflection of the public's fears and anxieties. He stated, "We harbor unspoken anxieties about the possibilities of disablement, to us or to someone close to us. What we fear we often stigmatize and shun and sometimes seek to destroy" (p. 32).

As early as 1985 Zola (p.8) observed that in films people with disabilities were most often portrayed as victims, relatively seldom as heroes or villains, which are two metaphorical traits that can be found often in the coverage of able bodied athletes (cf. Hall, 1997). Nelson (1994) listed seven major stereotypes as they were shown in the American media: the person with disabilities as "pitiable and pathetic" (p. 5), as "supercrip" (p. 6), as "sinister, evil, and criminal" (p. 6), as "better-off dead" (p. 7), as "maladjusted" (p. 8), as "burden" (p. 8), and as "unable to live a successful life" (p 9). From a semiological perspective Woodill (1994) distinguished different types of metaphors of disabilities in popular cultures, including newspaper presentations: The humanitarian "disability as misfortune", the medical "disability as sickness", the outsider "disabled person as other", the religious "disability as divine plan", the retribution "disability as punishment", the social control "disability as threat", and the zoological metaphor "disability person as pet, disability as entertainment" (p. 209). Of interest is the fact that Clogston (1994) divided newspaper coverage of people with disabilities into two distinct types: the traditional and the progressive models. The traditional model "views persons with disabilities as dysfunctions in a medical or economic way" (p. 46) and as such they must be cared for medically or economically by society. Another attitude of the traditional perspective is to regard them as "supercrips" for the way they master their fates (Sandfort, 1982; Clogston, 1994, Shapiro, 1993; Zola, 1985; Hardin & Hardin, 2004, Silva & Howe, 2012). The progressive model views "the major limiting aspect of a person's disability as lying in society's inability to adapt its physical, social, or occupational environment as well as its attitudes, to accept those who are physically different" (Clogston, 1994, p.47). A progressive coverage of people with disability would consider individuals as different, accepting their otherness as part of a cultural pluralism and thereby applying a pluralistic rationality (cf. Lyotard, 1983, p. 13), whereas the traditional discourse considers individuals with a disability as different and inferior to the hegemonic mainstream, thus exerting an excluding rationality (cf. Foucault, 1961).

Coverage of Sport for Individuals with Disabilities in the Media

Studies about media coverage of sport activities of people with disabilities are still relatively rare but there seems to be a growing interest for this topic (cf. Génolini, 1995; Kauer & Bös, 1998; Schantz & Marty, 1995; Schantz & Gilbert 2001, Schantz & Gilbert, 2008). Schimanski (1994) conducted one of the most important studies. When comparing German and North American journals for the period from 1984 to 1992 he found an increasing coverage of sport for persons with disabilities and observed that this coverage moved progressively from other headings to the sports pages. These findings were partly confirmed by the results of Schantz and Marty (1995) who analyzed the French daily sports journal *L'Équipe* and observed increasing frequencies of articles about sport for people with disabilities during a seven-year period from 1987 to 1993. But this evolution did not really improve the rather marginal role of sports for individuals with disabilities in this newspaper. The authors also observed that the articles often showed pity[2] for the athletes or focused on the way the people were coping with their fate instead of referring to the athletes and their performances in a sport specific manner. Paralympic athletes, as we know, would prefer to be reported for their physical feats and not their disability (Schantz & Alberto 1999).

Génolini (1995) analyzed newspaper clippings concerning physical activities for people with intellectual disabilities collected by French sports associations from 1979 to 1986. He found that these persons were portrayed as "gentle monsters" (p. 60), an image that is in-between the beast (mythical aspect) and the child (aspect of educability). The medical model still seems to dominate media coverage. Journalists contribute to perpetuate the biomedical model of disability as they often use medical terminology to describe and to locate the disabilities of athletes (Smith & Thomas 2005; Thomas & Smith, 2003; Howe, 2008; Schell & Duncan, 1999; DePauw, 2000).

Sport Coverage and Discrimination Based on Severity of Disability

The print media coverage of sport for individuals with disabilities appears to privilege some specific types of disabilities: The main group of individuals with a physical disability, which was by far the most over-represented, is the wheelchair fraternity (cf. Schantz & Marty, 1995; Schimanski, 1994). This is perhaps because the public's perception of the athlete with disabilities is historically that of individuals in wheelchairs. Lachal (1990a; 1990b) who analyzed regional French newspapers from 1977 and 1988 found that in 1988 about half (49%) of the articles about disabilities concerned physical (motor) disabilities, 29% disability in general, 11.5% sensorial disabilities, 7% intellectual deficiencies, and 3.5% "other" disabilities (Lachal, 1990a, p. 39). Topics concerning athletes with a mental disability figured rarely in the French *L'Équipe*, studied by Schantz & Marty (1995). In their content analysis of TV coverage of the Atlanta Games, Schell and Duncan (1999, p. 44) found that CBS featured less visible, war induced, or acquired disabilities more likely than others.

---

2. Persons with disabilities need respect, recognition and rights: Pity may be a first step for individuals and later lead to a form of regression if recognition, respect, and rights are lacking. Indeed, "Not its weakness, but its limits make pity questionable; pity is never enough" (Nicht die Weichheit, sondern das Beschränkende am Mitleid macht es fragwürdig, es ist immer zu wenig Horkheimer, Adorno 1989 [1947], p.121]. Cf. Also Gill (1994), a disability activist, who asks for recognition and respect of difference.

Sport Coverage and Discrimination Based on Gender and Race

Gender bias reporting in the media is another important area which requires further research in the Paralympic arena. Although in the able-bodied print media there have been relatively great numbers of researchers who have focused on gender biased media coverage (e.g. Duncan et al., 1991; Duncan, 1990; Eastman & Billings 2000; Haller, 2000; Hardin & Hardin, 2005; Hardin, 2003; Jones et al., 1999; Pappous et al., 2011; Smart, 2001; Urquhart & Crossmann, 1999; Wann et al., 1998). In an analysis of German newspaper coverage of the Olympics from 1952 to 1980, Pfister (1989) found that for female Olympic participants appearance beauty was of "central importance" (p. 11.29). Tuggle & Owen (1999) examined the amount of NBC's coverage given to female athletes at the 1996 Olympic Games and found that only women's individual events were covered extensively while the coverage of team competitions focused much more on men. Thomas and Smith (2003, p. 177) found a bigger media interest in male Paralympic athletes than females.

Female athletes with a disability are in fact subjected to multiple discrimination concerning gender, disability severity and race (cf. DePauw, 1994; DePauw & Gavron, 1995; Sherrill 1993). Analyses undertaken of the 1996 Paralympics by Sherrill (1997) and Schell & Duncan (1999) confirmed greater discrimination against female Paralympians than their male counterparts.

Studies on race or culture biased media coverage on disability sport are almost non-existent. According to C. A. Riley II (2005, p. xiv) "disability is the all-inclusive minority – it is completely race - and culture-blind". The contribution of Brenda-Kammel Atuona (chapter 18) in this volume is one of the first studies taking into consideration the variable of race while analyzing the media coverage of Paralympic sports.

Cross-cultural Differences

Researchers clearly indicate the influence of culture on the attitudes towards people with disabilities even though there was no consensus concerning the explanation of these differences (cf. Cloerkes, 1997; Ingstad & Whyte, 1995). Indeed, Schantz & Gilbert (2001) found significant differences in coverage of the 1996 Paralympic Games in Atlanta by French and German newspapers. Overall from a cultural perspective the awareness of Paralympic sports appears to be higher in the German speaking press than in the French.

Media Coverage of the Paralympic Games

Studies relating to media coverage of the Paralympic Games are quite rare. However, Enting (1997) compared the Atlanta Paralympics coverage in a nationwide, a regional and a tabloid German newspaper (*Frankfurter Allge-*

meine Zeitung, Rhein-Zeitung Koblenz and *Bildzeitung*). These newspapers offered respectively 10%, 7.5% and 0.3% of their sports pages to this event. Schell and Duncan (1999) made a content analysis of American television coverage of the Atlanta Paralympics and found that beside some empowering comments, athletes were portrayed as "victims of misfortune, as *different*, as Other" (p. 27). They observed an absence of sport specific commentaries, like information about rules, comments on strategies or physical abilities. Others found that the media interest in the Paralympics is much less important than in the Olympics (Golden 2002; 2003). Contrary, to Olympic coverage, where defeats were considered as catastrophes (Duncan, 1986), the defeat of Paralympic athletes were described from patronizing perspectives (Schell & Duncan 1999).

Extraordinary performances were portrayed as heroic achievements by using the "super-crip" stereotype (Schell & Duncan 1999; Goggin & Newell 2005, p. 87). According to Shapiro (1993) this "super crip" myth harms the average people with disabilities because it suggests that only heroic performances of persons with disabilities should be respected. Goggin & Newell who analyzed the 2000 Paralympics coverage in different Australian newspapers found that there is increasing skepticism regarding perceived notions of disability, producing complex, contradictory media texts. However, many stories still draw on stock stereotypes of 'brave, elite athletes', 'special people', 'remarkable achievers' (Goggin & Newell, 2005, p. 86).

Schantz & Gilbert (2001) compared the print media coverage of the 1996 Atlanta Paralympics, and found that the different newspapers focused much less on sporting results than on scandals and national issues. It is interesting, when referring to the Paralympic ideals, that Schell and Duncan (1999) found, that "war and the hope for peace among people of different nationalities was a recurrent theme" and that "spectators were shown the debilitating results of war and the political barriers that may be dissolved through friendly sport competition" (p.43).

Zeros or Heroes, or is there an in-between?

As the review of the research literature shows, there are still two dominating attitudes in the media towards Paralympic sports: either to ignore more or less these sport events or to construe the myth of the supercrip, the freaky cyborg or the hero who overcame his terrible fate.

Despite the claim of the official representatives from the International Paralympic Committee and the International Paralympic Committee, that the Paralympic Games and the Olympic Games are parallel Games, there is a huge gap in between these events. The symbolic and financial capital of the Olympic Games is enormous and cannot be compared with the Paralympic Games. The Olympics are selling a dream which corresponds to the ideals of today's mass culture: to be fit, fine-looking, and famous.

Both movements however, create heroes: the Olympic hero is mostly a dramatic creation of the sporting contest, the Paralympic hero is a product of the real life drama. The first-one generates envy or offers an identification model, the second-one calls for admiration or engenders pity. The role model potential of the disabled hero has to be considered with care. The common sense argument, that Paralympic athletes serve the empowerment of the community of people with disabilities is an ambiguous one. Indeed, the Paralympics show the prowess these people are able to achieve, but at the same time they make believe, that every person with disabilities can achieve success provided he or she is dedicated and hardworking enough. Many people with disabilities, however, have to struggle enormously in order to achieve daily routines like dressing, shopping, or travelling. The percentage of those able and willing to practice any sport is rather marginal. The success of a few disadvantaged athletes hides the failure of the great majorities who try but fail (Sage, 1990; Eitzen, 2009).

What sportswomen and men with disabilities probably need is media coverage in between the zero and the hero, a coverage which respects them as full and equal members of the sporting community. They do not need pity, neither heroic stories based on their disabilities; they need the right to play sports, an accessible sport world, and respect for their sporting performances. By describing and showing a realistic and respectful picture of the sport activities of people with disabilities, the media could help to challenge obsolete cultural norms and to prepare an inclusive sporting world, respecting the broad diversity of the physiques and abilities of humans. This book will hopefully add to the literature in this area and engender further research and understanding of the media – Paralympic – disability conundrum.

Chapter Anthology

This book 'Heroes or Zeros: The Paralympics and the Media' provides an anthology of chapters which when viewed as a whole constitutes the most up-to-date writings on the relationship between Paralympic and disabled sport and the media. The chapters have been written by academics from across the world and as such the work is global in its reach and framework. We have attempted as much as possible to integrate original research with sociological underpinnings with practical examples of this torrid relationship between media and the Paralympic movement. As such what follows represents varied views, opinions and ideas which have come together in this period of time to represent an anthology which we hope will become the starting point for further research into the social, political and comparative aspects of the Paralympics and the media's role in promotion and reporting of the Games. This book is the first of its kind and we have been supported admirably by our peers and colleagues who have not failed to respond to our many and varied request for further information, slight changes in chapter outline and in some cases total rewrites. Because of their professional commitment we have been able to organize chapters herein into three distinct sections in order to further simplify the task and to enable sense to be made of the content of the book.

Part I, *'National Narratives and Paralympic Sport'* has been developed in order to place the media and its relationships to the Paralympics into a scaffolding framework which is nation state and trans-nationally grounded in order to draw comparisons between issues of coverage and reporting of the Paralympics by adding cross-cultural dimensions to the text. This section reviews issues which are critical to the understanding of how the media works in the Paralympic context and offers lessons from the past and suggestions for the future of the tenuous relationship between media, Paralympians and the Paralympic movement. Chapter 2 titled *'The Media Coverage of the Paralympic Games from 1960 to 2004 by the Sport Newspaper 'L'Equipe': Change in Event and Participation Representation'* by Fréderic Reichhart and Aggée C. Lomo Myazhiom provides a good start to the book by referring to the methodological perspectives of researching the media and the Paralympics. This is followed by notions of visibility, social exclusion and recognition of the institution of the Paralympics. In this well-crafted chapter the writers tackle the difficult issue of politics and the stresses and strains which that places on the athlete. Finally they argue through the benefits's and understandings of the community of having disabled athletes perform at a separate Games and in this section they ask the important question as to whether the media views the athletes as athletes first and disabled second or vice versa. Chapter 2 *'An International Comparison of the Role of Public Service Broadcasters when Reporting on Disability Sports'* by Natasha Rother, Inga Oelrichs and Nina Geske provide a good understanding of the meaning of this text by arguing that public service broadcasting (PSB) providers have in particular a great social responsibility and they explore the extent to which public broadcasting is bound by legal stipulations to balance the private media deficits in reporting on disabled people and the positions of those responsible for programming. They consider and interpret the programming mandates of the public service providers in Great Britain, Germany and Switzerland and comment that while reporting on disability sports, and particularly the Paralympics, is an excellent opportunity for PSB providers to fulfil their programming mandate to support integration, thereby legitimising their financing through license fees. There is still a need for more research in this area in order to provide a full picture of the worth of PSB providers in the Paralympic realm. In comparison Chapter 4 written by Christoph Bertling and titled *'Disability Sport in the German Media'* provides a thorough analysis of research projects in the area of athletic beauty myths and forms of disability as described in the media. He argues that the criteria for selection of photographs and articles is purely arbitrary and also a comparison of the coverage of the Olympic Games and the Paralympics has shown that the World Games of disabled sport are not only neglected in forms of quantity but are also produced in an insufficient quality by the media. He concludes by reminding us that despite improvements in the past disabled and non-disabled still don't connect in everyday life and in this situation the media is often the only, and not to be underestimated, informative source about life and the capabilities of disabled people. We suggest that society relies on the media for positive information and knowledge regarding Paralympic athletes and the Paralympics. Chapter 5 in keeping with the theme of 'National narratives' has been written by Sue Bertschy and Jan Reinhardt. Their chapter titled *'Disability Sport in the Swiss Media'* provides a candid look at the relationship between the media, disability and the Paralympics from a Swiss perspective. They are interested principally in the relationship between high performance sport and the media in local and national Swiss newspapers and report on a study which they performed where they reviewed the papers. They found clear results that highlighted the one-sided nature of the reporting and interestingly, this nationalistic trend was not found when researching the Olympics. Julia Lebersorg and Maria Dinold in Chapter 6 titled *'The Austrian Press: Media Coverage during the 2008 Beijing Paralympic Games'* write on the Austrian media coverage of sport and in particular disabled and Paralympic sport. They review the local newspaper coverage of the Beijing Paralympics from qualitative and quantitative research perspectives. In its conclusive section the study indicated that the Austrian press is very interested in reporting about disability and Paralympic sport although the diversity and the volume of that reporting depends solely on the selected daily newspaper and its political persuasion and editorial staff. Chapter 7 written by Nicole Raab and Simone Janda is particularly interesting from a German perspective and their title *'Coverage of the Beijing Paralympic Games on German Television'* reflects the nature of their work. In this chapter they argue that both German public broadcasting stations were responsible for the increased public interest in the Paralympic Games and consequent rise in their prestige and public attention in the last eight years in Germany. In this chapter they question the media coverage by reviewing the social acceptability of the news reporting to the public and what sports were shown and their aesthetic accountability to the German public. Finally, they put forward some comments regarding the visual attractiveness of the coverage and supported this with data which provided indication that some sports are more popular - like athletics, wheelchair-basketball, swimming and table-tennis, and that the broadcasting of well-known and socially accepted disability athletes like wheelchair sportsmen and women, the visual impaired, and several paraplegics was commonplace. On the other hand Chapter 8 titled *'French Perspectives on the Media and Paralympics'* by Anne Marcellini is a well-researched chapter which highlights an historical perspective regarding the relationship between the media and the Paralympics. In this chapter she deals with an in-depth analysis of gender issues and new thoughts on visual documentation and the media's treatment of French Paralympic athletes - which she argues does not amount to much as coverage of the Paralympics and disability sport in general is very poor in France. Ian Brittain maintains the international theme by writing in Chapter 9 specifically about the *'British Media Portrayals of Paralympic and Disability Sport'*. In this well written piece Ian puts forward arguments which cover a short history of the media and the Paralympics in the British context and the value of Paralympic and disability sport in the U.K. He discusses the issues related to achievement of better coverage and speaks succinctly about the relationship between the London 2012 Games and the new host broadcaster all the while drawing comparisons from across the rest of the world to support his arguments. In his final comments he is optimist for the future and notes that it would appear the British media, or at least certain parts of it, are leading the way when it comes to raising the profile of disability and Paralympic sport and increasing its profile in a positive and constructive manner. In Chapter 10 Anna Fong and Sid Katz write candidly about the relationship between Canadian and U.S.A. media coverage of the Paralympic Games. In their chapter titled *US vs. Canada: An Analysis of Media Coverage of Paralympic Athletes* they found in an analysis of the Athens and Vancouver Paralympics that Canadian and American reporters admitted they knew the Paralympics had less coverage but said the reasons were not personal. They were a result of budget restrictions and the limited space allocated for each section. There chapter also covers issues related to the Paralympics and media nexus such as types of disability coverage, types of stories and the role of the International Paralympic Committee in the development of sound media practices. The following Chapter 11 titled *A Way Forward: Researching International Perspectives on Media and the Paralympics* by Eric de Léséleuc discusses issues in relation to which ways academics research the media and the Paralympics. He provides methodological and academic structures which he believes we should all work within in future research in the area.

Part II titled *'Visibility of Disability'* develops some of the themes which were relevant in the previous section. It delves deeper into the particular aspects of photography, perception and disability. Chapter 12 is the first in this section and is carefully written by Capucine Germain and Julie Grall. The work *'Analysing Disabled Athletes' Photographs: The Case of the 2008 Beijing Paralympic Games'* provides a well-developed set of arguments which discuss the visibility of sport, the notions of disability and performance as well as difficult issues of disability and compassion. Later in the chapter Germain and Grall challenge preconceived ideas of disability and conscious resistance and through a series of studies highlight the nature of disability, the Paralympics and the term polemology, which they argue consistently supports the building of social realities between the media and sport. Chapter 13 however, is slightly different and provides a philosophical perspective on the relationship between the media and the Paralympics. Louise Charbonnier and Cristina Popescu in this chapter *'Disabled Heroes in the Media'* highlight some specific issues relating to future of the multiple hero, the notion of a sentimental community, a pathos based discourse, invisibility of the athlete and instinct of mind control over the disabled body. There work is excellent and provides a clear understanding of the problematics of applying a discursive framework to the work on disability and the media. This coupled with the three principles which undercut their work provides us with a differing perspective which is clearly grounded in the philosophy theory. Following on from this in Chapter 14 Gregor Wolbring's work titled *'Media coverage of Pistorius: What are the angles? What is missing?'* emphasises the need for the media to understand the actual capabilities of the Paralympic athlete. He achieves this by presenting a short history of the media attention given to Pistorius over the past few years and also its portrayal of the athlete. He argues that there are several issues arising from the coverage and not the least are those which are left out or missing. In short it appears as though the media deliberately left out some important aspects of the Pistorius case and that they have a fascination with the cyborg body but are unsure as to how they can report on it or how they portray the trans-human nature of the Paralympics. This leads us nicely to Chapter 15 *'Post-modern perspectives of the media and disability'* by Emily Coutant who sets the scene by highlighting issues of spirituality, ethics and aesthetics where she notes that there is an imagined world of the Paralympics which is conjured up by the media. To this end she further argues that Paralympians and disabled athletes are becoming prototypes for humans of the future and that the real reach of the Paralympics has not yet been perceived. Furthermore she argues that perhaps the Paralympics is a giant laboratory where ideas and life-saving technology can be trialled. Her final point is a strong one and Emily imagines Paralympians as heroes who by essence would offer the possibility of believing in the impossible, would allow us to imagine that we can always push farther, higher and stronger the limits of the human's organic potential, thanks to their courage and the exercise of the will. This is an excellent chapter which redefines the nature of Paralympic technocracy. Chapter 16 by Cynthia Barounis takes a close look at the film *Murderball* and discusses issues of alternative masculinities and Paralympic athlete's sexuality. It is an interesting slant on the Paralympians relationship to the media and is perhaps a slice of life which we need to follow in more detail in our future research.

In contrast Chapter 17 by Donna de Haan is a measured piece titled *'Paralympic athletes' perspectives of media coverage: Whose story is it?'* and is the first chapter in Part III of the book. This section is headed *'Reconceptualising Paralympic Sport, Disability and the Media'*. In this chapter de Haan makes a good attempt at listening to the conversations of Paralympic athletes regarding their experience with the media. This is an original and interesting take on research and we feel that there needs to be more research of a narrative kind in the future. In this chapter she argues for sport specific coverage and that all sports should have equal time and paper space and at the core of this chapter was her desire to ask athletes what their ideal sport media coverage would look like. This she achieves quite well. This chapter leads into Chapter 18 written by Brenda-Kammel Atuona who poses some vexing question on race, the media and Paralympic sport. Her chapter *'Paralympic Sport, British Media and the Absence of Black Faces'* is clearly the first of its kind and very enlightening. In this chapter Kammel-Autona argues that historically there have been and there are few black Paralympic athletes represented in the media. Her writings centre round the notions of disability, society and the media, the absence of disabled athletes black faces in the media and that the oppression of black athletes is qualitatively different in kind to that of their white counterparts. It's a very good chapter grounded in theory and takes us into Chapter 19 by Maxine Newlands titled *'Debunking Disability: Media Discourse and the Paralympic Games'*. In this chapter she argues strongly against the complex classification system employed by the International Paralympic Committee as it acts as a stumbling block for future relations between the media and the Paralympics. She argues that it is far too difficult to understand and most media representatives can't be bothered to learn the systems for two weeks every two years. Newlands asks what are the exact messages which the media are trying to purvey and how do they come across in the light of pre and post Paralympic Games understanding by the public? She argues from a discursive approach that the media discourse changes every Paralympic Games and most reporters have little understanding of how to write about disabled individuals.

The last two Chapters are 20 *'An Implosion of Discontent: Reconceptualising the Rapport between the Media and the Paralympic Movement'* and Chapter 21 *'The Epilogue'* by the editors of Heroes or Zeros by Otto Schantz and Keith Gilbert, attempts to synthesize the previous chapters and add to them in a significant manner so that some sense can be made out of the relationship between the media and Paralympic sport. Their findings are profound, direct and novel and important questions are asked which if acted upon could change the relationship between the Paralympics and the media. To this end the above three parts are a gathering of academic work in the area of media and Paralympics which we hope will provide a basis and grounding for further research. Along with research this book offers new and refreshing ideas to all academics and practitioners in the media in order that they might improve the ways in which the Paralympics, Paralympians and disabled athletes are perceived in society.

References

Albright, A. C. (1997). *Choreographing difference. The body and identity in contemporary dance.* Hanover, NH: Wesleyan University Press.

Baudrillard, J. (1991, March 29). La guerre du Golfe n'a pas eu lieu. *Libération.*

Becker, P. (1983). Sport in den Massenmedien. *Sportwissenschaft 13* (1), 24-45.

Bell, A. (1991). *The language of news media.* Oxford, UK, Cambridge MA: Blackwell.

Berelson, B. (1960). Communication and public opinion. In W. Schramm (Ed.), *Mass communications* (pp. 527-543). Urbana: University of Illinois Press.

Berghaus, M. (1999). Wie Massenmedien wirken. *Rundfunk und Fernsehen 47* (2), 181-199.
Bette, K.-H. (1999). *Systemtheorie und Sport*. Frankfurt a. M.: Suhrkamp.
Blinde, E. M. & McCallister, S. G. (1999). Women, disability, and sport and physical activity: The intersection of gender and disability dynamics. *Research Quarterly for Exercise and Sport, 70*, 303-312.
Borcila, A. (2000). Nationalizing the Olympics around and away from "vulnerable" bodies of women: The NBC coverage of the 1996 Olympics and some moments after. *Journal of Sport and Social Issues, 24* (2), 118-147.
Bourdieu, P. (1994). Les Jeux Olympiques. Programme pour une analyse. *Actes de la Recherche en Sciences Sociales, 103*, 102-103.
Bourdieu, P. (1996). *Sur la télévision*. Paris: Liber.
Chambre des Communes (1988). *Pas de nouvelles, mauvaises nouvelles*. Premier rapport du Comité permanent de la condition des personnes handicapées. Ottawa: Chambre des Communes.
Cloerkes, G. (1997). *Soziologie der Behinderten*. Heidelberg: Schindle.
Clogston, J. S. (1994). Disability coverage in American newspapers. In J. A. Nelson (Ed.), *The disabled, the media, and the information age* (pp. 45-53).Westport, CN: Greenwood Press.
Coakley, J. J. (1994). *Sport in society. Issues and controversies*. St. Louis: Mosby
Cole, C.(1999, August, 27). Faster, higher, poorer. *National Post*, Canada.
Dearing, J. W. Rogers, E. M. (1996). *Agenda setting*. London: Sage.
DePauw, K. (1997). The (in)visibility of disability: Cultural contexts and sporting bodies. *Quest, 49*, 416-430.
DePauw, K. (2000). Social-Cultural Context of Disability: Implications for Scientific Inquiry and Professional Preparation. *Quest 52*, 358-368.
DePauw, K. P. (1997). The (In)Visibility of DisAbility: Cultural contexts and "sporting bodies". *Quest, 49*, 416-430.
DePauw, K., & Gavron, S. (1995). *Disability and sport*. Champaign: Human Kinetics.
Donsbach, W. (1991). *Medienwirkung trotz Selektion. Einflußfaktoren auf die Zuwendung zu Zeitungsinhalten*. Köln: Böhlauer.
Donsbach, W. (1992). Die Selektivität der Rezipienten. Faktoren, die die Zuwendung zu Zeitungsinhalten beeinflussen. In W. Schulz (Ed.), *Medienwirkungen. Einflüsse von Presse Radio und Fernsehen auf Individuen und Gesellschaft* (pp. 25-71). Weinheim: VCH.
Duhamel, A. (1985). *Le complexe d'Astérix*. Paris: Gallimard.
Dummer, G. M. (1998). Media coverage of disability sport. *Palaestra, 14* (4), 56.
Duncan, M. C. (1986). A hermeneutic of spectator sport: The 1976 and 1984 Olympic Games. *Quest, 38*, 50-77.
Duncan, M. C. (1990). Sports photographs and sexual difference. The images of women and men in the 1984 and 1988 Olympic Games. *Sociology of Sport Journal, 7*, 22-43.

Duncan, M. C.; Messner, M., & Williams, L. (1991). *Coverage of women's sports in four daily newspapers*. Edited by W. Wilson. Los Angeles: AAF publications. Retrieved January 27, 2000 from the World Wide Web: http://www.AAFLA.org/Publications/ResearchReports/ResearchReport1_.htm.

Eastman, S. T. & Billings, A. (2000). Sportcasting and sports reporting. The power of the gender bias. *Journal of Sport & Social Issues, 24* (2), 192-213.

Eco, U. (1997). *Cinque scritti morali*. Milano: Bompiani.

Eilders, C. (1997). *Nachrichtenfaktoren und Rezeption. Eine empirische Analyse zur Auswahl und Verarbeitung politischer Information*. Opladen: Westdeutscher Verlag.

Eitzen, S. D. (2009). *Fair and Foul. Beyond Myths and Paradoxes of Sport*. Lanham: Rowman & Littlefield.

Elias, N. & Dunning E. (1970). The quest of excitement in unexciting societies. In G. Lüschen (ed.). *The cross-cultural analysis of sport and games* (pp. 31-51). Champaign, IL: Stipes.

Enting, B. (1997). *Die Berichterstattung über die Paralympics 1996 in Atlanta - dargestellt in ausgewählten Printmedien*. Unpublished master's thesis, Sport University Cologne, Köln, Germany.

Erbring, L., Goldenberg, E., & Miller, A. (1980). Front pages news and real world cues: A New Look at Agenda-Setting by the Media. *American Journal of Political Science, 24* (1), pp- 19-49.

Farnall, O. & K.A. Smith (1999). Reactions to people with disabilities: Personal contact versus viewing of specific media portrayals. *Journalism and Mass Communication Quarterly, 76* (4), 659-672.

Fiske, J. (1993). *Power plays, power works*. London: Verso.

Foucault, M. (1961). *Histoire de la folie à l'âge classique*. Paris: Gallimard.

Früh, W. (1994). *Realitätsvermittlung durch Massenmedien. Die permanente Transformation der Wirklichkeit*. Opladen: Westdeutscher Verlag.

Galtung, J. & Ruge, H. (1965). The structure of foreign news. *Journal of Peace Research, 2*, 64-91.

Gebauer, G. (1994). Le nouveau nationalisme sportif. *Actes de la Recherche en Sciences Sociales, 103*, 104-107.

Génolini, J.P. (1995). L'expression euphémique du handicap mental dans les messages de presse sur le sport. *Revue Européenne du Handicap Mental, 2* (8), 54-63.

Gill, C.J. (1994). Questioning continuum. In B. Shaw (Ed.), *The ragged edge: The disability experience from the pages of the first fifteen years of The Disability Rag* (pp. 42-49). Louisville, KY: Avocado Press.

Goggin, G. & Newell, C. (2005). *Disability in Australia: Exposing a Social Apartheid*. Sydney: UNSW Press.

Golden, A. (2003). An Analysis of the Dissimilar Coverage of the 2002 Olympics and Paralympics: Frenzied Pack Journalism versus the Empty Press Room. *Disability Studies Quarterly 23*, (3/4) (www.dsq-sds.org).

Golden, A. (2002). An Analysis of the Dissimilar Coverage of the 2002 Olympics and Paralympics: Frenzied Pack Journalism Versus the Empty Press Room. Media & Disability Interest Group, Association for Education in Journalism and Mass Communication Annual Meeting, Miami, Fl.

Greenberg, B.S. & J. S. Brand (1994). Minorities and the mass media: 1970 to 1990. In J. Bryant & D. Zillmann (Eds.), *Media Effects: Advances in Theory and Research* (pp. 273-314). Hillsdale NJ: L. Erlbaum.

Guttmann, A. (1996). *The erotics in sport.* New York: Columbia University Press.

Guttmann, L. (1949). The second national Stoke Mandeville Games of the paralysed. *The Cord,* 3, 24.

Guttmann, L. (1979). *Sport für Körperbehinderte* [Textbook of Sport for the Disabled]. München: Urban & Schwarzenberg.

Hackforth, J. (1988). Publizistische Wirkungsforschung: Ansätze, Analysen und Analogien. In J. Hackforth (Ed.), *Sportmedien und Mediensport* (pp. 15-33). Berlin: Vistas.

Hackforth, J. (1994). Behindertensport in den Medien. In: Behinderten-Sportverband Nordrhein-Westfalen (Hrsg.). *Gesellschaft* (pp. 46-48). Duisburg: BSVNW.

Hall, S. (1997). The spectacle of the 'other'. In S. Hall (Ed.). *Representation. Cultural representations and signifying practices* (pp. 223- 290). London: Sage

Haller, B. (2000). If they limp, they lead? News representations and the hierarchy of disability images. In D. Braithwaite & T. Thompson, (Eds.), *Handbook of Communication and People with Disabilities* (pp. 273-288). Mahwah, NJ: Lawrence Erlbaum Associates.

Hardin, M. (2003). Marketing the acceptably athletic image: Wheelchair athletes, sport-related advertising and capitalist hegemony. *Disability Studies Quarterly,* 23(1), 108-125.

Hardin, M. M. & Hardin, B. (2004). The 'Supercrip' in sport media: Wheelchair athletes discuss hegemony's disabled hero. *sosol* 7. Retrieved January 10, 2005 from: http://physed.otago.ac.nz/sosol/v7i1/ v7i1_1.html.

Hiestand, M. (July 25, 2000). Paralympics online to test live market. *US Today,* C.9.

Holicki, S. (1993). *Pressefoto und Pressetext im Wirkungsvergleich. Eine experimentelle Untersuchung am Beispiel von Politikerdarstellungen.* München: Fischer.

Horkheimer, M., & Adorno, Th. W. (1989 [1947]). *Dialektik der Aufklärung. Philosophische Fragmente.* Leipzig: Reclam.

Howe, D. (2008). From Inside the Newsroom: Paralympic Media and the "Production" of Elite Disability. *International Review for the Sociology of Sport, 43* (2), 135-150.

Ingstad, B. & Whyte, S. R. (1995). *Disability and culture.* Berkley: University of California Press.

International Olympic Committee (1996). *Olympic charter*. Lausanne: I.O.C.
International Paralympic Committee (2000). *IPC constitution*. Retrieved February 1st, 2000 from the World Wide Web: http://www.paralympic.org
Internenettes (Eds.) (2000). *Représentations des femmes dans la vie politique française*. Retrieved April 2nd, 2000 from the World Wide Web: /femmes/politique.html
Jamieson, K. H., Campbell, K. K. (1997). *The interplay of influence. News, advertising, politics, and the mass media*. Belmont, 4th edition. CA: Wadsworth.
Jones, R., Murrell, A. J. & Jackson J. (1999). Pretty versus powerful in the sports pages. *Journal of Sport & Social Issues, 23* (2), 183-192.
Kauer, O., & Bös, K. (1998). *Behindertensport in den Medien*. Aachen: Meyer & Meyer:
Keller, C. E., Hallahan, D. P., McShane, E. A., Crowley, E. P., & Blandford, B.J. (1990). The coverage of persons with disabilities in American newspapers. *The Journal of Special Education, 24* (3), 271-282.
Kellner, D. (1995). *Media culture- Cultural studies, identity and politics between the modern and the postmodern*. London: Routledge.
Kepplinger, M. H. (1986). Begriffe und Modelle langfristiger Medienwirkung. In W.A. Mahle (Ed.), *Langfristige Medienwirkung* (pp. 27-38). Berlin: Wissenschaftsverlag Volker Spiess.
Klapper, J.T. (1960). *The effects of mass Communication*. Glencoe, Ill.: Free Press.
Krüger, A. (1993). Cui bono? Die Rolle des Sports in den Massenmedien. In A. Krüger, & A., Scharenberg (Eds.), *Wie die Medien den Sport aufbereiten - Ausgewählte Aspekte der Sportpublizistik* (pp. 24-63). Berlin: Tischler.
Kuhn, R. (1995). *The media in France*. London: Routledge.
Lachal, R.-C. (1990a). La presse française et les personnes handicapées de 1977 à 1988. In Institut de l'Enfance et de la Famille (Ed.), *Handicap, famille et société* (pp. 39-44). Paris: IDEF.
Lachal, R.-C. (1990b). Les personnes handicapées vues par la presse régionale française. Constantes et évolutions de 1977 à 1988. *Handicaps et Inadaptations - Les Cahiers du CTNERHI, 51/52*, 1-29.
Lazarsfeld, P.F., & Merton, R. K. (1948). Mass communication, popular taste and organized social action. In L. Bryson (Ed.), *Communication of ideas* (pp. 95-118). New York: Harper & Bros.
Lazarsfeld, P.F., Berelson, B., & Gaudet, H. (1968). *The people's choice* (3rd ed.). New York: Columbia University Press.
Levine, S. (2000). Narrowing the perception gap. *The Quill, 88* (3), 35.
Longmore, P. K. (1985). Screening stereotypes: Images of disabled people. *Social Policy, 16* (1), 31-37.
Luebke, B. (1989). Out of focus. Images of women and men in the newspaper photographs. *Sex Roles, 20* (3-4), 121-133.

Luhmann, N. (1996). *Die Realität der Massenmedien* (2nd ed.). Opladen: Westdeutscher Verlag.
Lyotard, J.-F. (1983). *Le différend*. Paris: Editions de Minuit.
Maguire, J. (1993). Globalization, sport development and the media/sport production complex. *Sport Science Review, 2* (1), 29-47.
McCombs, M. (1994). News influence on our pictures of the world. In J. Bryant, & D. Zillmann (Eds.), *Media effects. Advances in theory and research* (pp. 1- 16). Hillsdale, NJ: Lawrence Erlbaum.
McQuail, D. (1993). *Mass Communication Theory*. London, Thousand Oaks, New Dehli.
Merten, K. (1995). *Inhaltsanalyse*. Opladen: Westdeutscher Verlag.
Münch, R. (1993). *Die Kultur der Moderne. Band 2: Ihre Entwicklung in Frankreich und Deutschland*. Frankfurt a. M.: Suhrkamp.
Nelson, J. A. (1994). Broken Images: Portrayals of those with disabilities in American media. In J. A. Nelson (Ed.), *The disabled, the media, and the information age* (pp. 1-17). Westport, CN: Greenwood Press.
Noelle-Neumann, E. (1994). Wirkung der Massenmedien auf die Meinungsbildung. In E. Noelle-Neumann, W. Schulz, & J. Wilke (Eds.), *Publizistik, Massenkommunikation* (pp. 518-571). Frankfurt a. M.: Fischer.
Oakes, P. J., Haslam, A., & J. C. Turner (1994). *Stereotyping and social reality*. Cambridge, MA: Blackwell.
Oehmichen, E. (1991). Sport im Alltag - Sport im Fernsehen. *Media Perspektiven, 11,* 744-758.
Pappous, A., Marcellini, A., & Léséleuc, E. de (2011). Contested issues in research on the media coverage of feamle Paralympic athletes. *Sport in Society,* 14(9), 1182-1191.
Peltu, M. (1985). The role of communication media. In H. Ottway, & M. Peltu (Eds.), *Regulating industrial risks: Science, hazards and public protection* (pp. 128-148). London.
Pfister, G. (1987). Women in the Olympics (1952-1980): An analysis of German newspapers (beauty vs. gold medals). In *The Olympic movement and the mass media* (pp. 11.27–11.37). Calgary: Hurford.
Riggs, K. E., Eastman, S.T., & Golobic, T. S. (1993). Manufactured conflict in the 1992 Olympics: the discourse of television and politics. *Critical Studies in Mass Communication, 10* (3), 253-272.
Riley II, C. A. (2005). *Disability and the Media. Prescriptions for Change*. Hanover, London: University Press of New England.
Robertson, R. (1992). *Globalization: social theory and global culture*. London: Sage.
Rowe, D. (1999). *Sport, culture and the media. The untruly trinity*. Buckingham, UK: Open University Press.
Sage, G. H. (1990). *Power and Ideology in American Sport: A Critical Perspective*. Champaign, Ill.: Human Kinetics.

Sandfort, L. (1982). Medien-Manifest. Forderung behinderter an die Medien. In: H. J. Kagelmann & R. Zimmermann (Eds.). *Massenmedien und Behinderte. Im besten Falle Mitleid?* Weinheim, Basel: Beltz Verlag.

Schantz, O. (1999). La mise en scène du corps extraordinaire - Freak show ou implication éthique de l'esthétique. In Centre de Recherche en Education Corporelle (Ed.). *La danse, une culture en mouvement* (pp. 67-74). Strasbourg: UMB.

Schantz, O., & Alberto, C. (1999). Coping strategies of Paralympic athletes. In *12° Congreso Mundial de Actividad Fisica Adaptada - COMAFA '99, 4-8 de Mayo de 1999 Barcelona - Lleida*. Resumenes. Barcelona: Institut Nacional d'educació Física de Catalunya, pp. 95-96.

Schantz, O. J. & Gilbert, K. (2001). An ideal misconstrued: Newspaper coverage of the Atlanta Paralympic Games in France and Germany. *Sociology of Sport Journal 18*, 69-94.

Schantz, O. J. & Gilbert, K. (2008). French and German Newspaper Coverage oft he 1996 Atlanta Paralympic Games. In K. Gilbert & O. J. Schantz (Eds.). *The Paralympic Games. Empowerment or Side Show?* (pp. 34-56).Maidenhead: Meyer& Meyer.

Schantz, O., & Marty, C. (1995). The French press and sport for people with handicapping conditions. In I. Morisbak, & P. E. Jørgensen (Eds.) *Quality of live through adapted physical activity* (pp. 72-79). Oslo: Hamtrykk.

Schell, L.A., & Duncan, M. C. (1999). A content analysis of CBS's coverage of the 1996 Paralympic Games. *Adapted Physical Activity Quarterly, 16* (1), pp. 27-47.

Schimanski, M. (1994). *Behindertensport in der deutschen und amerikanischen Tagespresse 1984-1992. Unter besonderer Berücksichtigung der Paralympics. Eine Analyse anhand ausgewählter Printmedien*. Unpublished master's thesis, Sport University Cologne, Köln, Germany.

Scholz, M. (2010). *Presse und Behinderung*. Wiesbaden: Verlag für Sozialwissenschaften.

Schönbach, K. (1992). Transaktionale Modelle der Medienwirkung: Stand der Forschung. In W. Schulz (Ed.), *Medienwirkungen. Einflüsse von Presse Radio und Fernsehen auf Individuen und Gesellschaft* (pp. 109-120).Weinheim: VCH.

Segrave, J. O. (1988). Toward a definition of Olympism. In J. O. Segrave & D. Chu (Eds.). *The Olympic Games in transition* (pp. 149-161). Champaign, IL: Human Kinetics.

Shapiro, J. P. (1993). *No pity: People with disabilities forging a new civil rights movement*. New York: Times Books.

Sherrill, C. (1993). Women with disabilities. In G. Cohen (Ed.), *Women in sport: Issues and controversies* (pp. 238-248). Newbury Park, CA: Sage.

Sherrill, C. (1997). Paralympic Games 1996: Feminist and other concerns: What's your excuse? *Palestra, 13*, 32-38.

Silva, C. F. & Howe, D. P. (2012). The (In)validity of Supercrip Representation of Paralympian Athletes, *Journal of Sport & Social Issues* (online first January 26), 2012, 1-21.
Smart, J. (2001). *Disability, Society, and the Individual*. Gaithersburg: Aspen Publishers.
Smith, A. & Thomas, N. (2005). The "inclusion" of elite athletes with disabilities in the 2002 Manchester Commonwealth Games: an exploratory analysis of British newspaper coverage. *Sport, Education and Society, 10* (1), 49-67.
Stautner, B. K. (1989). *Abweichung - Behinderung - Sport in der modernen Gesellschaft. Eine Bestandsaufnahme und systemtheoretische Neuformulierung*. Unpublished doctoral dissertation. Julius-Maximilians University, Würzburg.
Sutton, J. (Jan 5, 1998). Sponsors shy away from Paralympic Games. *Marketing News, 32* (1), 21-22.
Thomas, N. & Smith, A. (2003). Preoccupied with Able-Bodiedness? An Analysis of the British Media Coverage of the 2000 Paralympics Games. *Adapted Physical Activity Quarterly, 20*, 166-181.
Tuggle, C. A. & Owen, A. (1999). A descriptive analysis of the centennial Olympics: the 'Games of the Women'? *Journal of Sport and Social Issues, 23* (2), 171-182.
Turner, B. S. (1998). Foreword. In W. Seymour, *Remaking the Body. Rehabilitation and Change* (v-viii). St Leonards: Allen & Unwin.
Urquhart, J. & Crossman, J. (1999). The Globe and Mail coverage of the winter Olympic Games. *Journal of Sport & Social Issues, 23* (2), 193-202.
Wann, D. L., Schrader, M. P., Allison, J. A. & McGeorge K.K. (1998). The inequitable newspaper coverage of men's and women's athletics at small, medium, and large universities. *Journal of Sport & Social Issues, 22* (1), 79-87.
Waxman, B. F. (1994). It's time to politicize our sexual oppression. In B. Shaw (Ed.), *The ragged edge: The disability experience from the pages of the first fifteen years of The Disability Rag* (pp. 82-87). Louisville, KY: Avocado Press.
White, D., M. (1950). The »Gatekeeper«: A case study in the selection of news. *Journalism Quarterly, 27*, 383-390.
Wilke, J. (1994). Presse. In E. Noelle-Neumann, W. Schulz, & J. Wilke (Eds.), *Publizistik, Massenkommunikation* (pp. 382-417). Frankfurt a. M.: Fischer.
Woodill, G. (1994). The social semiotics of disability. In M. H. Rioux & M. Bach (Eds.). *Disability is not measles. New research paradigms in disability* (pp. 201-226). North York, Ontario: Roeher.
Yoshida, R. K., Wasilewski, L., & Friedman, D. L. (1990). Recent newspaper coverage about persons with disabilities. *Exceptional children, 56*, 418-423.

Zola, I.K. (1985). Depictions of disability – Metaphor, message, and medium in the media: A research and political agenda. *The Social Science Journal, 22* (4), 5-17.

Part I
National Narratives and Paralympic Sport

Chapter 2
Media Coverage of the Paralympic Games from 1960 to 2004 by the Sport Newspaper 'L'Equipe'

Change in Event and Participation Representation

Fréderic Reichhart & Aggée C. Lomo Myazhiom

Introduction

Apart from recounting events, the media is a fundamental lever of public opinion. In this context, we are sometimes tempted to think that "the newspaper leads the world" as it never commands but always suggests and all the while gives us the appearance of being free. However, it has an ever stronger influence over us. Indeed, many people actually have similar opinions to those of the writers in the newspaper. "Tell me who you read, and I'll tell you who you are!"[1]. The newspaper then is a system of communicating that happens between 'the crowd opinion' and 'media calendar'. As early as 1901, Gabriel Tarde in *L'Opinion et la Foule*, indicated that the crowds were inundated by the press and that the latter "tries to accomplish the task of merging between personal and local opinions with national opinion" and "Transforming personal opinion into a social opinion, to 'the' opinion is due to

---

1. *Le Cameroun Catholique*, Douala edition, 3rd year, n°1, 1939, Arch. CSSp, Boîte 281-B.

public speech in the Antiquity and the Middle Ages, and due to the present day press" (Trade, 1989. P.41). This sees the dawn of the social functions of the press as a service: "information, entertainment, psychotherapy and social inclusion" (Albert, 2001, p.25). In this chapter, we will take interest in the last two points mentioned. Pierre Albert puts emphasis on the psychotherapeutic role and notes that "reading the press has a clear but very complex influence on readers' psychology". It often is a contributing factor to balancing readers' psyche: purification of profound instincts, making up for frustration and identifying with stars on the news headlines (Albert, 2002, pp. 27-28). Pierre Albert continues to show that "the fourth function (...) is that of social integration of the individual into the social body. Reading the newspaper provides some sort of dialogue that opens invisible doors to the world, helping the individual to belong to his local, regional and national environment, it also strengthens his or her affiliation to the different small professional groups or other groups and various cultural, spiritual or political communities. Newspapers are agents of an individual's socialisation; they break his or her isolation and encourage him or her to take part in group activities" (Albert, 2002, p. 28). This influence and interrelation has been increasing overtime so much so that it has entered into every sector in society, and indeed, mass media has turned our planet into a "global village" (McLuhan, 1977; Balle, 1985). It also supports the participation in social life of special categories (often times neglected[2]) which play a very unique role in the study of sports movement and how it is linked to the rest of society.

As components shaping public opinion, the printed press, television and radio have a very important effect on how a sport is developed and practised. The victory of an athlete or a sports team can increase the number of members joining a sports federation. Today it is impossible to think of a major sporting event without the media. For example, the 'Tour de France' and the FIFA World Cup are international sporting events that reflect the importance and volume of media coverage in the printing press, radio and television.

The Paralympics Games as covered by L'Équipe: methodological issues and insights

Our work takes shape around the media coverage of the Paralympics Games by the sports newspaper *L'Equipe* that has a monopoly[3] on the French media landscape. This is the only national sports daily, with an average circulation of 300,000 copies daily[4]; and its large print run gives it legitimacy both in-

---

2. Mainly affinitarian media.
3. In recent years all attempts to compete have been unsuccessful. The last being in 2008 the *10 Sport* yielded to the monopoly and became a weekly.
4. See *Associations pour le Contrôle de la Diffusion des Médias* (OJD), *Observatoire 2010 de la Presse* : as well as in the 2009 media podium *L'Equipe* is placed 4th behind *Ouest France, le Figaro and le Parisien*.

side and outside the sports world. The influence of *L'Équipe* is significant in the sports movement, both nationally and internationally. As emphasized by Guy Lionel Loew, "the French newspaper does not wait for major sporting events, it creates them" (Loew, 2007, p.102). Beyond an exploration for "meaning of sport in the media" and a case of "the influence of the daily" *L'Équipe* in the media coverage of the Paralympics Games[5], assuming that "the media play a key role in the production and reproduction of social representations, as well as strengthening standards and attitudes in the making in our societies", analysis of media coverage of *L'Équipe* "is a measure of prominence given to disabled people in society" (Léséleuc, Marcellini, & Pappous, 2004). The task at hand involves analysing and describing ways in which an event and its participants are presented and put on show by this specialised newspaper in order to grasp and "understand, like one would through a prism, the change and continuity logic that are at work in the collective representations on disabilities" (Léséleuc, Marcellini & Pappous, 2004).

Therefore, the first section of the chapter questions the Paralympics athlete and how he/she is presented. What are the characteristics highlighted in the texts and pictures? Do these characteristics depict the athlete as a sportsman or do they refer to his/her impairment? Is the athlete subject of hero making process on the back drop of a performing body? What kinds of values are used to represent and describe the athlete?

The research hypotheses that we developed are two-fold[6]. On the one hand the individual's impairment overshadows completely his/her status as an athlete and a sportsman. Attention is paid, primarily, on the biologically deformed body and organic alteration. On the other, there is a hero-making kind of process that surfaces but it seems to result from the impairment: it is not performance as such that it is admired but the will and the all-out effort that drives a person to surpass himself given the impairment: admiration comes as a result of outdoing oneself rather than the resulting fulfilment from doing sports.

Secondly, a second section focuses on this expression as an organization of sporting events. How is it described? Do the factors focused on match up to a sporting event? What points are highlighted by the press? From which view point is the event presented: 1. A meeting? 2. A group of impaired people? 3. A freak show? 4. A sporting event?[7] Our corpus corresponds to the media coverage of the newspaper *L'Équipe* from 1960 to 2004

---

5. In order to study the press influence in media coverage on sports events, one can read for example Michaël Attali (2010) and Evelyne Combeau-Mari (2007).

6. It will be referred to the work from Stéphanie Metz. She studies the process of normalisation of athletes with disabilities in the media coverage of the summer Paralympics Games from Foucauld's point of view (Metz 2005). See also Sylvain Paillette, Bernard Delforce and Fabien Wille (2002).

7. Otto Schantz (2005) notes a similar reaction as far as spectators participating in Paralympics games are concerned.

in total 162 items address or talk about the Paralympics Games during this period. Item sources are different; mainly comprised of articles (139 articles) and news flashes (25) supplemented by photos (7) or drawings (1) as well as advertisement (2). In the first results of an on-going research that we have presented here, we chose a content and iconography analysis[8].

Representation of the Paralympic Games in the newspaper L'Équipe

In 1960 the sports newspaper *L'Équipe* devoted 4 articles to the Rome Paralympic Games. These were very short articles in the form of "news flashes"[9]. The first step, far from prevalent stereotypes, the Games were presented as a sports competition, the competition results were shown (fencing, archery, basketball), indicating the overall results and the list of winners in the French team. Although the Games were designated as the "Games for the paraplegic"[10] in the paper, neither the nature nor the extent of the disability was given in details.

In 1964, in Tokyo, a significant development was the first biographies of athletes[11] (this will be discussed later) and in *L'Équipe* articles referred to the athletes as "physically challenged" or "paraplegic". This shows that while the Games were presented as a major sporting event, the ambiguity and discomfort when referring to the participants still remained. One title written by Christian Montaignac on November 20th, 1968 speaks for itself; it reads "They are called the physically challenged". The author who advocates a change in mentality, shines light on the exclusion and differentiation impaired persons are faced with. Doing sports is asserted as a way out of this situation, it illustrates how the disabled are struggling to fight discrimination and marginalisation. Sport became a pillar of social inclusion, a tool in the fight against exclusion, a symbol of equality and normality. Christian Montaignac wrote: Sport is not the prerogative of an 'unimpaired' man. Furthermore, he takes the example of Philippe Berthe[12] for whom sport embodies a reflection of the humanity of the disabled person and becomes a common denominator with the normal. A strong "signal was also an asset in accelerating the integration process". Taking part in the Games is a way of making the disabled more visible and a conquest of a whole identity, in

---

8. One can note on our corpus that since 1992, the number of articles has increased, 10 articles written in 1992 and 22 articles in 1996. In the same year, newsflashes and photos are printed. Secondly advertisement dates back to 2004.

9. September 20th/22nd/26th and 28th

10. See news flash titles for September 20th 1960: "*Début des neuvièmes jeux pour paraplégiques*" "Start of the 9 edition of games for the paraplegic" September 28th 1960: "*Quatre médailles d'or pour les paraplégiques français !*" Four gold medals for the French paraplegic".

11. This trend would accelerate in the competitions that followed.

12. A war amputee and founder of the Sports Association for the mutilated in 1954 which would later give birth in 1977 to the French Federation of Disabled Sports.

order to overcome marginalisation. "Personally, [P.Berthe points out] there are no disabilities, there are only men (...) what dominates is the human value of the individual. And human value is found in each one of us. We can feel it. Sometimes, we get the impression we are a bother". Medals won by the French participants in the Paralympics should be held in high esteem alongside other athletes (no more, no less) and their achievements should (which is not the case) get the same media coverage.

During the entire period (1960-2004), results from the different sporting events were presented, while not always commented upon and records broken were also announced. With the naming of the first special correspondent, Eric Lahmy, the number of countries, spectators as well as participants are mentioned; a medal chart lends the event an international perspective and add a competitive edge to it (among different countries). In the end, the Paralympics receive better coverage in L'Equipe: Before 1992, the average number of items per day was approximately 1 (an average of the past 9 Paralympics). In 1992 it remained at the same average of 1 per day but rose to about 3 (2.75) in 2004 (Metz 2005, p.52).

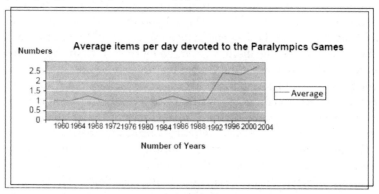

In the overall development of the Paralympics, it is worth noting that the appearance of leading figures and of different officials from international organizations added much needed legitimacy and recognition. Opening and closing ceremonies act as a beacon. Therefore, in 1964 in Tokyo Japanese officials were present. As a result, *L'Équipe* relates the Tokyo games from a very formal point of view concentrating on the presence of the Crown Prince Akihito and his wife Princess Michiko. The presence of the royal family further strengthened the legitimacy and recognition for the Games. The 1980 Games in Arnhem were inaugurated by Princess Margaret of the Netherlands. Ronald Reagan paid tribute to the Games in the same way in the 1984 Paralympic Games. During the Games in Barcelona an article talked about the participation of the Swedish queen who came to support a Swedish weight-lifter and finally the Atlanta Paralympics in 1996 were inaugurated under the auspices of Vice-president Al Gore.

Events uncovering political issues and strain

Several Paralympics survived various contemporary political strains and issues. The first geopolitical factor was the 1968 Games in Israel in which Arab countries and countries from the Eastern block refused to take part. This was as a result of the conflict in the Middle East in which the region has been engulfed since the 1940s. One of the key issues was the 6 day war that pitted Egypt, Jordan, Syria and Iraq against Israel. Israel won the war and Egypt accepted a cease fire signed on June 8th 1968. A *L'Équipe* news flash on November 4th 1968 read "Neither the Arab countries nor the Eastern Bloc countries are represented". In Toronto in 1976 it was the strained relations between the Non-Aligned countries and countries from the West concerning Apartheid in South Africa. It is only after the Afro-Asian conference in Bandoeng 1955 and the emergence of the third world countries that saw the spirit of universalism and brotherhood among people regardless of their differences, switch from the assertion rule of former colonial powers. The Paralympics Games are no exception to this process of emancipation of the people and the fight against discrimination. South Africa and its apartheid system was in the sights of Non-Aligned and the Eastern bloc during the Cold War period. So the *L'Équipe* article on August 9th 1976 read "4th day of the 5th Games for the disabled, marked by the return of the Polish athletes who had walked out of the Games on Friday in protest of the presence of the South African delegation. This so called 'walk-out' did not have any effect on the other eight countries that had withdrawn or had chosen not to participate for the same reason (Cuba, Hungary, India, Jamaica, Kenya, Uganda, Sudan and Yugoslavia). Upon its return to the Etobicoke stadium (Toronto suburb), the Polish delegation requested that South Africa be suspended. The President of the International Federation, Sir Ludwig Guttmann, rejected Poland's request, stating that South Africa respected the rules of the Games for the disabled, presenting a mixed team [sic] (30 white athletes and eight black athletes)"[13]. It should be noted that political strains cannot be reduced to the Paralympics only which, like the Olympics Games, has gone through a lot of political rivalry (since the second half of the 20th century) from world powers and different ideological blocs that resulted from World War II. In 1984 in Los Angeles, the Games were deep in the Cold War climate between the East and West. On June 28th, 1984, one news flash dares mention the defection of the USSR and Cuba[14]. Later in 1992, *L'Équipe* reported disturbances that had affected the closing ceremony

---

13. See, «22 médailles d'or pour la Hollande», August 9th, 1976.
14. The article signalled cracks in the Eastern Bloc countries with participation the participation of some countries e.g; Hungary, Bulgaria, Romania and Poland.

of the games. Thousands of Catalan nationalists whistled during part of the show in front of Spain King Juan Carlos who left his seat momentarily in the VIP stand[15].

About the participants at the Games: From 'misshapen' bodies to asserted athletes

The first portrait makes its way through the first games. It takes its shape around the disabled who do sport from a medical or integrative perspective: the disabled person is subject to a biographical representation that paints a tragic and unfortunate picture characterized by exclusion and stigmatisation. Being disabled means that socially the person is dead and the only way to resurrect is by doing sport. The disabled athlete's effort and personal devotion are seen as a form of resilience (Cyrulnik, 2004) or coping (Lazarus R.S. & S. Folkham, 1984) aimed at functional rehabilitation and subsequently, social integration of the person. Therefore, the underlying idea of self-transcendence, courage, the will of people with disabilities who intend to overcome their handicap by practising sport, backs sport as physical therapy and as a means of integration.

For example, Robert Colombini's story (November 3rd 1964) is based on a dramatisation of the biography of the disabled which highlights the values of courage and self-transcendence channelled in sport. He describes French participants, Aimé Planchon and Serge Bec referring to their record of achievements in sports for the disabled (who were world champions last year) and comparing them with renowned athletes like Magnan and Arabo. He mentions the athletes in a narrative that recounts misfortune and tragedy in their case that with courage and bravery results in social, sporting and professional success, synonymous with integration. These are men who "out-did themselves" and "who have given us bravery lessons". Here the writer dramatises the biography of the disabled athlete and underlines the qualities associated with courage and surpassing oneself as reflected through sport: she is a 'superhuman'. A lot of emphasis is put on practising sport, it is depicted as medical treatment embodying functional rehabilitation and acting as a social integration tool. If it were to be further analysed, sport represents the "breath" that helps the athlete to have a new social life; in this respect, it is the "main instrument in their resurrection", in that they come back to life through sport.

Athlete...at last...or the quest for performance?

The first figure changes gradually. It gives way to another portrait. The disabled athlete summons up courage, surpassing himself while practising sport, not as a sign of resilience in order to overcome his or her disability,

---

15. See, "Perturbations à la clôture des Paralympiques", Disturbances at the closing ceremony of the Paralympics Games in *L'Equipe*, September 16th 1991.

but in order to achieve his performance in sport. The purpose of the investment that drives the person in sport is focused on technical mastery and the development of physical potential, by training to get good results.

In this regard, we can mention the jump of 1.86 m from one-legged, Arnie Bolt who was the subject of a laudatory article August 10th 1976. In the same vein, in 1992 two athletes were put forward: a swimmer, David Foppolo[16] who compensated for his lack of arms with the effectiveness of his kicking.

The journalist described him as an autonomous person, who drinks a Coke with his feet. Laurent Giammartini, wheelchair-tennis, is described as an accomplished "disabled sportsman". The *L'Équipe* special correspondent Eric Lahmy, spares no superlatives to describe him in his article on September 9th, 1992: as "The wheel-chaired fortress"." He has the technical characteristics needed in tennis coupled with wheelchair manoeuvring and positioning, and the skilfulness, exceptional fitness and brilliance that a good tennis player possesses. Finally, as in all sporting events when the drive for success is high, cheating and doping are not far away. Significant change for these sportsmen and women in search of records and the increasing media exposure, is the systematic introduction, in 1992 of doping checks. Following this introduction, 4 cases of doping were reported at the Barcelona[17] Games and a dozen positive tests performed in 2004 in Sydney (including nine on weightlifters)[18].

By way of conclusion: from a hero-making process to a process normalising athletes

If the Games are a showcase of staging of the disabled body and making visible with a high prevalence of the "social function of the champion" (Hochepied, 2007, pp. 225-244), gradually, the idea of turning these bodies seen as "different", bodies that are "more than competitive" into "mythical heroes" was making its way up. In the 2000's (which equally coincides with the growing importance of the framework in social handing of acknowledgement of rights for persons with disabilities worldwide[19]), accepting their bodies and their identity, in proportion to performance in sports, gave way to real sports competition. To illustrate this, we will give two examples from the newspaper *L'Équipe*.

---

16. "Le roi DAVID et son dauphin" "King David and his heir apparent" in *L'Equipe*, September 16th 1992.
17. See, "Deux nouveaux cas de dopage" "Two new doping cases", in *L'Equipe*, September 17th 1992.
18. For the 600 spot-checks done.
19. See here the various international conventions on disability.

BY WAY OF CONCLUSION

In the year 2000 during the Sydney games, an article presented wheelchair rugby as a contact and manly sport "Those who haven't been spared by life, are not there to give gifts" it describes a very violent contact game that has caused many injuries (fractures, lacerations to the face, black eyes) following numerous collisions of wheelchairs speeding at up to 30km/h with several people ejected from their wheelchairs. Members of the Australian team, known as steelers (men of steel), are bad boys, very reckless and known for their daredevil attitude. This description goes beyond mere virilisation of the athlete: While acknowledging his 'disability' it also reckons his fearlessness, boldness and heroism. An even more striking phenomenon is the involvement of advertise in this process. In the 2004 Paralympic Games in Athens, Chronopost and EDF advertisement with insets depicting some athletes as heroes who have performed feats of sporting excellence. For Chronopost International, this is a great page dedicated to four champions part of its "Athléteam Handisport"[20]: Aladji Ba, Joël Jeannot, Dominique André et Assia El Hannouni. It reads "Well done athletes of the Athléteam Handisport Chronopost International for their participation and the medals won at the Athens Paralympics Games". The photo shows the four athletes including Joël Jeannot sitting in his racechair.

20. "The Athléteam Handisport Chronopost International' won nine medals during the Paralympics.

Similarly, "EDF commends its athlete agents who put a lot of energy into the Athens games". The poster features; swimmer Ludivine Loisean close-up on his smiling face in the pool (gold medal), wheelchair basketball player Frédéric Guyot basketball in one hand and his chair visible, Emeric Morning, table tennis (silver), close-up with his bat, Mor Cyril, fencing, two gold medals and one bronze medal, sitting in his chair claiming victory Marc Soravella in table tennis; Emmanuel Assam, bronze medal, trunk and face, with his foil, Gilles de la Bourdonnaye, table tennis, silver medal, we see his amputated arm while hitting a backhand; Pascal Pinard, swimming, gold medal and two bronze medals, close-up on the pool, Anne Cécile Lequien, two bronze medals in swimming, close-up on breathing in front crawl, Alain Pichon, table tennis, silver medal, hitting a forehand. Here, pictures of athletes in the act of effort in sport are shown, disability is not hidden, the field and awards are given for each participant with his/her full name. Ultimately, all this strives to "normalise" in some way the "disabled" athlete: we shift from "charity business" to "sports business". The "disabled" athlete becomes a brand like any other athlete. He is regarded as a sportsman "in his own right" and not a "sportsman with disabilities".

References

Albert P. (2002 [1968]). *La presse.* Paris: PUF.
Attali, M. (2010). (Ed.). *Sports et médias. Du XIXe siècle à nos jours.* Paris: Atlantica.
Balle, F. (1985). *Médias et société.* Paris: Montchrestien.
Combeau-Mari, E. (2007). (Ed.). *Sport et presse en France (XIXe-XXe siècles)*, Paris: Le Publieur.
Cyrulnik, B. (2001). *Les Vilains Petits Canards.* Paris: Odile Jacob.
Hochepied, F. (2007). La naissance du journal de l'UGSEL 1946-1950 : une vision militante du sport catholique. In E. Combeau-Mari (Ed.), *Sport et presse en France (XIXe-XXe siècles)* (pp. 225-244). Paris: Le Publieur.
Lazarus, R. S. & Folkam S. (1984). *Stress, appraisal and coping.* New York: Springer.
Léséleuc, E. de, Marcellini, A., & Pappous, A. (2005). Femmes/Hommes : la mise en scène des différences dans la couverture médiatique des Jeux Paralympiques. *Sciences de l'Homme et Sociétés,* 73, 45-47.
Loew, G.-L. (2007). *L'amateurisme dans la presse internationale. Les Jeux Olympiques d'Hiver de Sapporo 1972,* Unpublished doctoral dissertation, University Marc Bloch, Strasbourg.
McLuhan, M. (1977). *Pour comprendre les médias (les prolongements technologiques de l'homme).* Paris: Seuil.

Metz, S. (2005). *Analyse du traitement médiatique des personnes handicapées dans le journal « L'Equipe » de 1960 à 2004 : Exemple des Jeux Paralympiques d'été*. Unpublished master's thesis, UFR STAPS, University of Strasbourg.
Paillette, S. Delforce, B & F. Wille (2002). La médiatisation des Jeux Paralympiques à la télévision française. *Les cahiers du journalisme*, 11, 184-199.
Schantz, O. (2005). Leistungsentwicklung bei den Paralympischen Spielen. In R. Burger, D. Augustin, N. Müller, & W. Steinmann (Eds.). *Trainingswissenschaft. Facetten in Lehre und Forschung* (pp. 74-89). Niedernhausen: Schors Verlag.
Tarde G. (1989[1901]). *L'opinion et la foule*. Paris: PUF. Retrieved from: http://www.uqac.uquebec.ca/zone30/Classiques_des_sciences_sociales/index.html

Chapter 3
An International Comparison of the Role of Public Service Broadcasters when Reporting on Disability Sports

Natascha Rother, Inga Oelrichs & Nina Geske

Introduction

Mass media provide important information sources for the public and their impact is growing rapidly, and as such they hold increasing influence in modern society. Through media highlighting, smaller social domains can be picked out and garner the benefits of publicity and attention which they would otherwise have great difficulty attracting. Social areas that are ignored or marginalised in the media can, on the other hand, lose much of their relevance over the middle to long term. Many studies indicate that media representation of people with disabilities is to be characterised as deficient, both quantitatively and qualitatively (Kemper & Teipel, 2008; Bertling, Dyrchs, Giese & Schierl, 2004; Schantz & Gilbert, 2001; Schell & Duncan, 1999; Schierl, 2008; Scholz, 2009; Mürner, 2003). This lack of attention stands in close relation to the economic premises of a highly competitive media market – as it appears that other media contents generate audiences that are more valuable from the advertising perspective.

Under these conditions public service broadcasting (hereafter PSB) providers in particularly have a great social responsibility. They are expected to use their programming mandate to create publicity and attention for socially marginal groups – such as people with physical disabilities – in order to support their integration into society. Of course PSB providers must compete on a dual media market and measure themselves against private broadcasters. They cannot make products that completely ignore the market and must fulfil consumer expectations. Correspondingly, in such strongly competitive media markets with a dual broadcasting character, one must be wary of public broadcasters increasingly focussing on economic concerns and becoming neglectful of their original programming mandate. Two central questions follow from this situation: What is the programming mandate exactly? To what extent are public broadcasters generally obliged to report on people with disabilities and their sporting activities?

This chapter explores the extent to which public broadcasting is bound by legal stipulations to balance the private media deficits in reporting on disabled people and the positions of those responsible for programming. The comparison between the ARD, ZDF[1], BBC[2] and SF[3] is oriented towards the following questions: To what extent is the thematic consideration of people with physical disabilities a mandate in programming and how do the broadcasters themselves understand this mandate and put it into practice? In a first step attention will be drawn to the special importance of sports as an instance of intermediation between people with and without disabilities. In a second step we will reflect on and interpret the basic service agreements in Great Britain, Germany and Switzerland. The third step will be the exploration, through interviews with those in charge of programming, of their own understanding of the integration mandate.

The importance of sport as an intermediary between people with and without disabilities

Sports' reporting provides the opportunity to present disabled people in a positive, performance-oriented light within the programming schedule.

---

1. The ARD and ZDF are Germany's only public broadcasters. The ARD (Arbeitsgemeinschaft der öffentlich-rechtlichen Rundfunkanstalten der Bundesrepublik Deutschland – Association of Public Broadcasting Corporations in the Federal Republic of Germany) is organised federally and comprises a total of nine of the German states. Whilst the ZDF (Zweites Deutsches Fernsehen – Second German Television) is organised centrally.

2. The BBC (British Broadcasting Corporation) is Britain's largest PSB provider as well as the world's largest broadcaster. It was founded in 1926 as the first public service broadcaster and was the example used by many European countries when organising their own PSB providers (Karmasin, 2010).

3. The SF (Schweizer Fernsehen – Swiss Television) belongs to the SRG (Schweizerische Radio- und Fernsehgesellschaft – Swiss Broadcasting Corporation) and broadcasts their German-speaking television programming.

Sport is intimately connected with concepts like fair play, equal opportunity and international understanding. The degradation of prejudices, fear of contact and general social distance as well as an increase in acceptance, tolerance and cooperation can also be promoted (Scheid, 2008). Through reporting and the media multiplier effect, the publicly discernable evidence of the extraordinary physical capabilities of disabled people can support their integration into society. "[...] It [can] be made clear to the public that people with disabilities are a self-evident and highly capable part of society as a whole and are capable of participating in all (even physically challenging) areas of non-disabled life" (Schierl, 2008, p.84). Sport as a subject for reporting is not only an excellent way to form positive connotations in society, it is also well suited to media creation. Hence, from a producer's perspective, it is easy to capture a simple, authentic representation of athletes with a disability.

The Paralympics play a particularly important role as a major media event. "Major sporting events [have] to a large extent become a matter of national ambition, national pride and national identity. Especially live transmissions of sporting events which give the viewer the feeling of participating directly in the experience, thereby creating an emotional investment in winning or losing. Through identification with a team or individual, sports broadcasts can have polarising or integrating effects, whether locally, regionally or nationally. Thus, sport provides an important linking point for a broad range of societal communication" (Dörr, 2000, p.40).

The athletes of the German Disabled Sports Association also see great potential in reporting (as cited in Keuther, 2000, p.168): "We require the active and committed support of the media to show the world that handicapped sportspeople are not second class athletes. Exciting competitions, outstanding results and open human encounters are our contribution to the normalisation of the interaction with disabled people".

Consideration and interpretation of the programming mandates in Great Britain, Germany and Switzerland

PSB providers should pay attention to and take note of relevant circumstances, create transparency, publicity and generate follow-up communication and orientation. In order to fulfil these responsibilities the PSB providers need to supply the population with well-balanced media offerings, which should depict the full range of existing social realities and interests. Communicative diversity is, accordingly, a normative goal for the PSB-providers. It is the foundation of the freedom to develop an opinion in a pluralistic society. The only way for PSB providers offerings to have an integrative effect and provide society with a common foundation for information and communication, is by ensuring that all societal groups, majorities as well as minorities, have their say, and by representing society's full diversity.

In the context of the limited media exposure, of people with disabilities generally and disability sports specifically, we first considered the programming mandate of selected PSB providers, focussing particularly on their integrative function. In a second research step, we investigated the extent to which sports reporting is a legal obligation in the various countries. The results of the secondary analysis will, when taken with the expert interviews that we conducted, reveal the differences and commonalities in the understanding and implementation of the programming mandates.

Great Britain - BBC

The first example to be considered in relation to the integration of people with disabilities in society is Great Britain and its biggest PSB provider, the British Broadcasting Corporation (hereafter BBC). The BBC's mandate has been laid down in a Royal Charter. This means that the BBC's operation is not – as with most broadcasters – established through legislation, but granted through royal dispensation. The present Royal Charter went into force on 1st January 2007. The Charter is always valid for ten years and is renewed in an extensive public process, the Charter Review, in which the extent of the BBC's fulfilment of its mandate is appraised. Besides stipulating its obligations and authority, it also contains the BBC's programming mandate (Latzl, 2010).

The basic framework of the programming mandate is constructed from six Public Purposes as laid down in Article 4 of the Royal Charter (Department for Culture, Media and Sport, 2006a):

The Public Purposes of the BBC are as follows:
- sustaining citizenship and civil society
- promoting education and learning
- stimulating creativity and cultural excellence
- representing the UK, its nations, regions and communities
- bringing the UK to the world and the world to the UK
- in promoting its other purposes, helping to deliver to the public the benefit of emerging communications technologies and services and, in addition, taking a leading role in the switchover to digital television.

In addition to the Charter, the BBC has an Agreement with the Secretary of State for Culture, Media and Sport. It fills out the BBC's legal framework and defines exact goals for each of the Public Purposes, known as the Purpose Remit (Department for Culture, Media and Sport, 2006b, §10; Latzl, 2010).

Sport plays an important role in the BBC's programming mandate. According to public purpose "Bringing the UK to the world and the world to the UK" (Department for Culture, Media and Sport, 2006b, §10) sports transmissions are as much a part of the BBC's programming mandate to inform the domestic audience on international affairs or different cultures and views from outside the UK, as news, documentaries or educational programmes. In the Public Purpose Remit on "Stimulating creativity and cultural excellence" sport of minority interest is explicitly referenced, on which sufficient reports are to be made (BBC, 2007).

The ninth Royal Charter, in 2007, set out a new strategy for the BBC, which, though not redefining the company entirely placed the core competence of public service broadcasting in the foreground through the motto: "Building Public Value" (Troxler, Süssenbacher & Karmasin, 2011; Karmasin, 2010). According to Karmasin (2010) this aspires to create greater value for all, in order to achieve such societal goals as democratic plurality of opinion, participation in or mediation of culture and education, which cannot be achieved through pure market-economic conditions, entirely or in part. In this way the BBC is attempting to actively work against the danger that media might become a pure commodity without intrinsic social or cultural meaning (Kaumanns et al., 2007).

Although the programming mandate does not explicitly mention the integration of people with a disability or reporting on disability sports, the new strategic directions do set concrete goals when it comes to the consideration of people with a handicap. In order to generate public value and thereby meet their public mandate, the BBC's goals include (2004, p. 14):

- in network services on TV and radio, seek to foster greater audience understanding of cultural differences across the UK population – in ethnicity, faith, sexuality, ability/disability and age; show particular sensitivity in reporting issues and events which may be socially divisive

- faithfully reflect modern Britain's diversity in mainstream as well as specialist programmes; set new targets for the on-air portrayal of ethnic minorities, those with disabilities and those from other minorities; monitor usage of, and attitudes to, the BBC by the UK's minorities, listen to their concerns and priorities, and reflect those concerns in the future development of services.

Beyond this, the BBC wishes to be more open to its audience and as a result are encouraging greater contact to ethnic minorities and people with disabilities (BBC, 2004).

Sport is also ascribed an important role in the new strategy (BBC, 2004). The BBC considers their function as a sports reporter to encompass not only premium sports but also support for minority sports, such as the Snooker World Championships and the London Marathon. In the course of boosting minority sports it also takes account of disability sports and reporting on the Paralympics in its scheduling (BBC, 2004). Even if the integration of people with disabilities and disability sports are not referred to directly in the BBC's programming mandate, i.e. the Royal Charter, or in the Agreement, the publication of the BBC's strategic goals indicates that the broadcaster is clearly aware of its responsibility to consider and support minorities and people with disabilities and makes a concerted effort to include them in its programming.

Germany – ARD and ZDF

The BBC shaped the mould for Public Service Broadcasting that the public service systems in other countries were designed after in certain ways (Woldt, 2005). Germany's public service broadcasting systems were also founded in imitation of the BBC model after the end of the Second World War. By organising the broadcasting service into independent public institutions the perceived danger of having a central, state-controlled broadcaster, comparable to the Reich's Ministry of Propaganda, was avoided. This fundamental legal decision still holds for Germany's public broadcasters (Lucht, 2006).

In Germany, the broadcaster's mandate is chiefly organised on two levels. The first is a comprehensive state contract on broadcasting for all federal states and the other is structured through broadcasting laws and state broadcasting contracts, by which individual broadcasting institutions were created for one or more federal states (ARD, 2004). The most vital legal foundation for the dual broadcasting system in the Federal Republic of Germany is the Interstate Broadcasting Treaty (Rundfunkstaatsvertrag) laid down on 31st August 1991[4] (ARD, 2010a). Articles 1 to 5 of this document contain the ARD's state mandate, the ZDF's state mandate, the state licence fee mandate and the broadcasting financing mandate, it thereby sets the basic structure for the public service as well as the private broadcasters (ARD, 2010a).

According to the Interstate Broadcasting Treaty, the public service broadcasting institutions are obliged to create and distribute their content as a medium and factor in informing individuals and the public with an end to supporting their free development of an opinion (LFK, 2010, §11). In this manner they are to fulfil society's democratic, social and cultural needs. Through the comprehensive overview of international, European, national and regional happenings in all important areas of life they are also intended to encourage international understanding, European integration and societal bonds within the Federal Government and its federal states. They are to contribute to education, culture, information, advisory service and entertainment. In carrying out this mandate the public broadcasting institutions are expected to meet the necessary standards of objectivity and impartiality in reporting, providing content that reflects the plurality of opinions and balanced consideration.

The integration and participation of disabled people is presented as a cross-functional responsibility in the ARD's guidelines (2008), which it fulfils in accordance with its mandate. As such, the ARD sees it as "a duty to encourage disabled people, to take account of them in their programming, and to expand their already extensive range of barrier-free programming and offerings for people with disabilities" (ARD, 2008, p. 102). Beyond this, they

---

4. To date the Interstate Broadcasting Treaty has been changed fourteen times. The present, 15th Amendment to the Interstate Broadcasting Treaties was signed on 21st December 2010.

refer to reports and shows by the ARD that consider the lives of disabled people and seek out their participation as an example of the ways in which they fulfil their responsibilities towards disabled viewers (ARD, 2008). In their own mission statement, ZDF also repeatedly affirms the obligation of public broadcasters to support integration, though here more attention is given to the integration of immigrants than to people with disabilities (ZDF, 2008; ZDF, 2010).

In Germany, the much disputed question of basic service provision by public broadcasters means that their related task of sports reporting as a part of this basic service is likewise unclear. The concept of basic services was introduced in 1986 by the Federal Constitutional Court in its 4th judgement on broadcasting and describes "the essential functions of the broadcaster for democratic order as well as for cultural life in the federal republic" (ARD, 2010b). The idiosyncrasy of the public service broadcaster is legitimised by the basic service provision. Basic services are thereby clearly not limited to minimal service provision, but include the entire range of programming in the areas of education, information and entertainment and thereby confirm the comprehensive "classical mandate" of the broadcasting institutions (ARD, 2010b; Lucht, 2006). According to the judgements of the Federal Constitutional Court, public broadcasters play the central role in a dual system when it comes to ensuring comprehensive and balanced information on all areas of society. Sports reporting is included in this special position, since sport provides opportunities for identification in both the local and national levels, making it a necessary part of comprehensive reporting in the court's view.

The importance of sports reporting in terms of integration, identification and value orientation is considered independently by both the ARD and the ZDF in their programming guidelines or mission statement respectively – though with varying aims. The preamble to the current ARD guidelines (2008) contains the introductory premise that public service broadcasters must fulfil a necessary societal function through the entirety of their offerings and services. Implementation of the programming mandate connects the ARD to standards of quality that are grounded in values like human dignity, tolerance and protection of minorities. These high quality standards prevail for all the core areas laid out in the Interstate Broadcasting Treaty and established in the ARD's principles, i.e. information, education, advisory service, entertainment and culture. Thanks to its function in integration, identification and example, the ARD sees sports reporting as not only entertainment, but also as an important and socially relevant part of their mandate to inform (ARD, 2008, p. 77). The broadcaster will therefore "continue to seek out creative solutions for making reports on marginal, recreational and disability sports even more attractive to a large audience" (ARD, 2008, p. 78).

The ZDF's mission statement also considers sports reporting as an important part of their programming in its own right. Besides the transmission of bigger national and international competitions and events the ZDF considers itself to be obliged to make provision for sport's individual and societal functions. It is emphasised that national and international sporting events as well as recreational sports are among those events and activities that can forge societal bonds regardless of age groups, classes and environments (ZDF, 2008). Though it is also increasingly the case that sports in a globalised world are subject to external, commercial and political influences, which could relativize its integrative importance. Concrete events which are to be reported on in Germany include the football World and European Cup as well as the women's football World Cup and both the Summer and Winter Olympics. The Paralympics or other disability sporting events are not considered individually (ZDF, 2010; ZDF, 2008).

Switzerland – SF

Since 1st January 2011 Swiss Television (Schweizer Fernsehen - SF) and the Swiss Radio DRS have merged to become Swiss Radio and Television (SRF). With three television and six radio channels as well as additional multimedia offerings, this, in turn, is the largest branch of the Swiss Radio and Television Corporation (SRG, 2011). The SRG as an association, more specifically a private industry association, is organised privately and run with a public broadcasting license in accordance with stock corporation law (Dumermuth, 2003). The SRG takes 75 percent of its financing through the license fee, public money in other words. This is why the SRG is called a public corporation, privately organised (Dumermuth, 2003).

The SF's public mandate derives from the Federal Constitution (Bundesverfassung), the Radio and Television Law (Radio- und Fernsehgesetz), the Radio and Television Act (Rundfunk- und Fernsehverordnung) and the SRG's concession (Konzession). The mission statement, programme charter and business strategy of the SRG lay down guidelines for the SF. As such, Switzerland's so-called Service Public is provided by the SRG (Schweizer Fernsehen, 2008).

The Federal Constitution defines legislation on radio and television as a matter for the federation, whilst also offering the SRG autonomy when it comes to programming. Furthermore, article 93 of the Federal Constitution stipulates that Radio and Television are to contribute to education, cultural development, free development of opinion and entertainment. They are also expected to portray events appropriately and accurately show the multiplicity of views.

The concession adds detail to the SRG's mandate and reflects the demands and expectations of politics and society (SRG, 2009). It also follows overarching goals, which the SRG are to fulfil through their publicised offerings. The concession also mentions the SRG's integrative function, though this is targeted at foreigners living in Switzerland rather than the integration of people with disabilities. The SRG's programmes are also intended to encourage understanding, solidarity and exchange between areas, language communities, cultures, religions and social groups.

The SRG's programming charter provides values on an internal constitutional level, which are then worked out in greater detail operatively in the individual business units' guidelines. They are expected to ensure that programmes meet high standards of content and form, contributing to the value creation that the SRG must supply as a public service company. Similarly to the BBC's programming charter, the chief editor leads a committee of programme makers in an internal review once a year (SRG, 2006). The company strategy states explicitly that it is to orient its actions towards fulfilling its public service mandate and not towards financial goals. The SRG's activities cannot be operated by the market and its mechanisms alone and are of existential importance to the proper functioning of society and democracy (SRG, 2010b).

The mission statement that SF added to the SRG's general principles and guidelines lays down the fundamentals of the company's mandate, values and actions for all SF employees to follow. According to the mission statement, the SF sees itself as a company "in the service of the public, which considers the interests of majorities as well as minorities" (Schweizer Fernsehen, 2008, p. 7). In order to achieve its goals, it orients itself towards "the highest professional and ethical standards and stands on the pillars of information, entertainment and integration" (Schweizer Fernsehen, 2008, p. 7). Though the PSB provider's integrative function is referenced here, there is no explicit mention of the integration of people with disabilities.

The SRG considers sports to play an important part in its public service mandate. Sport is said to have the potential "to unify people across the boundaries of language and culture" (SRG, 2009, p. 38). Furthermore, particularly diverse sports reporting is aspired to, considering traditional sports that continue to lose importance on the globalised market, like athletics, gymnastics and rowing, besides premium sporting events like the Olympic Games and the Football World and European Cups. The sports reporting strategy rests on its own three-pillar model: to show Swiss athletes, to report on sports events in Switzerland and to broadcast key international events (SRG, 2009).

These main focuses are repeated in the SF's mission statement. The importance of diversity in the content and form of sports offerings is also highlighted, and is to be found on the daily news, in-depth analyses and exciting live broadcasts. Furthermore, integration and societal unity is to be supported through a multicultural programme, which is internationally focussed, yet locally rooted (Schweizer Fernsehen, 2008). SF placing itself "at the service of a tolerant society, which integrates minorities, rather than marginalising them" (Schweizer Fernsehen, 2008).

In summary we can conclude that the integrative function is clearly anchored in SF's public service, but that neither the programming mandate nor their own mission statements make any reference to including people with disabilities in programming. Neither disability sports in general, nor specific reporting on the Paralympics are considered.

Interviews with managers of programming

Analysis of the programming mandates and mission statements of PSB providers in Germany, Great Britain and Switzerland make it clear that some general guidelines are provided for addressing the topic of people or athletes with disabilities, though there are no concrete stipulations concerning the manner and means by which this is to be accomplished. This leaves a lot of room for the broadcasters to act. In order to get reliable statements on the PSB providers' own understanding of their integrative function expert interviews were conducted with representatives of the ARD, ZDF, BBC and SF – all have, or had at the time of interviewing, significant involvement in programming decisions and representation criteria for reporting on the Paralympics.[5] What follows are their main statements:

ARD

As a PSB provider, the ARD considers itself obliged to provide a faithful reflection of the diversity of sports, including disability sports, without taking viewing figures or market share as their only standards. This is the only way to differentiate oneself from the private broadcasters with primarily economic goals and to meet the legally binding integration mandate. Nevertheless, the ARD has noticed increasing public interest in reports on the Paralympics, leading to their decision to increase programming volume on this front.

The guiding concept followed by the ARD when it comes to the Paralympics is much like that used for the Olympics, placing the competitions and the performance of the athletes centre stage. The broadcaster feels that this concept is in line with the needs of athletes with disabilities. "They [the athletes with disabilities] would of course like to be perceived as competitive athletes as any other, so the question must be, who wins the medals, who finishes in which position", said the ARD representative. Though he also emphasised that beyond this, background information is important for the viewers, e.g. competitive class and percent rules, in order to engender a feeling for the performance of the athletes with disabilities. For this reason, the ARD works with experts on location among others, who, like leg-amputee Alexander Spitz, can give direct insights and first hand information as a result of their own disability. Their declared goal is to reach as many viewers as possible, including those without any prior experience of Paralympics reporting. Bridges can be built by integrating this reporting into transmissions on established sports or in the news or magazine feature formats.

---

5. The interviews were conducted with Wolf-Dieter Jacobi (ARD), Peter Kaadtmann (ZDF), Tony Garrett and Paul Cox (both BBC) as well as Notker Ledergerber (SF) in 2010. Therefore the Vancouver Paralympics were one topic of the interviews.

ZDF

To the ZDF reporting on people with disabilities not only fulfils the programming mandate and their own mission statement, but is also the logical consequence of the broadcaster's decades long support of those with disabilities.[6] Disability as a theme is taken up in a wide variety of contexts including sport. Here, the main opportunity taken is the Paralympics, this being the world's biggest and most meaningful disability sports event.

The ZDF representative also emphasised that athletes with disabilities should above all be viewed as competitive athletes in the reports. The point of interest must not be the disability, but the sporting achievement. For the viewer, who is rarely, if ever, faced with disability sports, there is a greater need for clarifying information than in many other sports. This need can be filled within the context of the sporting competitions and by showing the athletes as accomplished personalities.

BBC

As a PSB provider, the BBC also sees itself as being able to deal with topics that commercial broadcasters do not show due to the lack of viewing figures. The BBC can thereby provide impetus and generate interest – as was the case with its Paralympics broadcasts in previous years[7]. But other competitions like the IPC Swimming World Championships, where swimmers with a disability compete, are also shown. Growing interest in disability sports has been observed in the population, which has, in expectation of the Paralympics 2012 being held in Britain, been growing continually the closer the date of the big event draws.

Yet coverage of the Winter Paralympics has been reduced. These did not have enough internal intensity to garner much interest. On the one hand this was due to the lack of British successes[8], on the other there were too few athletes with fascinating personalities or life stories. A choice was made to produce a few, high-quality contributions, rather than many

---

6. In 1964, on the ZDF's initiative, the social organisation "Aktion Sorgenkind" – "Troubled Child Campaign" (now: "Aktion Mensch" – "Human Campaign") was founded. It is funded by lottery and donations and has, among other goals, the intention of increasing public utilities for people with disabilities.
7. The International Paralympic Committee has awarded the BBC with the Paralympic Media Award on several occasions for their reporting on the Paralympics.
8. A look at the contestant and medal statistics supports these claims. Only 12 athletes started for Great Britain in 2010 (British Paralympic Association, 2010), great results were not to be expected. This can be concluded from the medals awarded at the Paralympics 2006 in Turin (GB: Position 17) and 2002 in Salt Lake City (GB: no medals) (Paralympic Movement, 2002; Paralympic Movement, 2006). Great Britain, for climatological and geographic reasons among others, also lacks a marked winter sport tradition.

weaker ones. The alternative would be more likely to damage the image of disability sports than to serve it – images without successful domestic athletes or interesting personalities would hardly speak to the viewers.

The BBC rather likes to cover the athletes' personal stories, which is an easy way for the viewers to identify with the actors. Images of the sporting activities may carry the concealed danger of misunderstandings. For most viewers it is hard to comprehend why, as a result of the various classes of disability, someone who crosses the finish line third might win the gold medal, whilst first place only gets bronze.

SF

Thanks to SF's peculiar position of having a quasi-monopoly over the Swiss TV market, the channel has the unique opportunity among European broadcasters to have all the available rights at their disposal. In principle they could show everything. Of course, in practice, some selection must take place and this orients itself towards internationally important sporting events in which Swiss athletes participate, and sports that have a strong domestic tradition, including marginal sports.

Disability sports are considered less important in this context and are only shown – if at all – during the Paralympics. Since over ten years the Winter Paralympics have only been covered in summaries and a few magazine features covering several sports. Here the athletes were mostly only shown in emotional stories, where the sport was simply used as the context. Since the Swiss competitors are usually not particularly successful[9], there is little pressure to include the day's results in the SF's daily news. "If someone performs badly it may be mentioned briefly, if at all. We want to measure these things by the same standards", said the SF representative, meaning the same standards as athletes without disability. The viewing figures for the Paralympic review revealed little interest among the population, making more in-depth reporting unnecessary.

Conclusive statements

In conclusion, through the comparison of PSB providers legal foundations in Great Britain, Germany and Switzerland, several important differences and similarities between the programming mandates and guidelines can be highlighted. It is clear that the organisational structure and programming mandates are very similar across all the PSB providers. All the broadcasters are obliged to fulfil a public mandate, which could not be fulfilled in the same way by private companies operating under the conditions of a pure market economy. They wish to contribute to free, public development of opinion and improve social solidarity through their programmes in the

---

9. On the medal table for the 2006 Paralympics in Turin, Switzerland took 13th place in Salt Lake City in 2002 this was place 7 (IPC, 2002; IPC, 2006).

fields of information, education and entertainment. Furthermore, an important part of the programming mandates of all PSB providers is their function towards integration. The BBC's and ARD's guidelines even mention the integration of people with disabilities explicitly; the ZDF and SF (as part of the SRG) emphasise the integrative function of the media in reference to immigrants.

Sports reporting plays an important role for all the PSB providers with marginal sports or minority sports requiring airtime besides the top sports. Whilst the BBC and the German PSB providers, ARD and ZDF, actually explicitly include reporting on disability sports in their target agreement, the SF places more importance on traditional sports like athletics and gymnastics, which are losing ever more media interest. The importance of domestic events and participation of domestic athletes is also emphasised. Nevertheless the SF's guidelines also considers integration of minorities to be essential, though it is not stipulated which minorities in particular.

With regard to the main question of this article, the results of the literature analysis would lead one to conclude that, considering the similarity between the PSB providers' programming mandates – which emphasise the integrative function of public broadcasting companies – their programming choices would take account of the Paralympics as a socially relevant global event. Yet the results of the expert interviews reveal clear differences in relation to the reporting of disability sports, or the (Winter) Paralympics specifically. ARD and ZDF consider reporting on the Paralympics to be primarily a matter of fulfilling their integration mandate, SF base their coverage choices more on the expected viewer interest and success of domestic starters in medal winning. Particularly the Winter Paralympics are considered a form of marginal sport by them, lacking sufficient newsworthiness to be dealt with in any detail.[10] The Winter Paralympics are less important for the BBC as well due to their lack of winter sport traditions. However, the BBC usually tries to fulfil its integration mandate by showing other disability sporting events.

From the way in which German channels describe their reporting protocols for the Paralympics, it is clear from their focus on the performance and success of the athletes that they wish to emphasise their integrative potential. Though for them equal importance must be accorded to basic and background information on the athletes, the sports and the modalities of the competition, so that they can appeal to the broadest possible range of viewers and not just to experts or small interest groups. Despite the fact that SF is not limited in terms of broadcasting capacities and the availability of rights, and would as a result be capable of reporting on the Winter Paralympics in depth with live coverage, it has, for a long time, implemented a

---

10. A study by the Institute of Communication and Media Research at the German Sport University Cologne, in which the German, British and Swiss PSB providers' programming structures and contents for news and magazine features were studied during the 2010 Paralympics, is almost completed. A first comprehensive publication is expected in 2012.

reporting concept that limits itself to a summary and a few magazine features. The main emphasis is on human stories of the individual participants, for which the sporting event simply serves as a backdrop. There is less an intention to show the athletes as a part of a performance-oriented society, than to create an emotional attachment. The BBC takes a similar approach, considering the performance of the British athletes at the Winter Paralympics too weak to merit airtime, so that – if they show anything at all – the athletes are considered as personalities with interesting stories.

Finally, we can conclude that reporting on disability sports, and particularly the Paralympics, is an excellent opportunity for PSB providers to fulfil their programming mandate to support integration, thereby legitimising their financing through license fees. There is nevertheless no guarantee that disability sports will be shown by public service broadcasters. They do not have a unified understanding of the extent to which their public programming mandate should be seen as an obligation to report on the Paralympics. This is clear from both the broadcasters' own programming guidelines and the managers of programming interviewed. It will be interesting to observe how the PSB providers in the researched countries evolve their transmissions on the Paralympics and other disability sporting events going forward. Sustainable development in the integration of people with disabilities will only be possible if the broadcasters institutionalise on-going reports on disability sports rather than covering them only on exceptional occasions.

References

ARD (2004). Rechtsgrundlagen. Retrieved January 10, 2011 from: http://www.ard.de/intern/organisation/rechtsgrundlagen/-/id=54434/13b80qd/index.html

ARD (2008). Bericht 07/08. Leitlinien 09/10. Retrieved January 10, 2012 from: http://www.daserste.de/service/ARD-Leitlinien08-2.pdf

ARD (2010a). Rundfunkstaatsvertrag. Retrieved January 10, 2012 from: http://www.ard.de/intern/organisation/rechtsgrundlagen/rundfunkstaatsvertrag/-/id=54384/tpmigr/index.html

ARD (2010b). Grundversorgung. Retrieved January 10, 2012 from: http://www.ard.de/intern/organisation/rechtsgrundlagen/grundversorgung/-/id=54408/1cm440t/index.html

BBC (2004). Building Public Value. Renewing the BBC for a digital world. Retrieved February 27, 2011 from: http://downloads.bbc.co.uk/aboutthebbc/policies/pdf/bpv.pdf

BBC (2007). BBC Public Purpose Remit: Stimulating creativity and cultural excellence. Retrieved February 27, 2011 from: http://www.bbc.co.uk/bbctrust/assets/files/pdf/about/how_we_govern/purpose_remits/creativity.pdf

Bertling, C., Dyrchs, S., Giese, S. & Schierl, T. (2004). Die überregionale Berichterstattung der Paralympics in Sydney und Salt Lake City. Ein medialer Vergleich zu den Olympischen Spielen. In I. Herwald-Schulz (Ed.), *Innovatives Sportsponsoring: Behindertensport als Marke* (pp. 23-36). Düsseldorf: VDM Verlag.

British Paralympic Association (2010). Team Handbook Vancouver 2010. Retrieved February 27, 2011 from: www.paralympics.org.uk/core/core_picker/download.asp?id=1224&filetitle=Vancouver-+2010+Team+Handbook

Department for Culture, Media and Sport (2006a). Broadcasting. Copy of Royal Charter for the continuance of the British Broadcasting Corporation. Retrieved February 27, 2011 from: http://www.bbc.co.uk/bbctrust/assets/files/pdf/about/how_we_govern/charter.pdf

Department for Culture, Media and Sport (2006b). Broadcasting. An Agreement Between Her Majesty's Secretary of State for Culture, Media and Sport and the British Broadcasting Corporation. Retrieved February 27, 2011 from: http://www.bbc.co.uk/bbctrust/assets/files/pdf/about/how_we_govern/agreement.pdf

Dörr, D. (2000). *Sport im Fernsehen: Die Funktionen des öffentlich- rechtlichen Rundfunks bei der Sportberichterstattung* (Volume 8). Frankfurt a. M.: Peter Lang Europäischer Verlag der Wissenschaften.

Dumermuth, M. (2003). Regulierung des öffentlichen Rundfunks in der Schweiz – Erfahrungen und Perspektiven. In P. Donges & M. Puppis (Eds.), *Die Zukunft des öffentlichen Rundfunks: Internationale Beiträge aus Wissenschaft und Praxis* (pp. 292- 310). Köln: Herbert von Halem.

IPC (2002). Medal Standings. Retrieved February 27, 2011 from: http://www.paralympic.org/Sport/Results/reports.html?-type=medalstandings&games=2002OPWG&sport=all

IPC (2006). Medal Standings. Retrieved February 27, 2011 from: http://www.paralympic.org/Sport/Results/reports.html?-type=medalstandings&games=2006PWG&sport=all

Karmasin, M. (2010). Public Value: Zur Genese eines medienstrategischen Imperativs. In M. Karmasin, D. Süssenbacher & N. Gonser (Eds.), *Public Value: Theorie und Praxis im internationalen Vergleich* (pp. 11-25). Wiesbaden: VS Verlag für Sozialwissenschaften.

Kaumanns, R., Siegenheim, V. & Knoll, E. (2007). *BBC – value for money and creative future: Strategische Neuausrichtung der British Broadcasting Corporation*. Munich: Reinhard Fischer.

Kemper, R. & Teipel, D. (2008). *Selbst- und Fremdkonzept von Leistungssportlern mit Behinderung*. Cologne: Sportverlag Strauß.

Keuther, D. (2000). Zur Bedeutung des Leistungssports im Deutschen Behinderten-Sportverband & National Paralympic Commitee Germany. In V. Scheid & H. Rieder (Eds.), *Behindertensport – Wege zur Leistung: Optimierung der Leistungsentwicklung im Behindertensport im Sinne der Rehabilitationsziele* (pp. 165- 181). Aachen: Meyer und Meyer.

Latzl, D. (2010). Großbritannien. In R. Christl & D. Süssenbacher (Eds.), *Der öffentlich-rechtliche Rundfunk in Europa. ORF, BBC, ARD & Co auf der Suche nach dem Public Value.* (pp. 201- 242). Vienna: Falter.

LFK (2010). Staatsvertrag für Rundfunk und Telemedien (Rundfunkstaatsvertrag - RStV-). Retrieved February 27, 2011 from: http://www.lfk.de/fileadmin/media/recht/04-2010/13.RStV-April2010.pdf

Lucht, J. (2006). *Der öffentlich-rechtliche Rundfunk: ein Auslaufmodell? – Grundlagen – Analysen – Perspektiven.* Wiesbaden: VS Verlag für Sozialwissenschaften.

Mürner, C. (2003). *Medien- und Kulturgeschichte behinderter Menschen: Sensationslust und Selbstbestimmung.* Weinheim: Beltz Verlag.

Schantz, O. J. & Gilbert, K. (2001). An Ideal Misconstrued: Newspaper Coverage of the Atlanta Paralympic Games in France and Germany. *Sociology of Sport Journal*, Vol. 18, 69-94.

Scheid, V. (2008). "Behinderte helfen Nichtbehinderten" – eine ungewöhnliche Initiative mit beachtlicher Wirkung. In F. Fediuk (Ed.), *Inklusion als bewegungspädagogische Aufgabe. Menschen mit und ohne Behinderung gemeinsam im Sport* (pp. 143-158). Baltmannsweiler: Schneider.

Schell, L. A. & Duncan, M. C. (1999). A Content Analysis of CBS's Coverage of the 1996 Paralympic Games. *Adapted Physical Activity Quarterly*, Vol. 16, 27-47.

Schierl, T. (2008). Dreamteam Medien und Sport? Chancen und Risiken der Kommerzialisierung des Mediensports. In M. Schweer (Ed.), *Sport in Deutschland. Bestandsaufnahmen und Perspektiven* (pp. 75-94). Frankfurt/Main: Peter Lang.

Scholz, M. (2009). *Presse und Behinderung. Eine qualitative und quantitative Untersuchung.* Wiesbaden: VS Verlag für Sozialwissenschaften.

Schweizer Fernsehen (2008). Leitbild. Retrieved February 27, 2011 from: http://www.srgssr.ch/fileadmin/pdfs/Leitbild%20SF.pdf

SRG (2006). Programmcharta. Retrieved February 27, 2011 from: http://www.srgssr.ch/fileadmin/pdfs/Programmcharta%20der%20SRG%20SSR.pdf

SRG (2009). Service Public – Für Sie erbracht. Für Sie erklärt. Retrieved February 27, 2011 from: http://www.srgssr.ch/de/publikationen/service-public/

SRG (2010a). Gesetzgebung über Radio und Fernsehen. Retrieved February 27, 2011 from: http://www.srgssr.ch/de/srg/rechtliche- grundlagen/gesetzgebung/

SRG (2010b). Unternehmensstrategie 2011: Kommentierte Fassung. Retrieved February 27, 2011 from: http://www.srgssr.ch/fileadmin/ pdfs/Unternehmensstrategie%20SRG%20SSR%202011.pdf

SRG (2011). Unternehmenseinheiten. Retrieved February 27, 2011 from: http://www.srgssr.ch/de/srg/unternehmensstruktur/unternehmenseinheiten/

Troxler, R., Süssenbacher & D., Karmasin, M. (2011). Public-Value- Management als Antwort auf die Legitimationskrise und Chance für neue Strategien der Mehrwertgewinnung. In H. Gundlach (Ed.), *Public Value in der Digital- und Internetökonomie* (pp. 121-143). Köln: Herbert von Halem.

Woldt, R. (2005). Öffentlich-rechtlicher Rundfunk im internationalen Vergleich. Fragestellungen, Methoden, Fallbeispiele. In C. Ridder, W. Langenbucher, U. Saxer & C. Steininger (Eds.), *Bausteine einer Theorie des öffentlich-rechtlichen Rundfunks* (pp. 293-310). Wiesbaden: VS Verlag für Sozialwissenschaften.

ZDF (2008). Selbstverpflichtungserklärung des ZDF 2009-2010. Retrieved February 27, 2011 from: http://www.unternehmen.zdf.de/fileadmin/files/ Download_Dokumente/DD_Das_ZDF/Selbstverpflichtungserklaerung_Programm_Perspektiven_2009_2010.pdf

ZDF (2009). ZDF-Staatsvertrag vom 31. August 1991, in der Fassung des Zwölften Staatsvertrages zur Änderung rundfunkrechtlicher Staatsverträge. Retrieved Retrieved February 27, 2011 from: http://www.unternehmen.zdf.de/uploads/media/zdf- staatsvertrag_neu.pdf

ZDF (2010). Selbstverpflichtungserklärung des ZDF 2011-2012. Retrieved February 27, 2011 from: http://www.unternehmen.zdf.de/fileadmin/files/Download_ Dokummente/DD_Das_ZDF/Fernsehrat/ ZDF_Selbstverpflichtungserklaerung_Programmperspektiven_2011-2012.pdf

Chapter 4
Disability Sport in the German Media

Christoph Bertling

Introduction

Like most other world media organizations the sports sections of the German media almost always concentrate on the beautiful and seemingly perfect athletic sports bodies for reporting and so called entertainment purposes. While keeping the above point saliently in mind this chapter attempts to highlight what happens in respect to beauty and the experience of beauty when we deal with sports that have superficially less aesthetic appeal in the media and in society in general. In relation to this argument questions need to be asked. Do such sports become devalued? Indeed, what happens when, precisely, imperfection and not beauty is foregrounded through media representations? In response to these and other questions this chapter will present some basic theories and also some of the most important findings of research projects in the area of athletic beauty myths and forms of disability.

Describing the relationship between the Paralympics and the Media

Following the empirical research already completed on the presentation of the Paralympics in the German media[1], one can draw the following conclusion: although disabled sport is not totally neglected, the coverage of the Paralympics, especially in the German print media, is deficient in quality and quantity (Kauer-Berk/Bös 2004; Herwald-Schulz 2004; Schierl *et.al.* 2004, Bete 2005) as compared with the reporting of able-bodied sport. A larger study in support of these studies and completed by the author analysed quantitative and qualitative aspects of the coverage of both Olympic and Paralympic sport events in Sydney 2000 and in Salt Lake City 2002 in the daily newspapers *Die Welt, Frankfurter Allgemeine Zeitung* and *Süddeutsche Zeitung*[2]. All articles published during the Olympic Games and the Paralympics in Sydney and Salt Lake City were analysed. The data gained from the coverage of the two Olympic Games served as a benchmark and a total of 2,047 articles were included in the research (Bertling *et.al.* 2004).

The analysis of number and length of the articles lead to some decisive findings. While almost 2,000 articles were published on the Olympics and Paralympics, only a total of 82 focused on the Paralympics. The articles on the World Disabled Games were considerably shorter: while an average article about the Olympic Games was about 90 lines long, the average length of an article about the Paralympics was only 57 lines. This indicated that the Paralympics only received about 2.7 percent of the overall Olympic Games and Paralympic Games time coverage.

The emphasis on results displayed in the coverage of the Paralympics assumes an inadequate view of the Paralympic Games that is primarily cost-orientated. A coverage that concentrates primarily on results can be produced inexpensively. This kind of reporting is "fed" by news agency information and is therefore economically efficient, thereby usurping complex and costly research which is not required. While some very important sport events, which are highly attractive for recipients, are worth an individual coverage for the purpose of image creation and differentiation, compared to other competitors, and are therefore worth a higher effort in expense and staff, the analysed quality newspapers did not seem to view the need and justification for similar effort for the coverage of the Paralympics. The coverage of the World Disabled Games is in fact dominated by the journalistic presentation forms known as "news notice" and "report". Whereas almost half of the press coverage on the Olympic Games used these styles, they made up almost 2/3 of the articles within the coverage of the Paralympics.

---

1. There is almost no coverage of disability sports in Germany. Therefore I will in this chapter concentrate on the media coverage of the Paralympics.

2. There are few larger empirical works examining the TV-coverage of the Paralympic Games. However, one such study is currently in process at the Department of Mass Media and Sports at the German Sports University Cologne (DSHS).

The use of photos is a further indication for the meaning of the Paralympics as media content in the press. Pictures attract attention, perception, emotion and involvement. In sport coverage press pictures primarily have an emotional, entertaining and/or illustrative function and often use eroticism, general aesthetics (especially athletic body composition) or even humour (sarcasm). Indeed, because of the meaningful and serious nature of disabled sport, press coverage aimed at visual presentation of eroticism, aesthetics and entertainment does not seem suitable in broad journalistic understanding. These thoughts lead to a differentiated approach, in quantity and quality, when dealing with Paralympics press photos.

Pictures are in fact implemented very scarcely in the coverage of the Paralympics. Only a quarter of the articles are accompanied by pictures, whereas every second article about the Olympic Games received visual support. A closer quantitative inspection revealed that even if press photos were used they tended to cover the disability or keep it in the background. Shadow techniques or similar artificial effects are commonly used to distract from disabilities; or people and portrayals are chosen that don't picture the disability.

Plate2: Press Picture of a Paralympics wheelchair athlete

Source: Süddeutsche Zeitung [16.3.2003; 12.3.2002]

For the print media, it has been proven that even quality newspapers cover the Paralympics inadequately; this is despite the increasing social importance of disability in the German cultural contexts. For example, in the areas of sport politics, sport organisation and sports sponsorship the coverage uses mainly economic production patterns and language.

Criteria for Selection as used by Sport Journalists

The question arises then as to why journalists strongly neglect disabled games in the mass media despite their increasing social relevance? One possible explanation – as already mentioned – might be found in the perceived discrepancy between the entertainment and aesthetic value of disabled sport. In other words as the presentation of sport is increasingly orientated on affective public needs the appearance of disabled sport might be seen as a cause of irritation or limited entertainment value and therefore not suitable for editorial concepts in the sport department of a newspaper.

Other studies have revealed that sport journalists in particular when compared to their colleagues in other departments feel uncomfortable when dealing with disability. In actuality, Kauer-Berk/Bös (2004) points out that visible physical disability regularly causes 'psycho-physical' reactions such as fear, affective excitement and discomfort among non-disabled people. This might be a root cause of the problem with reporters.

In mass communication which is normally characterized by entertainment and advertisement, physical and mental disablement and individuals with physical handicaps are rarely seen and almost classed as 'taboo'. Infact, our society is dominated by a constant search for entertainment and the honouring of the near perfect and beautiful body, and therefore any disability is viewed as a loss of the basic right of perfection. Imperfection is thus not totally tolerated by the media in our society.

One might expect that the perception of discrepancy towards disabled bodies would emerge as especially powerfully with sport journalists who produce pictures of perfect, idealized bodies as part of their professional routine. Kauer-Berk/Bös speak of an "aesthetic-sexual aversion" that some viewers feel and that mainly appears when disabilities related to face, skin or cerebral paretic paralysis are visible.

The apparent helplessness to include disabilities in a sport context is problematic and serious. A questionnaire among sport journalists has shown that 7.2 percent are of the opinion that high-performance sport of disabled people should be abolished and while asked by the German disabled sport youth and the University of Mainz only three percent of athletes during the Paralympics in Sydney 2000 judged the coverage as "very good", whereas twelve percent marked the media presentation as "very bad/insufficient". In order to better comprehend the criteria of selection used by sport journalists in the press and therefore find an answer to the question whether or not a problem between media sport and disability really exists, the German *'department of sport and media'* conducted telephone interviews with 41 sport desks at German daily newspapers (Schierl/Bertling 2006). The questionnaire covered the following three main areas of interest:

1. Do sport journalists themselves judge the coverage of the Paralympics as being deficient?
2. Do sport journalists assume interest among readers or do they regard the Paralympics as uninteresting for their readership?
3. Do sport journalists find an aesthetic and entertaining presentation of disabled sport in the media problematic/difficult?

The interviews revealed that sport journalists themselves claim that the coverage of the Paralympics is deficient and stereotyped. When answering the question: What a good coverage of the Paralympics might look like? 82.9 percent of the journalists saw the necessity of using all journalistic forms of presentation within a good coverage. However, the results of the content analysis pointed out that only the styles "news notice" and "report" are actually used. A further highly interesting finding is that sport journalists see that a main criterion for good coverage of disabled sport is fulfilled when a priority is set on the athlete's personal history. This result gains importance when the questioning of athletes revealed that disabled sportsmen do not want to be subjects of the media because of their history, but rather for their sporting results. This signals a discrepancy in understanding between disabled athletes and journalists. Or putting it more concretely: A good coverage of the Paralympics in the eyes of the journalists would be considered partly discriminatory by the majority of disabled athletes, as they would be presented as disabled and not as world class athletes with a disability.

Another interesting result concerns the interest of readers: It has even been shown that sport journalists produce inadequate presentations of the Paralympics however; they consider their readers to be highly interested. Indeed, 70 per cent responded positively to the question: Do you think your readers are interested in a detailed coverage of the Paralympics? Taking both the previous results into consideration, a conclusion concerning the disproportion between entertainment and disability can be drawn because the press presents the World Disabled Games as deficient and stereotypical in spite of the fact that sport journalists assume high interest among their readers. One reason for this discrepancy may be found in the fact that journalists find it problematic to introduce disabled sport into the concept of media sport which mainly emphasizes aesthetic and entertainment aspects.

This assumption is supported by the answers to the interview question: Do you think problems concerning aesthetic/entertaining aspects exist in disabled sport? More than half approved this question. Keeping the aspect of social desirability in mind one can assume that a number of journalists would tend to negate the use of photos than approve to it – so that probably far more than 50 percent of the journalists are aware of a problem considering aesthetics and entertainment. If that's the case then why are they not doing anything about changing their work practices?

Valuation of press photos by Journalists, Readers and Disabled Athletes

While the two previously mentioned studies only looked at the communication perspective and therefore merely considered the recipient's view anticipated by the communicator a third study has analysed how the photo journalistic presentation of various aspects of disabled sport is valued by journalists, recipients and especially by the disabled sportsmen themselves. So the question is: Can we evaluate photo journalism as "good" and "less good" or "adequate" and "less adequate" in relation to visual presentations of disabled athletes or does the evaluation of a quality journalistic photo vary among the differing groups?

For this research an online survey was answered by 30 participants from each of the following groups: readers of sport sections, disabled athletes and sport journalists from German daily newspapers (Schierl/Bertling 2006). A document with 50 professional photos of the Paralympics was attached to the questionnaire. The participants were asked in accompanying letters to grade the pictures of the World Disabled Games for their suitability for presentation of the Paralympics. The newspaper journalists, sport section readers and athletes graded the pictures from their personal point of view concerning the information and entertainment value using the common German school grading system (1 to 6). Grade 1 describes "very well suitable" and grade 6 "not at all suitable". Participants were explicitly informed that the apparent technical quality of the picture was to be ignored.

The criteria of evaluation then served as data basis for a cluster analysis that aimed at sorting the pictures into specific groups according to the above mentioned evaluation. The cluster analysis was utilised as it is an explorative model of data analysis in order to create groupings within research objects that reveal the highest possible homogeneity concerning those characteristics on which the research is based. The clusters should however, differ from one another as much as possible concerning the mentioned characteristics. This kind of analysis is explorative as the content structure of the cluster is assumed as a *priori* but created with the help of the data itself. The clusters were:

Cluster 1	*Still, static*
Cluster 2	*Disability visible (unconventional perspective)*
Cluster 3	*Dynamic*
Cluster 4	*Long Jump*
Cluster 5	*Emotions*
Cluster 6	*Cheer*

Comparing the groups that judged the photos reveals that the evaluation of the clusters 1, 3, 4, 5 and 6 was very homogenous among the groups. Especially between journalists and recipients, even different tendencies were not apparent in the evaluation and the evaluation by disabled athletes did not significantly differ from the other groups – with the exception of cluster

2. A significant difference between the questioned groups only appeared in cluster 2. The photos showing the disability of the pictured athlete very clearly and openly were graded far more positively by the athletes than by journalists and recipients who expressed a certain aversion towards those pictures that either emphasised the disability more or showed it from an unconventional perspective. This result correlates with the findings of the first study: that sport journalists prefer to cover disabilities or leave them in the background just as they prefer to show those pictures with 'conventional disabilities'.

However, in my opinion a more important finding was gained by evaluating each cluster showing that those clusters containing pictures that are entertaining and create emotion and excitement are preferred by all three groups in comparison to static and informative clusters. This clearly marks the real problem in visual presentation of disabled sport: the perception of sport is – maybe because of common use of media and its offers – set equally at the same level as gratification such as entertainment, aesthetics and (primarily positive) emotions. Sport transmitted by the media is supposed to entertain and the same is expected from disabled sport. But on the other hand entertainment is not simply produced with the basic materials of 'disabled sport', as this has decisive features that cause disturbance. This calls for definitely more innovative and creative strategies that combine the media attention – also required by the athletes – and the necessary respect towards the protagonists and their matters of concern.

Conclusions

The studies presented herein convey first hints about the common and maybe also the desired visual presentation of disabled athletes in the media. I would like to emphasize that we have considered the presentation of disabled sport at the Paralympics and have therefore analysed *the top event* on the world disabled sports calendar. Keeping this in mind it is a truism to point out that disabled sport on a lower level largely remains without any kind of publicity what-so-ever.

The results lead to the claim that it is viewed as problematic when media sport increasingly focuses on its combination of entertainment and aesthetics as socially important subsystems of sport because disabled sports are systematically discriminated against. A comparison of the coverage of the Olympic Games and the Paralympics has shown that the World Games of disabled sport are not only neglected in forms of quantity but are also produced in an insufficient quality by the media.

The results of the second research reveal that disabled sport's devaluation in quality and quantity has already had great effects on sport journalists' selection. Sport journalists are already aware of a high discrepancy of disabled sport in comparison to "normal" media sport as it has considerable deficits in their opinion within the constantly increasing aspects of entertainment and aesthetics.

Even if an adequate presentation of disabled sport is intended, insufficient knowledge can seem to cause inadequate presentation in many cases. 40 percent of the journalists are of the opinion that good coverage will focus on the athlete's personal history. However, this does not support the social acknowledgment of world class athletes with disabilities, but rather opposes their efforts to be accepted as efficient and equal members of society. Talking about the consequence of focusing on achievement too much as well as focussing on the personal fate Peter Radtke, the president of the *Working Group Disability and Media* (ABM) points out:

> "On the one hand people with disabilities are presented who, from a common point of view, accomplish extraordinary achievements. Reports about results of disabled sport events such as the Paralympics subjecting single action (e.g. "Blind person conquers the Nanga Parbat", "Single legged cycles around the world") belong to this category. [...] Standards for non disabled are here used for people who are usually seen outside of these standards. On the other hand the people are mainly presented as dependent on help, appealing consciously or not consciously for the sympathy of the non involved."
>
> (Radtke, 2003 p. 9)

Different quality criteria within the visual presentation of top athletes with disabilities refers to the fact that great discrepancies already exist between the sport journalists' and top disabled athletes' views. While groups agree that photos displaying disabled sport should be dynamic and emotional, there are severe differences in the presenting the disabilities.

It is significant that the picture of disabled athletes in the media is deficient both in quantity and quality. Radtke further points out that between able bodied and disabled there remains 'parallel worlds which still exist in society'. Despite improvement in the past disabled and non disabled still don't connect in everyday life. In this situation the media is often the only, and not to be underestimated, informative source about life and the capabilities of disabled people. Whatever the so called non disabled in society learn about people with disabilities, they usually learn from the media and under these circumstances the picture of mankind being conveyed by the media is crucial to the future of Paralympic and disabled sport.

References

Bertling, C., Dyrchs, S., Giese, S., & Schierl, T. (2004). Die überregionale Berichterstattung der Paralympics in Sydney und Salt Lake City. Ein medialer Vergleich zu den Olympischen Spielen. In I. Herwald-Schulz (Ed.), *Innovatives Sportsponsoring. Behindertensport als Marke* (pp. 23-36). Düsseldorf: VDM.

Blödorn, M. (1988). Das magische Dreieck: Sport – Fernsehen – Kommerz. In W. Hoffmann-Riem (Ed.), *Neue Medienstrukturen – neue Sportberichterstattung?* (pp. 100-129). Baden-Baden/Hamburg: Nomos.

Bosshart, L. (1984). Fernsehunterhaltung aus der Sicht von Kommunikatoren. *Media Perspektiven*, 8, 644-649.
Bosshart, L. (2000). Models und 'Mäuse'. Die Symbiose von Sport, Ästhetik und Ökonomie. In J. Wermke, (Ed.), *Ästhetik und Ökonomie. Beiträge zur interdisziplinären Diskussion von Medienkultur* (pp. 153-162). Wiesbaden: Wesdeutscher Verlag.
Bryant, J., Comisky, P.W., & Zillmann, D. (1977). Drama in Sports Commentary. *Journal of Communication*, 3, 140-149.
Bryant, J., Brown, D., Comisky, P.W., & Zillmann, D. (1982). Sports and Spectators: Commentary an Appreciation. *Journal of Communication*, 1,109-119.
Cloerkes, G. (2001). *Soziologie der Behinderten*. Heidelberg: Schindele.
Früh, W. (2002). *Unterhaltung durch das Fernsehen. Eine molare Theorie*. Konstanz: UVK.
Früh, W. (2003): Triadisch-dynamische Unterhaltungstheorie (TDU). In W. Früh, & H. J. Stiehler (Eds.). *Theorie der Unterhaltung. Ein interdisziplinärer Diskurs* (pp. 27-56). Köln: Herbert von Halem Verlag.
Gleich, U. (2000). Merkmale und Funktionen der Sportberichterstattung. *Media Perspektiven* 11/2000, 511-516
Gumbrecht, H. U. (2005): *Lob des Sports*. Frankfurt am Main: Suhrkamp.
Gumbrecht, H. U. (1998). Die Schönheit des Mannschaftssports: American Football – im Stadion und im Fernsehen. In G. Vattimo, & W. Welsch (Eds.). *Medien-Welten Wirklichkeiten* (pp. 201-228). Paderborn: Wilhelm Fink.
Haselbauer, T. (2004). *Olympiastadt Athen – Ein Sport- und Reiseführer*. Göttingen: Die Werkstatt.
Herwald-Schulz, I. (Ed.) 2004. *Innovatives Sportsponsoring – Behindertensport als Marke*. Düsseldorf: VDM.
Kauer-Berk, O. & Bös, K. (2004). Behindertensport in den deutschen Medien. In I. Herwald-Schulz (Ed.). *Innovatives Sportsponsoring – Behindertensport als Marke* (pp. 13-20). Düsseldorf: VDM.
Korf-Sage, K. (1999). *Medienkonkurrenz auf dem Werbemarkt*. Berlin: Erich Schmidt Verlag.
Kroeber-Riel, W., & Weinberg, P. (1999). *Konsumentenverhalten* (7th ed.). München: Franz Vahlen.
Radtke, P. (2003). Zum Bild behinderter Menschen in den Medien. *Aus Politik und Zeitgeschichte* 8/2003, 7-12
Schierl, T., Bertling, C., & Giese, S. (2003). Paralympics und Olympische Spiele 2000 und 2002 im medialen Vergleich. Institut für Sportpublizistik (unpublished manuscript). Sporthochschule Köln, Cologne.
Schierl, T. (2004a): Ökonomische Aspekte der Sportberichterstattung. Mögliche Strategien der ökonomisch motivierten Mediatisierung des Sports. In T. Schauerte, & J. Schwier (Ed.): *Die Ökonomie des Sports in den Medien*. Köln: Herbert von Halem Verlag.

Schierl, T. (2004b): *Visualisierung des Sports*. Köln: Hernert von Halem Verlag.
Schierl, T. (2005): Ästhetik als Mehrwert journalistischer (Sport-)Fotographie. In M. Lämmer, & T. Nebelung (Ed.): *Dimensionen der Ästhetik*. (pp. 170-185). Sankt Augustin: Academia Verlag.
Schierl, T., & Bertling C. (2006). Die Thematisierung von Behinderung im Rahmen der visuellen Sportkommunikation. *Zeitschrift für Kommunikationsökologie und Medienethik*. Ausgabe 1/2006, 49-56.

Chapter 5
Disability Sport in the Swiss Media

Sue Bertschy & Jan D. Reinhardt

Introduction

A total of 4,200 athletes from 148 countries competed for 472 medals at the Summer Paralympics in Beijing 2008 and the Games saw a total of 279 new World records and a total of 339 Paralympic records broken and overall Swiss athletes won 11 medals of which 3 were gold. Altogether 5,600 representatives from the media visited Beijing and reported on the Paralympic Games. The above simple data indicates that the Paralympic Games have eventually become a regular sports and media event with a strong emphasis on the performance of individual athletes and nations which are supported by large scale sports media coverage. In this manner the way mass media represent elite athletes with a disability substantially affects the Swiss societal attitude towards those persons and persons with disabilities in general and thus may generate or reduce disability in a social sense (Barnes, Mercer, & Shakespeare, 1999).

The objective of the study as presented here in this chapter is to draw a representative picture of elite sports practiced by athletes with disabilities as it is depicted in the Swiss daily newspapers. We performed a newspaper content analysis, i.e. an eight month study of the Olympic and Paralympic daily newspaper coverage, was performed to analyze the coverage of the Paralympics in relation to the Olympics and the thematization of disability sports as high-performance sport. To specify and structure the reality of the Swiss media in this study the "news values-theory" (Emmerich, 1984; Schulz, 1990; Staab, 1990) and the agenda setting theory (McCombs & Shaw, 1991; Wernecken, 2000) were applied. At this juncture it might be wise and fortuitous to view the following brief quote by (Hug, 2009) who states quite categorically that:

> "I want to be respected as an athlete and not admired as a disabled person".
>
> (Hug, 2009)

High-performance Sport in the Mass Media

Can sports practiced by disabled athletes also be classed as high-performance sport? This question was answered by the Swiss disabled elite athlete Beat Bösch with a clear "Yes" and:

> "I would like to show that in spite of our disability we are competitive athletes"[1].

This comment was supported by Patricia Keller who commented:

> "I want to prove that I'm not a poor disabled girl - I can reach great sports achievements"[2].

Recognition for such athletic accomplishments seems to be a common desire among the respondents. Indeed, Hardin B. & Hardin M. (2004) ascertain that:

> "Talk about [that] person's athletic abilities or the team's athletic accomplishments, and it's OK to mention a disability, because that's what makes the person who he or she is, but you don't focus on it".

There are more or less large differences between sports news coverage as regards able-bodied and disabled athletes, because

> "(....) newspapers seem to have a rather low opinion regarding the media value of sports for persons with disabilities. Indeed, sports for such people is still marginalized and trivialized in most newspapers (Schantz & Gilbert, 2001)".

When reporting on the success or failure of athletes, sports journalists use specific categories such as the athlete's or the team's abilities, goals, training methods and family support, psychological aspects, as well as luck and coincidence. Content analyses of sports news coverage by Gleich (2000) indicates in the following quote:

> "....that journalists rely mainly on a standardized and reduced, primary explanation repertoire referred to the individual"[3].

---

1. Statement from Beat Bösch, 2 x Bronze medal winner at the Paralympics in Beijing 2008. (Bühler, 2008)
2. Statement from Patricia Keller, Junior World Champion. (Marti, 2008)
3. Own translation.

An extensive analysis of reasons for success or failure rarely takes place. Often, reasons are given that can be personally attributed to the athlete, such as motivation, psychological strength, and goals reached. Journalists usually attribute internally, i.e. referring to personal factors to justify athletic accomplishments; external factors are rarely used (Henning, 1990; Möller & Brandt, 1994).

Existing research indicates that sport reporting is focusing more and more on entertainment and visual/personal aspects of athletes and are therefore more often portrayed in the media than others (Beck & Kolb, 2009). This focus combined with the demand to satisfy the need for entertainment may be a reason for the systematic separation of news about sports of disabled athletes from other sports events. Studies clearly demonstrate that sports media not only neglect disability sports quantitatively, but also report on a qualitatively lower level (DePauw, 1997; Golden, 2002; B. Hardin & Hardin, 2004; M. Hardin, 2003; Kauer & Bös, 1998; Schantz & Gilbert, 2008; Schierl & Bertling, 2006; Schönau, 2008; Spanny, 2007). In addition, if the focus is placed on the personal destiny or fate of an athlete it does not promote the social value of an elite athlete with disability. Moreover, it obstructs the athletes' efforts to be noticed as a high performing member of the society.

Sports news coverage satisfies the need of entertainment; hence, the entertainment value of news coverage is of utmost importance; more especially, the elements of entertainment such as personalization, dynamics, or the aesthetic value of an event which clearly influences reporting about physically disabled athletes (Becker, 1983; Hackforth, 1987). The increasing 'shift of sports media coverage to include aesthetic and entertainment aspects contributes greatly to the neglect of specific domains like disability sports' (Schierl, 2004).

The following section of the chapter captures and describes the picture, which daily newspapers draw of disability high-performance sports in comparison to the high-performance sports of able-bodied athletes. The specific aims were to analyze how Swiss media reported on the Paralympic Games and how those reports differ from those on the Olympic Games; and whether the sports accomplishments of athletes with a disability are recognized by the media as high-performance sports.

Methods

The national and regional Swiss-German daily print newspapers were taken as the main observational unit. In order to make comparative statements about the reporting between the Olympic (OG) and Paralympic Games (PG) two clusters were formed and media contents were examined over a period of eight months. The selected time interval was six months before the Games, the month of the Games, and one month later. The articles were selected by drawing a stratified random sample considering 56 newspapers with national and regional range and a total number of 1,626 articles on Olympics and 467 articles on Paralympics were found. In total 280 articles were selected.[4]

Quantitative (Früh, 2007) as well as qualitative (Mayring, 2008) content analyses were chosen as part of the methodical approach. The category system (Rössler, 2005) was constructed theory driven and includes 78 variables. Different types of variables were developed:

- The first group represents general and formal variables, such as the date of publication and type of newspaper.
- The second group of variables assessed the specific content of the article assigning rubric, genre, subject, etc. as well as news value factors: ethnocentrism, dynamics and negativism, stereotype, prominence, sports career and type of sports.
- The third group contains variables to measure high-performance sports issues. These issues were coded qualitatively and different constructs were formed to identify high-performance sport and the analysis of sports accomplishment (e.g. high-performance sport: nutrition, training methods, professional, coach, manager, sponsors, sports psychologist and performance goals were evaluated).

Data collection and Analysis

The authors and two graduate assistants evaluated the news articles with regard to each major theme, coverage, achievement - and failure criteria. An inter-coder reliability test (Früh, 2007) yielded a 0.89 reliability rate for articles coded. Kappas ranged from 0.88 to 0.9 and Früh estimates a rate of 0.75 as a good outcome.

The differences regarding the newspaper reports on Paralympic and Olympic Games were analyzed with contingency tables (Chi square test and analysis of the association with Phi and Cramer's V). For metric variables t-tests were applied, if the conditions were satisfied. Otherwise, the Man-Whitney test was applied. The confidence level is, if not otherwise mentioned, $\alpha=0.05$. Statistical Package for Social Sciences (SPSS 14.0) was used for quantitative analysis.

Results

A total of 467 articles about the Paralympic Games and 1,626 articles about the Olympic Games were found in the Swiss-German daily newspapers from which 280 articles were randomly selected. Overall, in newspapers

---

[4]. For detailed information's about the methods consult the thesis of (Bertschy, 2009a).

with national coverage (e.g. NZZ; 20 Minuten) twice as many articles about the Olympic Games were found than articles about Paralympic Games, however, in the regional press it was equally reported on both events.

The article length is significantly (p=0.014) shorter in articles about the Paralympic Games. Accordingly, the average characters per article are 3,198 for the Paralympics and 3,726 for the Olympics. Interestingly, while the Olympic Games are reported only in the sports section of the newspaper, the Paralympic Games articles are sometimes published in local or regional sections of newspapers using this report form in two-thirds of cases.

Journalists very often wrote about both events in the Paralympic articles: While in the Olympics articles only 4% also refer to the Paralympics, 43% of the Paralympic articles share the attention with the Olympic Games and these findings are significant (Chi-squared test: 76.47, df: 1, p<0.001, Phi:0.529).

Table 1: Frequency table for reported sports

Months before Games	Month		Sports	
			1st mention	2nd mention
6	February	OG	Track-and-field	Different sports
	March	PG	No reports	
5	March	OG	Mountain Bike	Swimming
	April	PG	Handbike	Different sports
4	April	OG	Beach Volley	Canoe/Kayak
	May	PG	Handbike	Track-and-field
3	May	OG	Track-and-field	Wrestling
	June	PG	Track-and-field	Different sports
2	June	OG	Track-and-field	Mountainbike
	July	PG	Track-and-field	Different sports
1	July	OG	Track-and-field	Different sports
	August	PG	Track-and-field	Different sports
Games	August	OG	Different sports	Tennis
	September	PG	Track-and-field	Different sports
1+	September	OG	Different sports	Tennis
	October	PG	Handbike	Track-and-field

Contents were also evaluated in terms of their international, national and regional perspective and noticeably ethnocentric aspects about sports reporting are not identical for the Paralympic and Olympic Games. Reports with a national athlete focus are written in general by 46% of the articles. However, 10% more articles for the Olympics than for the Paralympics athletes with a national focus were written. Also 32 % of the articles on the Paralympics focused on the regional perspective and this is 9% fewer than those written about the Olympics. The Swiss media reported a wider variety of sports in their coverage of the Olympics than on Paralympics. For the latter, the focus was mainly on track-and-field events (see table 1). Whereas every victory by the Olympians was considered news-worthy in the Swiss press, not every medal was reported about Paralympic athletes, e.g. a bronze medal in archery was not reported or published in the Swiss media.

Interestingly, the majority of journalists use similar description forms to refer to "high-performance sports" throughout their reporting. In particular, the indicators "training", "professional", "coach" and "performance goals" dominate in the relative frequency analysis. Three indicators also revealed a significant difference between Olympic and Paralympic Games, e.g. "training", "professional" and "coach" were significant. Indicators requiring more detailed investigation such as nutritional habits of the athlete and professional sports support (manager, sponsor, sport psychologist) are mentioned rather marginally in all texts (see table 2 below).

Table 2: Indicator variable high-performance sport

High-performance sport	OG		PG		Phi, p (of Chi-Square)
Indices in %, n=185	yes	no	yes	no	
Nutrition	4.4	95.6	1.1	98.9	-0.103, p=0.162
Training	**42.9**	**57.1**	**25.5**	**74.5**	**-0.183, p=0.013**
Professional	**25.3**	**74.7**	**8.5**	**91.5**	**-0.224, p=0.002**
Coach	**27.5**	**72.5**	**14.9**	**85.1**	**-0.154, p=0.036**
Manager	4.4	95.6	3.2	96.8	-0.032, p=0.668
Sponsor	6.6	93.4	6.4	93.6	-0.004, p=0.954
Sport psychologist	2.2	97.8	1.1	98.9	-0.045, p=0.542
Performance goals	52.7	47.3	41.5	58.5	-0.113, p=0.125

Bold: Significant indicator

A sum index of terms used to describe high-performance sports per article was composed to compare the average number of criteria mentioned between the Paralympics and Olympics. The terms defined for high-performance sports are mentioned in Olympic articles on average with 1.66 criteria per article (sd=1.5), in Paralympic articles only with 1.02 (sd=1.25). This difference is highly significant (p=0.01).

Analysis of Sports Performance

Preparation for a competition, the competitive conditions, the climatic conditions, sports facilities and competitors themselves were frequently mentioned as success criteria in articles. Who were the main competitors and how well was the athlete prepared or why was he/she at all successful? From 11 evaluated criteria only two differ significantly, those of preparation and competition conditions. Whether someone has a disability pension and therefore does not have to work has never been brought up in an article (see table 3 for precise details).

Table 3: Indicator variable success criteria

Success criteria Values in %, n=185	OG yes	OG no	PG yes	PG no	Phi, p (of Chi-Square)
Preparation	28.6	71.4	10.6	89.4	-.226, p=0.002
Professionalism	9.9	90.1	6.4	93.6	-.064, p=0.382
Familial support	3.3	96.7	3.2	96.8	-.003, p=0.968
Character	8.8	91.2	6.4	93.6	-.046, p=0.536
Competition situation	16.5	83.5	4.3	95.7	-.201, p=0.006
Sport aid	2.2	97.8	3.2	96.8	-.031, p=0.677
Pension	0	100	0	100	no value
Association	7.7	92.3	8.5	91.5	0.015, p=0.838
Sponsor	3.3	96.7	3.2	96.8	-.003, p=0.968
Competitor	12.1	87.9	8.5	91.5	-.059, p=0.423
Convalescence	8.8	91.2	4.3	95.7	-.092, p=0.210

*Phi bold: Significant

As failure criteria the strongest competitors and the competition situation are often mentioned. Convalescence and professionalization in sports show significant differences between Paralympics and Olympics. Clear differences are observed under the criterion "convalescence": This topic is not as much reported as by athletes with a physical disability (3.2%) than non-disabled athletes (12.1%) (see table 4).

Table 4: Indicator variable failure criteria

Failure criteria Values in %, n=185	OG yes	OG no	PG yes	PG no	Phi, p (von Chi-Square)
Preparation	5.5	94.5	3.2	96.8	-.057, p=0.441
Professionalism	0	100	4.3	95.7	0.146, p=0.047
Familial support	1.1	98.9	1.1	98.9	-.002, p=0.982
Character	0	100	2.1	97.9	0.103, p=0.162
Competition situation	13.3	86.7	11.7	88.3	-.025, p=0.738
Sportaid	1.1	98.9	3.2	96.8	0.072, p=0.328
Pension	0	100	0	100	No value
Association	2.2	97.8	5.3	94.7	0.082, p=0.266
Sponsor	0	100	0	100	No value
Competitor	19.8	80.2	13.8	86.2	-.080, p=0.279
Convalescence	12.1	87.9	3.2	96.8	-.168, p=0.022

*Phi bold: Significant

Again a sum index for success and failure criteria was composed. For the Olympics an average of 1.01 (sd=1.6) criteria occur per article. For the Paralympics the occurrence is only 0.59 (sd=1.24) for success criteria (without assistance and pensions). This difference is not significant (p=0.101). For failure criteria the result is different, although still not significant (p=0.587). Thus for the Olympics an average 0.55 failure criteria are mentioned per article (sd=0.88) and for the Paralympics 0.49 (sd=0.99) are mentioned frequently.

Do Swiss newspapers report differently on the Paralympic Games than on the Olympic Games?

The evaluation shows that daily papers portray a rather one-sided picture of the Paralympic Games. Swiss-German daily newspapers published three times as many articles on the Olympics as on the Paralympics. This was particularly noticeable in national daily papers. One reason for this discrepancy is that the Olympic Games obviously hold a higher national interest. Shorter contributions tend to be written about the Paralympics rather than Olympic Games. However, some approximation of the article length may be assumed if we consider the results of a German study conducted in the year 2006 as baseline material (Schierl & Bertling, 2006). Our results are in line with studies conducted in other countries (Golden, 2002; M. Hardin, 2001; Schantz & Gilbert, 2008; Schierl, 2004; Spanny, 2007).

While articles on the Paralympics are almost exclusively written as reports or short messages, the spectrum of reporting formats was substantially larger in the case of the Olympics. Again, these results are in line with other studies. For example, Schimanski (1994) indicated that disability sports news coverage in American and German daily newspapers increased from 1984 to 1992. However, 80% of the articles about disability sports are messages and short messages. Furthermore, athletes from other countries receive consideration in Swiss daily newspapers. Indeed, every fifth report on the Olympic Games mentions athletes from other countries. The successes and records of Phelps and Bolt were mentioned extensively. The Paralympic sample does not show a similar tendency, with Swiss newspapers reporting almost exclusively on Swiss successes. Regarding news-worthiness the disabled athlete obviously has to be successful *and* Swiss.

In contrast to the results of the studies from Beck (2006) and Kauer & Bös (1998), the Paralympic sample rarely reports on swimming competitions. This can be attributed to the fact that only one Swiss swimmer participated in Bejing. However, again the journalists focused on specific types of sports with track-and-field events dominating. In Switzerland disabled athletes do not often receive appreciation for their efforts or an appropriate appraisal of their ambitious efforts and the sacrifices made to reach their goals which are similar to those of able-bodied athletes. Heinz Frei, Swiss elite disabled athlete, formulated this very accurately:

> "I don't have to defer myself behind a super league soccer player. My efforts are just as intensive and professional, possibly even more substantial. I cannot afford escapades. My body is my capital and therefore I have to manage daily life with discipline and responsibly".
>
> (Bertschy, 2009b)

The results clearly show that the performance aspects are less discussed in the investigated Paralympic sample. If these are discussed in reports, then it is with a focus on goals, training units and coaches. Nutrition habits, professional sports support (manager, sponsor and sport psychologist) were mentioned only marginally.

In summary, this pioneer study was limited to the Swiss-German press. For further research the study could be expanded to other media as well as increasing the time period to a longitudinal study which contains also non-Olympic/Paralympic years. An additional research area could be to what extent para-social relations (Beck, 2006) between disabled athletes and able-bodied recipients are possible. Which indicators play a role for para-social relations and can they be applied to both groups? Comparisons of future reporting about the Games 2012 in London with the base-line-results determined for Switzerland 2008 will be possible. Also a Monitoring of the UN-Convention (2006) is possible for appropriate "reporting over persons with disabilities in a consistent manner".

Conclusions

Based on this study and the reporting about the Olympic Games the Paralympic Game still have a shadowy media existence. There are clearly less articles about the Paralympic Games, and the article length is smaller and it is more focused on specific kinds of sports and athletes. Accomplishment, success and failure criteria from elite athletes with a disability are represented in an undifferentiated manner. The focus is still often on destiny and stereotypes.

It is still an open question as to whether Swiss sports news coverage is following the trend of standardization of press reports on the Paralympics and the Olympics as shown in some studies in other countries. Only the analysis of the reporting about London 2012 will prove to what extent a positive trend in Swiss reporting can be stated. It is hoped that the present study as highlighted in this chapter may contribute to this trend, by helping journalists to identify and overcome certain implicit categorizations and stereotypical conceptions in their reporting (destiny=report). The goal of the UN-Convention to achieve fair representations in the reporting about disabled people (athletes) which does not differ from the representation of other sub-populations, is still far away. Although, perhaps it now appears to be within sight.

References

Barnes, C., Mercer, G., & T. Shakespeare (1999). *Exploring Disability. A Sociological Introduction.* Cambridge: Polity Press.

Beck, D. (2006). *Der Sportteil im Wandel. die Entwicklung der Sportberichterstattung in Schweizer Zeitungen seit 1945.* Bern, Stuttgart, Wien: Haupt.

Beck, D., & S. Kolb (2009). (Eds.) *Sport & Medien.* Zürich/Chur: Rüegger Verlag.

Becker, P. (1983). Sport in den Massenmedien. Zur Herstellung und Wirkung einer eigenen Welt. *Sportwissenschaft, 13,* 34.

Bertschy, S. (2009a). *Die Presseberichterstattung über Sportler mit einer körperlichen Behinderung: Paralympics und Olympics im Vergleich.* University of Fribourg, Media & Communications Sciences.

Bertschy, S. (2009b). Interview with Heinz Frei. Nottwil.

Bühler, R. (2008, September 25). Medaillengewinner zeigen ihre Gefährte. *Neue Luzerner Zeitung,* p. 22.

DePauw, K. (1997). The (In)visibility of DisAbility: Cultural contexts and "sporting bodies". *Quest, 49*, 416-430.
Emmerich, A. (1984). *Nachrichtenfaktoren: Die Bausteine der Sensationen. Eine empirische Studie zur Theorie der Nachrichtenauswahl in den Rundfunk- und Zeitungsredaktionen.* Saarbrücken: Verlag der Reihe.
Früh, W. (Ed.). (2007). *Inhaltsanalyse Theorie und Praxis.* Konstanz: UVK.
Gleich, U. (2001). Sportberichterstattung in den Medien: Merkmale und Funktionen. In G.Roters, W. Klingler & M. Gerhards (Eds.), *Sport und Sportrezeption* (pp. 167-182). Baden-Baden: Nomos.
Golden, A. (2002). Analysis of the dissimilar Coverage of the 2002 Olympics and Paralympics: Frenzied pack journalism versus the empty press room. *Disability Studies Quarterly, 23* (3), 75-95.
Hackforth, J. (1987). Publizistische Wirkungsforschung: Ansätze, Analysen und Analogien (pp. 15-33). In J. Hackforth (Ed.), *Sportmedien & Mediensport. Wirkungen Nutzung Inhalte der Sportberichterstattung.* Berlin: Vistas.
Hardin, B. & Hardin, M.M. (2004). The 'Supercrip' in sport media: Wheelchair athletes discuss hegemony's disabled hero. *Sociology of Sport Online, 7*(1).
Hardin, M. (Ed.). (2001). *Disability and Sport: (Non)Coverage of an Athletic Paradox.* New York.
Hardin, M. (2003). Marketing the acceptably athletic image: wheelchair athletes, sportrelated advertising and capitalist hegemony. *Disability Studies 4*(23).
Hardin, M. (2006). Disability and sport: (Non)coverage of an athletic paradox (pp. 577-585). In A. A. Raney, & J. Bryant, (2006). *Handbook of sports and media.* Mahwah, NJ: Lawrence Erlbaum Associates.
Henning, A. (1990). Dem Spieler fehlte jegliches Selbstvertrauen. Ursachenerklärung des Sportjournalisten für sportlichen Erfolg und Misserfolg. *Brennpunkte der Sportwissenschaft, 4*(1).
Hug, M. (2009). Marcel. Retrieved February 2nd from: http:home.datacomm.ch/marcelhug/sport.html
Kauer, O., & Bös, K. (1998). *Behindertensport in den Medien.* Aachen: Meyer & Meyer.
Mayring, P. (2008). *Qualitative Inhaltsanalyse, Grundlagen und Techniken.* 10. Auflage. Weinhelm, Basel: Beltz.
Marti, W. (2008, 3 July). Ich will beweisen, dass ich keine arme Behinderte bin. *Blick,* p. 10.
McCombs, M. & Shaw, D. (1991). The agenda setting function of mass media. In D. Protess & M. McCombs (Eds.), *Agenda Setting. Readings on media, public opinion, and policymaking* (pp. 1726). Hillsdale, NJ: Lawrence Erlbaum Associates.
Möller, J., & Brandt, H. (1994). Personale und situationale Leistungsbegründung in Fernseh- und Zeitungsberichten. *Medienpsychologie,* 6(4), 266-277.
Rössler, P. (Ed.). (2005). *Inhaltsanalyse.* Konstanz: UVK.

Schantz, O. J., & Gilbert, K. (2001). An Ideal Misconstrued: Newspaper coverage of the Atlanta Paralympic Games in France and Germany. *Sociology of Sport Journal, 18*, 69-94.

Schantz, O. J., & Gilbert, K. (2008). French & German newspaper coverage of the 1996 Atlanta Paralympic Games. In K. Gilbert, & Schantz, O. J. (Eds.), *The Paralympic Games: Empowerment or Side Show?* (pp. 34-47). Maidenhead: Meyer & Meyer.

Schierl, T. (2004). *Die Visualisierung des Sports in den Medien.* Köln: Hernert von Halem Verlag.

Schierl, T., & C. Bertling (2006). Die Thematisierung von Behinderung im Rahmen der visuellen Sportkommunikation - Empirische Befunde zur Darstellung der Paralympics, den Weltspielen des Behindertensports in den Printmedien. *Zeitschrift für Kommunikationsökologie und Medienethik, 1*, 49-56.

Schimanski, M. (1994). *Behindertensport in der deutschen und amerikanischen Tagespresse 1984-1992. Unter besonderer Berücksichtigung der Paralympics. Eine Analyse anhand ausgewählter Printmedien.* Unpublished master thesis, Köln: Sport University Cologne.

Schönau, C. (2008). *Behindertensport und Darstellung in den Medien. Medienanalyse der Winter-Paralympics 2006 Turin.* Saarbrücken: VDM Verlag.

Schulz, W. (1990). *Die Konstruktion von Realität in den Nachrichtenmedien.* (Vol. 2). Freiburg, München: Alber-Broschur.

Spanny, B. (2007). *Behindertensport: Medienpräsenz aus Sicht von Sportler und Journalisten.* Saarbrücken: Verlag Dr. Müller.

Staab, J. F. (1990). *Nachrichtenwert-Theorie. formale Struktur und empirischer Gehalt* (2nd ed.). Freiburg, München: Alber-Broschur.

UN (2006). *Convention on the Rights of Persons with Disabilities.* Available at: http://www.un.org./esa/socdev/enable/rights/convtexte.htm., accessed on 8th January 2009.

Wernecken, J. (2000). *Wir und die anderen... Nationale Stereotypen im Kontext des Mediensports.* Berlin: Vistas.

Chapter 6
The Austrian Press

Media Coverage during the 2008 Beijing Paralympic Games

Julia Lebersorg & Maria Dinold

Introduction

The history of Austrian disability sport activities began in the early nineteen fifties and the establishment of the parent organisation (ADSF) started at the time of the pioneers in 1958 and took its name 'the federation of the war invalids' (Österreichischer Versehrtensportverband – ÖVSV) from the individuals who had been wounded in the World War II. Previously and shortly after the end of the Second World War skiers with disabilities started to practise their sport despite their amputations and founded their own disability unit in the Austrian skiing federation (ÖVSV, 1988, p.11). After this period the movement continuously grew to maturity to a "time of perfection" and finally became the modern disability sports organisation which is now the "Austrian Disability Sports Federation" – hereafter the ÖBSV in 1989.

The ÖBSV is an association with several sections including sport for amputees, the blind, people with cerebral palsy, mental disability, hearing impairment, and wheelchair users. Today, the Federation includes about 7,000 members who are enrolled in 101 clubs. Since 2003 the ÖBSV has been a full member of the Federal Sports Organisation (BSO) and is funded by the state (ÖBSV, 2008, pp. 22-30). Twelve years ago in 1998 the Austrian Paralympic Committee was established in order to assist in the delegation for disability sport competitions and to get more funding and supporters.[1]

At the last summer Paralympics in Beijing 2008 Austria was represented by 38 athletes and 24 coaches or persons in support. The Austrian team competed in 8 sports: Athletics, Cycling, Table Tennis, Wheelchair Tennis, Sailing, Shooting, Swimming, and Equestrian. They were successful in getting six medals and finished thirty third in the medal standings and the most successful Austrian athlete was Thomas Geierspichler who won one gold and one bronze medal.[2]

Austrian Media Coverage

According to Schauerte (2007) television has a key function in media coverage in sports because it sets the focus on selected topics, by providing live TV-broadcasting. The main task of print media is often limited to reporting and commenting on the events. As such the media concentrates mostly on top class European sports such as skiing, ski jumping, tennis, car racing, football and athletics (Weigl, 1994, pp.65-66). All other sports appear in the media through their involvement at major sporting events for example during the Olympic Games. A study of the Austrian public television company during the years 2003 and 2005 suggested that the percentage of the sport reports in TV was between 5.3% and 6.6% (ORF, 2008). Compared to the print media –according to the sport chief editor Christoph Wikus, the newspaper 'Kronen Zeitung' did cover a percentage of 17.64% for sport reports in only one issue in 2009. Clearly it is not possible for the newspapers to keep up with the speed of the television coverage; however, the strength of the print media allows the possibility of in depth verbal analysis (Klemm 2007) which the television coverage does not always provide. Indeed, the main topics of the newspapers are dependent on the popularity of the sport, the number of members in a sport, the viewers at a television broadcast and their interest in a national sport star. Quality newspapers try to arouse interest in the reader by picking out new topics as a central theme (Schauerte, 2007).

---

1. Österreichischer Behindertensportverband 2006. Available at: (http://www.oebsv.or.at/de/menu_main/der-verband). (accessed 10th November 2008).

2. Österreichisches Paralympisches Komitee-Peking 2008. Available at: (http://www.oepc.at/peking2008_dev/Dasist Peking2008QQid-252-216.html). (accessed 12th December 2008).

In 1998 Bös and Kauer asserted that disability sport and media coverage are still at the beginning of their cooperation. These authors identified three ways of representing people with disabilities in newspaper publications. The first kind of reporting deals with the latent fear of anomalism and disability which is targeted in order to make the reports more interesting and more profitable, according to the motto 'sensations sell'. The second type of report focuses on the individuals with a disability and may be demonstrated on mainly two topic areas. One is the medical reason of the disability, which takes the centre of attention and from the second perspective the individual with a disability is presented as a victim who constitutes his/her right of existence with special achievements (Bös & Kauer, 1998).

In order to check the actual situation a comparative study was carried out regarding the manner of Austrian media coverage during the Paralympic Summer Games in Beijing 2008. The research wanted to find out how the themes and report styles vary in Austrian press today? The question refers to the situation whether it remains the same as in 1998, or if the focus, interests, and reporting styles have changed over the last 10 years.

Methodology of the study

The investigation compared the German and Austrian print and visual press during the time when the Beijing Paralympics 2008 took place in China. The main focus of the research was placed on how the reports about the events and about disability sport in general differentiated between the German and the Austrian media. Special attention was given to the reports and results of selected Austrian newspapers. The newspapers which were chosen for the investigation had been collected and surveyed with the support of several people, who were available at any time. The choice of independent Austrian newspapers differed significantly from each other as to provide some variation in the results. The main selection criteria to choose the newspapers for our study relied on the high numbers printed in each run. Therefore the newspapers 'Kronen Zeitung', 'Kurier' and 'Kleine Zeitung' where utilized for this study. The German papers were also selected accordingly to the above criteria. They were: 'Süddeutsche Zeitung', 'Frankfurter Allgemeine Zeitung' and the 'Bild'. The observation period of the six newspapers ranged from August 31st 2008 to September 21st 2008 as this seemed to be the time when most of the reports were published.

The most important perspective of the research was to generate relevant categories and this was viewed as a central element of the qualitative content analysis of the newspapers. In order to make an exact analysis of the data the material was divided into formal (quantitative) and content related (qualitative) categories. The decisions for choosing the categories were influenced by the criteria of general sport reports and more importantly in relation to disability sport reports.

The quantitative categories of the examined print media were:

- *Number of contributes during the specified time period* (counting the number of articles during the observation period).
- *Length of the articles* (measured by the number of words in the article).
- *Number of texts supported by pictures* (counting the number of pictures within an article).
- *Number of front pages* (counting how often the newspaper had a contribution about the Paralympics on their front page).
- *Departmental allocation* (possible departments were: politics, chronicle, culture, medicine, society, sport, album, front pages, "Tribüne").
- *Genre of the article* (possible genres were: report, comment, interview, coverage, announcement, newsflash, critical review, review, portrait).
- *Placement of the article in the respective part of the newspaper* (possible places: front part, middle part, back part).
- *Placement on the respective page* (central or border area)

The qualitative categories of the examined print media were:

- *Emotional effects*
  Emotions, compassion or feeling pity for the person specifically, which is often used in disability sport reports. Terms like "admirable", "poor", or the description of the accident, fate and similar notions appear regularly. This category considered passages in the texts where the journalist tried to arouse emotions in the reader.

- *National orientation*
  Sport reports in general are often more interested on sport events in their own country respectively and on their 'own' athletes rather than on other nationalities. It seemed interesting to find out if we have the same phenomenon in disability sport. The analysis was divided into national – international – China.

- *Success/Failure*
  This category evaluated if the the reports portrayed success success or failure or if the issue did not influence the report style.

- *Personal background information*
  Readers of popular newspapers expect that the reports include elements which show the athlete as a private person which was additional to sport specific information. The graduation was made between no private elements – few private elements – many private elements.

- *Report style*

A specification of report styles in this context is given by Bös & Kauer (1998):

1. "sensations sell" – playing with the fear of abnormity
2. "disability" – the essential thing is the medical reason of the disability

3. "special achievement" – the person with the disability renders his/her right to exist by a special achievement Additionally, a neutral rating was included in this category.
4. *Doping*
The doping reports were classified as whether the media mentioned the word doping or not.

In this context it is important to mention that doping in disability sport is categorized into four different kinds of doping: wrong classification, intake of illegal substances (doping agent), boosting (specific method of doping), and technical doping (Jahnke and Schüle 2006, pp.166-167).

Results

In this chapter it is possible to present only a selection of results of the study and to emphasize the most significant ones. It is the intention to show the tendencies of the Austrian newspapers with a side view to the selected German newspapers according the above quantitative and qualitative categories. It was interesting to check if Austrian newspapers followed a central line so as to indicate whether they differed much between each other.

Results according to the quantitative categories

The total number of articles which were included in the survey from Austria and Germany was 110. The Austrian newspapers had 53 articles during August 31st and September 21st 2008 and 57 articles were reviewed from the German newspapers. This comparison seems very balanced in a percentage of 52% (D) to 48% (A). With-out doubt, the proportion of the newspapers inside one country was less equal. The daily newspaper 'Kleine Zeitung' (28 articles) published more than the half of all contributions. This was also reflected in the category *length of the articles*: 4,800 words from totally 8,500 could be counted in "Kleine Zeitung".

Another interesting result was found in the *number of Paralympic articles on front pages*. Austrian newspapers had contributed three to four articles on front pages. All three articles were on the front page of 'Kleine Zeitung', furthermore on 21st of September the cover picture was dedicated to the gold medal success of Thomas Geierspichler. 'Kleine Zeitung' also dominated the categories *resort* and *genre*. These categories achieved their diversity through the newspaper. Most of the articles in *resort* were classified to the area of sports. 'Kleine Zeitung' had three more classifications called album, "Tribüne", and a front page report. At the category *genre* report and newsflash were the most dominant classifications which made altogether 86% of all contributions. The rest of the classifications were almost only from 'Kleine Zeitung'.

As mentioned previously the reason for the use of photographs was to focus the attention of the reader on the respective article. Indeed, pictures lose this effect if there are too many of them on one page, for example in the German newspaper 'Bild'. This paper had the fewest number of articles but the highest number of pictures were in selected German newspapers. In Austria 64 pictures could be counted in all three daily newspapers during the observational time period. This seems to be a good result compared to Germany with 56 pictures from all three newspapers. However, it is also important to mention that 47 of 64 pictures from the Austrian newspapers had appeared in 'Kleine Zeitung'. All contributes were accompanied by one picture per article, at least. Additionally, the placements of the articles were central and legible for the reader.

Results according to the qualitative categories

(Older) literature reports regarding disability in sport refers to the commiseration-problem. Therefore text passages of the category *emotions* were checked if they included expressions which should produce emotions and in particular aspects of commiseration. Keywords like 'fate', 'very poor' and 'accident reports' where used as indicator for such texts. Although the rating in this category can be seen as extremely dependent on the subjective perception of the evaluator such passages occurred rarely. As their frequency depends somehow on the length of the articles these key words were used in 'Kleine Zeitung', 'Süddeutsche Zeitung' and 'Frankfurter Allgemeine Zeitung' more often than in other publications.

The category *report style* indicated the same direction. Most reports were, as similar to regular sport reports, dominated by a neutral report style. Articles were classified to belong into the category *special achievement* when the amount of talking about specific performance was more detailed than usually used.

The category *personal background information* was almost non-existent and only a few reports contained private stories or more detailed personal background. The topic *doping* was not very often addressed in the selected Austrian newspapers. Just four Austrian articles enclosed the issue of doping, and if it occurred it was mentioned additionally. A few more articles about doping issues could be found in German press. The reason for this was probably a German doping affair during the Paralympics 2008.

National orientation and *success/failure* were interestingly identified as the two most important and significant categories. *National orientation* was subdivided into national, international and China related issues. Germany had a relatively equal distribution at this point. Indeed, 48% of all German contributions were about German athletes, the rest was subdivided into international articles and reports about China. 'Süddeutsche Zeitung', was clearly responsible for the balanced German result in this category. In Austria articles addressing national concerns reached 76% which is more than two thirds of all contributions. All three daily newspapers concentrated their sport reports on national athletes and among the 53 Austrian articles seven of them dealt completely with international athletes and four with Chinese content.

The category *success/failure* was relatively evenly spread in Austrian and German papers. In fact 50% of all Austrian articles promoted successful reports and only 10% of reports related to a failure. Indeed, 'Kleine Zeitung' published 12 success reports from all 29 articles. The other two Austrian newspapers 'Kronen Zeitung' and 'Kurier' concentrated most of the time on successful reports and it was evident that negative coverage was avoided. Only seven articles were published about failure and these articles just informed the reader about the defeat of the athletes without any criticism levelled at them.

Conclusions

In order to evaluate how the reporting style in Austrian print media has developed over time it is important to summarize that the only significant categories *national orientation* and *success/failure* may contribute to this assessment. The Austrian Press during the summer Paralympics of 2008 was primarily orientated towards the national participants and their results in the Games. To report about the success of "their own" athletes was indeed a dominant focus throughout and it appears as though the journalists liked to write about winning Austrian athletes.

Furthermore, it can be stated that there are big differences between the reportage of the daily newspapers in Austria more especially the 'Kleine Zeitung' which showed decisive differences when compared to the 'Kurier' and 'Kronen Zeitung', the 'Kleine Zeitung' which had more and longer articles and showed more diversity and higher priority to the articles which included photographs. In short this study indicated that the Austrian press is very interested in reporting about disability and Paralympic sport although the diversity and the volume of that reporting depends solely on the selected daily newspaper and its political persuasion and editorial staff.

References

Bös, K. & Kauer, O. (1998). *Behindertensport in den Medien*. Aachen: Meyer & Meyer.
Jahnke, B. & Schüle, K. (2006). *Entstehung und Entwicklung der Paralympischen Winterspiele: Örnsköldsvik 1976 bis Turin 2006*. Köln: Sportverlag Strauß.
Klemm, T. (2007). Sportjournalismus in den Printmedien. In T. Schierl (Ed.), *Handbuch Medien, Kommunikation und Sport* (pp. 324-339). Schorndorf: Hofmann.
ORF (2008). Statistik. Retrieved October 21, 2008 from: http://www.statistik.at

Österreichischer Behindertensportverband – ÖBSV (Ed.). (2008). *Golden Moments. 50 Jahre Österreichischer Behindertensportverband.* Wien: Österreichischer Behindertensportverband.
Österreichischer Versehrtensportverband – ÖVSV (Ed.). (1988). *30 Jahre ÖVSV.* Wien: Österreichischer Versehrtensportverband.
Österreichischer Behindertensportverband – Verband. Retrieved November 10, 2008 from: http://www.oebsv.or.at/de/menu_main/der-verband
Österreichisches Paralympisches Komitee – Geschichte. Retrieved November 27, 2008 from: http://www.oepc.at/peking2008_dev/DasistPeking2008QQid-252-216.html
Schäfermeier, A. (2001). *Berichterstattung über Behindertensport.* Unpublished master's thesis, Universität Wien, Fakultät für Grund- und Integrativwissenschaft.
Schauerte, T. (2007). *Was ist Sport in den Medien? Theorie-Befunde-Desiderate. Sport. Medien.* Gesellschaft Band 6. Köln: Sportverlag Strauß.
Weigl, M. (1994). *Sport und Fernsehen – Internationale Entwicklung und die Situation in Österreich.* Unpublished master's thesis, Universität Wien, Fakultät der Grund- und Integrativwissenschaften.

Chapter 7
Coverage of the Beijing Paralympic Games on German Television

Nicole Raab & Simone Janda

Introduction

The Beijing 2008 Paralympic Games have now become an inspiring reference point for all athletes, officials, spectators, and just about every person from around the world who were involved with them. From 6th-17th September 2008, the Chinese capital was host to what the President of the International Paralympic Committee (IPC), Sir Philip Craven, deemed the greatest Paralympic Games ever in his speech at the Closing Ceremony. The people of China did deliver an unforgettable and well-organized sporting event in Beijing, and it did change standards. In effect, this has been the marking of a large growth spurt for the Paralympic Movement. The Beijing Paralympic Games saw approximately 4,000 athletes from a total of 147 different countries, competing in 20 different sports, including rowing a new addition to the Paralympic programme. There were a total of 472 medal events, with 262 for men, 176 for women, and 34 were mixed events. The medal tally was topped by the host country, China, winning 89 gold medals. Following the Chinese Paralympic Team in the gold medal count were Great Britain with 42, USA with 36, Ukraine with 24 and Australia with 23. The Games saw a total of 279 new World records, and 339 new Paralympic records.

With regard to spectators, the Beijing 2008 Paralympic Games welcomed a total of 3.44 million people on site. Guiding the crowds on the Olympic Green and in the venues were more than 30,000 volunteers, mostly from China (cp. Klein 2008). During the past twenty years the Paralympic Games has developed into an event of giant dimensions which has been aided and developed in the 'Olympic' surroundings. It could be argued that broadcasters have been covering the Paralympic Games properly since Sydney 2000, and that the Paralympics are the most important event on the international disability sport event timetable.

In Beijing 2008 around 100 hours of Paralympic sport were televised (Schinzel 2008). Around 4,000 disabled athletes from 148 nations took part and the 170 athletes from Germany made up one of the largest teams. Thanks to technology the television channels were able to report immediately about all decisions in which German athletes were involved. (Schinzel 2008). In total 870,000 tickets were sold and 3.4 million visitors made the trip to the Paralympic Summer Games in Beijing 2008 which on the surface appeared to be the most successful ever. Indeed, never before have the World games for disabled been visited by so many people. Not only athletes represented Germany but also around 150 media people, who were responsible throughout for some attractive pictures[1] from China's capital.

Coverage of the Beijing Paralympics on German Television

In 1948 Ludwig Guttman rehabilitated WW II invalids with sport activities, and thus introduced the first disabled sport competitions and since the Paralympic Games of Seoul in 1988, there has been a continuing rise towards equity with the Olympic Games has been achieved. Indeed, the Paralympic sports performance level has become more and more professional and along with better performances has come even greater media interest which has grown enormously. The Paralympics of Beijing were a huge success with quality athletic performances comparable to the Olympic Games. The public broadcasts radically increased their qualitative and quantitative transmission power in comparison to their first operation at the Paralympic Games in Seoul in 1988. Both German public broadcasting stations were responsible for the increased public interest in the Paralympic Games and consequent rise in their prestige and public attention in the last eight years in Germany. Along with this came a new and improved transmitting concept, that of increased number of hours and minutes coverage, which also strongly supported the professionalization of Paralympic sports in Ger-

---

1. Taken from the actual media brochure of the public broadcasts

many. The large amount of media and television reporters and cameramen were able to provide attractive pictures from the Beijing Paralympic and altogether both channels broadcasted 30 hours, to an average of 870,000 recipients (cp. Wittstock, 2008) over the successful Beijing Paralympic Games period.

Questioning the Media Coverage

In this study there were five important questions regarding the Beijing Paralympic Games and their relationship to the German media. These were:

1. On what major sports will the focus of the television and media coverage be placed?
2. Will the Television coverage show disabilities that are obvious and socially acceptable/unacceptable for example: like athletes in wheelchairs, with amputations and visually impaired?
3. Which kinds of individual and team events will be shown?
4. Will German athletes be the focus of media attention in order to satisfy the public's perceived need for social group affiliation?
5. Were the highly performed, aesthetic sports performances of the disabled connected with the affective satisfaction of the spectators and readers needs or did it trail away into lurid/attention-grabbing reports?

The following describes the methodology and objectives of the study on the Beijing Games.

Method and objectives of the study

The following analysis is a standardized media content analysis. At first, it was important to define the main features. This method is preferred in social science orientated communication research (Rössler, 2005) and focuses on the reduction of complexity of the media contents by selecting its central clusters. These clusters are called contentual categories. These categories initially build the primitive form of the content of analysis. At the same time the categories should clearly indicate all decisive contents for the analysis, and should be arranged from general to specific. All individual categories must be disunited and must guarantee that they really measure different features and are clearly attached to one category.

The 'Object of investigation' of this empirical media content analysis was the coverage of the German public service broadcasting channels regarding the Paralympics of 2008 in Beijing. Alternately both channels broadcasted in the evening as "Paralympics extra "for half an hour, from 17.30 pm to 18.00 o'clock. This broadcast was shown over the period from 7th September until 17th September 2008. The eleven broadcasts were recorded on DVDs and videotapes and examined. The division of the articles happened in study-units and these were tagged with current numbers. In order to get a precise survey, the study-units were viewed twice. First the correct number of contributions and their visual illustration were examined. The data was determined on the basis of a questionnaire and this lead to the results by computation. The complete material was split into units, which were selected by the highlighted sports and the reports before and after the event. All in all 89 (49 by ARD and 40 by ZDF) contributions were numbered by this distribution. The total time of the contributions count was 4:14:16 hours and on average the individual contributions were 3:19 minutes.

Results

From 6th to 17th September 2008 both broadcasts reported in daily alternation regarding the XIII Paralympic Games from China's capital Beijing. In comparison to the Games of Sydney 2000 and Athens 2004, this is an absolute record from a German broadcaster: Altogether broadcasts and reports about sports, news and magazine channels made up a combined total of one hundred hours of quality broadcasting time. As argued by the news reporter, "One focus of the coverage will be the sports and especially the performance of the German athletes". (Pleßmann & Stange, 2008, p. 2). This was followed by other statements from the press such as:

[1] "..but in Beijing it will be even more detailed reporting, much more intensive, personally and technically much better organized than so far." and,

[2] "..the ultimate ambition is to produce sports programs, which only differ a little from Olympic broadcasts" (Pleßmann & Stange 2008, p. 7).

So what was the focus of the competition coverage?

The coverage was composed of 51% competition and 49% reports before and afterwards the Games time. The rate of the competitions stayed marginally ahead of the reports before and after and it shows a balanced coverage. During the coverage the sporting activity stood with circa 30% in front, but there still were other themes. With 18% the disability as the subject of conversation, following the starting classes with 12% and the rules with 10%. Themes, which were not sport related, were represented by 9%, with 8% centering on the equipment and the materials used making topical conversation. Subsequently, followed the theme of intellectual disability with 6%, training with 3%, sports medicine about 2% and finally doping with 1%. The theme "diversity" made the coverage very transparent and gave an insight into topics like classification starting classes, the sport disciplines and their rules.

Will the TV program show disabilities that are obvious and socially accepted?

When answering this question it became clear that a few telegenic kinds of sports, which are interesting for the channels, were shown and presented more extensively than others (Kauer & Bös, 1998). Persons with physical disabilities often create a sense of un-sureness (while interacting with able-bodied persons), of non-acceptance or disgust (cp. Kauer & Bös 1998). This happens unconsciously. It is well known, that the denegation is higher concerning clearly visible physical disabilities than regarding less visible kinds of disabilities for example like blindness. Consequently there is a ranking of disabilities. Athletes with disabilities do not fit in a world, in which a perfect body is the ideal. However, wheelchair-users or amputees, as we are used to see them, do not provoke much aversion in spite of their apparent disability. The main problems are the journalists' reservation and uncertainness. Furthermore the amount of starting classes keeps the journalists from reporting. Therefore, wheelchair users came first with 18% of broadcasting, followed by athletes with amputations and athletes with visual impairments.

Which type of sports will be shown?

Athletics was not just the most frequently but also the most shown sport with all in all 41:25 minutes of total broadcasting time. This was closely related to the fact, that athletics has the most events and starting classes. In second position were the following as the most shown sports: cycling, wheelchair-basketball, swimming, table tennis and riding. Wheelchair-basketball came directly behind athletics with 40:36 minutes. Furthermore, other telegenic sports were shown, which were not just interesting but also created suspense and presented well-exercised bodies. It is worth mentioning that goalball, judo and rowing were low down on the coverage of the Paralympics. These were shown with an average of 11 to 17 minutes of daily coverage.

Will German athletes be focused on satisfying the need for affiliation to a social group?

With 78% of the whole coverage, German athletes were presented to the viewing public much more than other nationalities. When mentioning other athletes it was interesting to note that they were often in close relationship to German athletes, either in competitions or in interviews, or they performed with phenomenal prowess. The most prominent person and only none German taking up viewing minutes was the South African Oscar Pistorius with six separate stories. The German media, like the rest of the world, were alerted by his spectacular victory within the 400m race where he broke the world record. Interestingly, Oscar Pistorius was under discussion by the media long before the Beijing Paralympics because he just missed out on the qualification for the South African Olympic Games team.

Were the highly performed, aesthetic sports performances of the Paralympic athletes connected with the affective satisfaction of the recipients' needs?

Overall, the coverage did not delve into lurid or attention-grabbing reports, but tried to establish a balance between sport specific and objective perspectives towards non-sportive themes. The results pinpoint the fact that the central thrust of the coverage was predominantly the sporting performance of the athletes. Explanation about the classification system and the rules of the different disciplines came a close second. Perhaps the main focus of the reports before and after the competitions was regarding athletes coping abilities, family background and the reason or cause for their disability. Interestingly, reports about Beijing's surrounding area were also kept in balance. The results indicated that the journalists attached great importance to the factual, and developed a professional attitude when writing critical reviews of the Paralympic athletes.

Discussion and Conclusions

The main issue of this chapter inquired as to how the coverage of the competitive sports of athletes with disabilities at the Paralympic Games of Beijing 2008 was presented on German Television (on public service channels). It seems to be clear from the results that in future we can expect the promised extensive coverage through aggrandised announcements, the high number of visitors and sold ticket. German broadcasters managed to keep a balance between competition coverage and preliminary and post competition reporting. In addition these reports were upgraded by varying interviews with athletes, studio guests and interesting news to provide real "infotainment" and credibility. Furthermore, the commentators attempted to explain the different classifications, the rules of the competitions by incorporating this information as a part of their interviews, news and comments. Throughout the commentators created a positive and friendly atmosphere and there were only few obvious headlines that focused on the German athletes only. The visual attractiveness of the coverage was provided by showing popular sports like athletics, wheelchair-basketball, swimming and table-tennis, and by the broadcasting of well-known and socially accepted athletes with disabilities like wheelchair users, the sportsmen and -women with visual disabilities, and several athletes with paraplegics. Some presentations were compensated by positive emotions where the disability of the athletes was marginally discussed in an informative and professional way without dominating the reporting. As a conclusion we can sum up that the German coverage of the Paralympics 2008 in Beijing leaned towards an informative, performance related and professional enterprise.

The audience gained more understanding and further transparency about the Paralympic Games by an increased amount of informative interviews and comments about the starting classes, rules, equipment and material used by the sportsmen and women from the reporters. The German coverage regarding the sports at the Paralympic Games we feel is about to reach an almost equal integration in television broadcasting as the Olympics. Equal in the sense of the amount of time broadcast on the event. In comparison to the previous years both German public-service channels increased their broadcasting time about seven-times up to one hundred hours. However, not just the broadcasting time was increased but also the amount of people involved from both channels was extended to an overall number of 150 media people in total. Of interest is the fact that the Olympic Organising Committee (OCOG) paid 9 million U.S. Dollars for broadcasting rights to the International Paralympics Committee (I.P.C.). Indeed, for the next Paralympics in London 2012 a sum of 14 million US Dollars is planned to cover broadcast rights (Löscher 2006).

"Nowadays sport for disabled is handled absolutely competitively in editorial offices" stated by the chairman of the 'Deutsche gesetzliche Unfallversicherung' (German compulsory insurance company; DGUV 2008, p. 8) who granted the 'German Paralympic Media Award 2008' for outstanding coverage regarding the Paralympic athletes. "The Paralympic sport is not seen as sport of a second class any longer, like in earlier days", Dr. Karl Quade[2] mentioned in an interview with ZDF online in advance of the Paralympics 2008. Noticeably, however, in spite of raised attention of the Paralympic Games and the very high number of visitors during the Beijing Games the Paralympics sports immediately disappeared from German television as soon as the Games had finished. Indeed, the sport for people with disabilities on television is still limited to the Paralympics, being repeated every two years. Earlier analysis indicated that the quantity of sports coverage in Athens was high but the quality still leaves a lot to be desired (Lenzen 2005). Further analyses has made us mindful that reports from Athens can perhaps be seen as comments belonging to the most popular sports, rather than being performance-related which is a step back rather than a step forward into integration/inclusion (Lenzen 2005). This statement does not apply four years later in Beijing as during this time a lot of effort has been invested to achieve a performance related and professional coverage by the German public broadcasters. Perhaps London 2012 will be different, but from the above analysis a clear step into a performance-related athlete centred approach will be required in order to make the German media presentations valid for the public and aspiring disabled athletes.

---

2. Vice president of German Disability Association since 1995. Quade was himself a participant of the Paralympic Games in 1984, 1988 and 1992.

Concluding Notes

In spite of this positive feedback from Beijing and the generally positive critics the Paralympic Games continue to be way behind its big brother the Olympic Games. Put simply the numbers and the audience/viewing rates tell us a lot. For example the opening ceremony of the Olympic Games was watched by around 7.71 billion people on the television in comparison to just 19 million who viewed the Paralympic opening ceremony.

Integration and equality of the Paralympic Games was the aim of the IPC up to the early 1990s and in 2001 and 2003 contracts were made between the International Paralympic Committee and the International Olympic Committee, which obviously optimize external conditions for the holding of the Paralympics, but these contracts also include a separation: different names, different topics and a different logo. One could exaggerate that the Paralympic Committee has sold their soul to the IOC and that the Paralympic Committee has been given money by the IOC to keep quiet and stop demanding integration for its athletes (Meyer & Schantz 2008).

In an interview on German television Verena Bentle, a German biathlete and cross-country skier, who has won medals four-times at the World Cup and twelve-times at the Paralympic Games, mentioned important differences between the Paralympics and the Olympic Games. First she mentioned that the support of the top team just works one year in front of the Games (but longer before the Olympic Games), there's also no occupational aid for the Paralympic participants and thirdly there's little support for the disabled youth. Another important fact that was mentioned is the money the athletes receive for a prize. Maria Riesch for example earned 15,000 Euro for her Gold Medal and in comparison to this Verena Bentle earns just 4,500 Euros for her Gold medal at the Paralympics. Arguments like smaller starting classes, consequently lower performance levels and thereby less advertising effect are the main reasons for this discrepancy.

References

DGUV - Pressestelle (10.11.2008). Bedeutung von Behindertensport in den Medien deutlich gestiegen: Retrieved March 24, 2010 from: http://www.dguv.de/inhalt/presse/2008/Q4/mediaaward/index.jsp

Die Paralympics in den Medien. Retrieved January 12, 2010 from: http://www.tagesspiegel.de/sport/Paralympics-Peking-TV-Programm;art17971,2606845

Guttmann, L. (1979). *Sport für Körperbehinderte*. München: Urban & Schwarzenberg.

Kauer, O. & Bös K. (1998). *Behindertensport in den Medien.* Aachen: Meyer & Meyer.

Klein, S. (2008). The Torch Relayed to Beijing. *The Paralympian* 8. Retrieved 12 January 12, 2010 from: http://www.paralympic.org/ export/sites/default/Media_Centre/News/Paralympian/ 2008_12_Paralympian_3_08.pdf

Lenzen, L. (2005). *Die mediale Inszenierung von Behindertensport in der Fernsehberichterstattung von ARD/ZDF während der Paralympics 2004 in Athen.*Unpublished master's thesis, Deutsche Sporthochschule Köln, Cologne.

Löscher, K. (2006). *Der Behindertensport in den Medien*. Unpublished master's thesis, Humboldt University Berlin, Berlin.

Meyer, F. & O.J. Schantz (2008). Das Paralympische Komitee hat seine Seele verkauft. Retrieved April 21, 2010 from: http://www.dradio.de/dkultur/sendungen/thema/842827/, Köln: Deutschlandradio Kultur.

Pleßmann, R. & T. Stange, (2008). Paralympics 2008 (Pressemappe ARD und ZDF). Hamburg: Norddeutscher Rundfunk.

Raab, N. (2009). *Die mediale Darstellung des Leistungssports der Menschen mit Behinderung in der Fernsehberichterstattung von ARD/ZDF während der Paralympics 2008 in Peking.* Unpublished master's thesis, University Koblenz-Landau, Koblenz.

Rössler, P. (2005). *Inhaltsanalyse*. Konstanz: UVK.

Schinzel, H. (2008). Die Paralympics 2008 in den Medien. Fernsehen, Rundfunk und Internet berichten über die Spiele in Peking. Retrieved March 26, from: http://tv-nachrichten.suite101.de/article.cfm/die_paralympics_in_den_medien

Wittstock, S. (2008, March 26). Re: Paralympics in the media. E-mail conversation with Swantje Wittstock, coordinator of ARD sport news. E-Mail address: swantje.wittstock@DASERSTE.de)

Chapter 8
French Perspectives on the Media and Paralympics

Anne Marcellini

Introduction

Little research has been conducted in France on the subject of media coverage of sport for the disabled. The rare existing research has been completed by a few sports sociologists who are particularly interested in the subject of disability and 'suitable' physical activities. In fact, social science research into Paralympic sport in France has remained, up to the present, quite radically separate from classic research into sports sociology. Thus, any French sociology and social-history papers on sport make no mention of sports for the disabled, indeed it is ignored, or more precisely, left to "specialists in suitable physical activities". A clear example of this discrimination was the joint paper *Sport et presse en France (XIXème-XXème siècle)* [Sport and press in France - nineteenth and twentieth centuries] (Combeau-Mari 2007), which despite being a landmark paper makes no mention of sport for the disabled.

Early research through the 1990's

The earliest paper on the media treatment of sport for the disabled was that of Jean-Paul Génolini (1995), followed shortly afterwards by an article by Otto Schantz (1995) analysing the discourse in the written press. René-

Claude Lachal (2000), without being specifically interested in sport, emphasised in his work the place accorded in media reporting to disability. Subsequently, Schantz and Gilbert (2001) initiated research into the media coverage of the Paralympics, highlighting some important points in a comparative study of press coverage in France and Germany during the Atlanta Paralympic Games in 1996.

Our team in Montpellier thus began work on the increasing volume of media discourse at the time of the Sydney Paralympic Games in 2000 (Marcellini & Léséleuc, 2002), examining press coverage of the event in France, Spain and England. For his part, Sylvain Paillette, working on a Master's degree in sports sciences (2001) started examining audio-visual productions, taking a special interest in French television broadcasts of the Paralympic Games from the date of the first Paralympics in 1960, up to 2004 (Paillette et al., 2005).

In general, all French research has been concerned with the issue of the relations between media treatment of sports for the disabled and social representations of the disabled. Research has reviewed both the gradual increase in media coverage accorded to sports for the disabled, through a quantitative analysis of treatment content (written matter, and oral discourse and including both still and moving images) and highlighting the qualitative dimension of such media productions and the connotations and denotations associated with disability and the disabled.

From the quantitative point of view, it quickly became apparent that France differed from other European countries in its very limited media coverage of Paralympic events. In fact, the study undertaken by Schantz & Gilbert (2001) showed that the French press produced only half the number of articles as the German press covering the Atlanta Paralympic Games of 1996. The comparative analysis conducted by Marcellini & Léséleuc (2002) confirmed the very limited cover of the Sydney Paralympic Games by the French and Spanish press by comparison with the British press, the latter giving three times as much space as the other two. Furthermore, it also shows that the French press is stands out for the virtual absence of photographs illustrating its articles on the Sydney Paralympic Games, while the British press showed numerous photographs of the Paralympic athletes at the Games. The iconographic poverty of French coverage had previously been reported by Schantz & Gilbert (2001) explaining in the corpus of their article on the 1996 Paralympic Games in Atlanta, that while the German press published 23 photographs the French press published just two.

Very soon therefore, on starting to make comparisons with other European countries, France became identified as the country with the least coverage of the Paralympic Games in the written press, almost overlooking the Games entirely as the French press gave a mere 64 cm^2; over the two weeks of the event in Sydney 2000. This statistical data led to questioning the sociological nature of the relationship of France with disability, and to put forward the hypothesis that the rationale of assimilating the disabled with the general population, which had historically prevailed in the national arena since the 1950s, might explain why these particular sporting events were virtually ignored.

Sylvain Paillette (2002), through a corpus developed from French audiovisual broadcasts over a long time span (1960 to 2004) showed that media treatment of the Paralympic Games varied at different periods. According to him, from 1960 to 1988, audio-visual media treatment remained limited and selective, relating merely to television news. From 1988 to 1994 there was a period when the premise of developing some form of media coverage of disabled sports in France was supported by the choice of France as a location for the Winter Paralympic Games which were held in Albertville in 1992. This author stresses the emergence between 1996 and 2000, of a media model for the Paralympic Games with an increase in televised reporting, the appearance of the subject in sports magazines In addition to televised news programs, the advent of a cult of hero worshipping some Paralympic athletes, the broadcasting of interviews with athletes, as well as the development of sports reporters specialising in covering the event.

In-depth development of gender issues and new thoughts on visual documents

This early research was to serve as the basis on which in-depth development of the subject and new issues of media coverage of the Paralympic Games are now treated in France. In particular this concerns the issue of gender, seeking evidence of any under-representation of women Paralympic athletes in press coverage, and raising the question of the image and photographic positioning of disabled sports people.

Indeed, early research findings showed that press coverage accorded only a small place for disabled sports women, thus suggesting that they were victims of double discrimination, or even a double penalty – being both a disabled person and a woman. The work of Pappous et al. (unpublished) and Léséleuc et al. (2010, awaiting publication) stresses that disabled sports women should not be considered as quantitatively under-represented in media coverage of the Paralympic Games, since their press visibility correlates with their contribution to the medals won. Nevertheless, through qualitative analyses of media cover the discourse on sports women finds them treated like children, trivialising them more than it does their male counterparts.

Another route for furthering French research on the media coverage of Paralympic Games is to examine the way photographs are used to illustrate press articles and to study the quantitative and qualitative changes in the press, particularly when reporting the Paralympics. In fact, taking part in sports activities is seen as social exposure of the body in movement, and thus the visibility of the disabled body is socially affirmed. Reproductions of press photographs of disabled athletes seem in this respect to merit attention in order to understand what is "provided visually" on the disabled in parallel with the verbal discourse. Pappous et al. (awaiting publication) showed that in France, as in other European countries, there was an increase in the number of published photographs of the Paralympic Games held in 2000 (Sydney) and 2008 (Beijing). This change has enabled substantial work to be accomplished on the corpus of the pictures, in which analyses of the messages imparted by them can be developed. In fact, the aim now became to understand the message these photographs communicate and to see whether they have changed over time. What is communicated by these media representations of disabled persons? In 2006, we published a first paper on "displaying the disabled sports body" which identified three principles present in the construction of these pictures: that of masking the impairment, that of *mimesis* (the imitative representation of human behaviour) by the disabled person, and finally that of biological and technological association (Marcellini, 2006). These premises led to sharing thoughts on specific epistemological and methodological work on pictures of able-bodied and disabled people (Lebel et al., 2010; Gorin, 2010; Stiker, 2010). A longitudinal study then identified changes in the way photographs of disabled athletes were published in Europe between 2000 and 2008 and showing an increase in the number of photographs masking impairment (Pappous et al., awaiting publication).

From the initial questions up to recent developments on the issues concerned, one question is raised by all French research concerning the "type of disability", or more precisely, the type of impairment that forms a focal point in press coverage of the Paralympic Games, or alternatively, tends to be overlooked.

The Paralympic Games: What is shown?

The diverse situations encompassed by the idea of disability, and more specifically, the types of impairment affecting Paralympic athletes, challenges media portrayals of them. The papers cited in the previous section above raised the issues regularly. Indeed, was there an over-representation of certain types of disability in the media coverage of Paralympic events?

In point of fact, in her study of television reporting, Combrouze (2003) found that in the corpus she examined 60% of cases concerned motor disabilities, 32% sensorial disabilities, while only 5% were affected by a mental disability. The phenomenon of representing only certain types of impairment also applies in general television programs, generally with no coverage of intellectual impairment and cerebral paralysis (Combrouze, 2000). Furthermore, some work has shown an over-representation of those in wheelchairs in media treatment of the disabled (Lachal, 2000).

Concerning the media coverage of Paralympic sports, this issue has been raised in French research. In fact, while initially Paralympic events were limited to people in wheelchairs, they have gradually extended to include other categories of impairment and disability. An analysis of European press articles reporting on the Sydney Paralympic Games in 2000 (Marcellini &

Léséleuc, 2002) indicated that a large proportion of the athletes taking part had some form of motor impairment. It also showed that Spain was the country most likely to give publicity to athletes with impaired sight, which may be understandable in the light of the social history of visual impairment in Spain. Furthermore, statistical data on the subject again shows that as far as women are concerned, the impairments covered by the press substantially correlate to the medals won and the number of athletes with a given category of disability who are taking part.

The situation of the people with intellectual disabilities however, deserves special attention. Jean-Paul Génolini stressed as early as 1995 the euphemistic expression for people with intellectual disabilities in the messages conveyed in the sports press. We have known moreover since the 1980s, that the people with intellectual disabilities are seen as the "fundamental figure of disability", bearing the heaviest stigma (Giami, 1988). In addition, the inclusion of the mentally impaired in the Paralympics movement occurred very late and was short-lived. In 1988 the new organisation of the International Paralympic Committee suggested opening all sports in Paralympic Games to the people with disabilities, whatever their type of impairment. The International Paralympic Committee, incorporating the INAS-FMH - the International Association of Sports for Persons with a Mental Handicap (which later became the INAS-FID - the International Association of Sports for Persons with an Intellectual Disability), and for the first time in 1996, at the Atlanta Olympics, 56 athletes with mental impairment took part in athletic events and swimming. But by 2000 in Sydney, fraud by the Spanish basket-ball team which included athletes without impairment resulted in suspension and the exclusion of the people with intellectual disabilities.

However, it is important to note that in the French media cover of the Sydney Games, there is no mention, either in writing or even in a less iconic form, advising the public that athletes with intellectual disabilities were taking part in competitions. Few mentions were found in the Spanish and British press. As Alain Kerlan (2007) suggests we might think that the "strength of photography is to be by nature a beginning of denial to the suppression of self at work in exclusion mechanisms," (Kerlan, 2007, p. 44) it can be asserted that the people with intellectual disabilities suffer effective exclusion through being ignored. The official re-inclusion of the mentally impaired in the Paralympic Games in London in 2012, after eight years of ineligibility, provides the opportunity to test this hypothesis. More generally, in the European press - to stay with "local" attitudes - the research conducted has enabled the contours of "invisible" images to be drawn, like negatives, the "reverse" of published photos. It is almost possible to draw the silhouette that is hidden in the darkness because it fails to reflect the *mimesis* of the sports body, and specifically by a driving force that evokes the *gesticulatio* and not the *gestus* (Schmitt, 1981). The *gesticulatio*, which implies large, rapid, energetic gestures and the idea of undisciplined energy, meaning there are "too many" gestures, is defined explicitly by Jacques le Goff and Nicolas Truong as *"gesticulations and other contortions reminiscent of the devil"* (op. cit., p.173). The *gesticulatio* denotes disorder and senselessness. It includes, in the world of Paralympics, both the mentally handicapped and those affected by cerebral paralysis (Marcellini, 2006, 2007). By contrast, the *gestus*, Jean-Claude Schmitt (1990, pp. 173-207) tells us, is both movement and representation; it is a sign, a symbol. The *gestus* involves action, with a practical purpose and body effectiveness and it also involves an attitude, a representation where symbolic dimension is bound to aesthetic dimension. The most frequently disseminated press photographs show the disabled body of the athlete, which can be qualified through recurrent indices, building an image of a controlled, efficient, active and technological body - in other words a body that is furnished with or even inserted into an engine. This athlete's body is most often shown taking part in an actual sport, corresponding to the typical example of classic sports photography, visibly exhibiting emotions of joy, and suffering and in perfect *mimesis* with the sports figure.

The connection achieved in sports photography (and sports images more generally, whether still or animated), between impairment and technology is of a figure that excels, that is completely in harmony with the sports figure. Thus the disabled sports figure incarnates the ideology of progress, the possibility of exceeding the biological limits and human "destiny" determined by the flesh, at the same time as increasing the reputation of techno-sciences. When In addition, a human figure thus equipped achieves remarkable performances, in other words of the same order as a fully able bodied athlete, which was the case of Oscar Pistorius, the press and media in general accord them an exceptional place. According to the Factiva data base, there were 5305 press articles mentioning Oscar Pistorius published in many different languages from January 2007 to December 2008. In France, in the two years, 2007 and 2008, 53 articles out of a total of 294 on the Paralympic Games, in other words 18% of the total, were devoted to him in five newspapers (Figaro, Midi Libre, Libération, Le Monde, Les Echos) (Marcellini et al., 2010). Of course, beyond the mimesis and the *gestus* showed in the numerous photographs published of him, the fact that his performance altered the established hierarchies between able bodied and disabled persons, and the controversy created by his later exclusion underpin this excessive media exposure.

Media and the Paralympic Games: Mirrors and Representation

French research into the media treatment of the Paralympic Games really seems to be a shared paradigm which questions the game of mirrors between social representations of the disabled, the sports they undertake and the press coverage of such sports competitions. Which facets of Paralympic sport are shown, and do they play a role in de-stigmatising the disabled?

While it is clear that sport is a special media prop for the disabled, and while various research projects have analysed the French press and TV coverage of Paralympics in quantitative terms, a qualitative analysis of content of the message shows that some sports categories are overlooked in favour of others. Moreover, the analysis of sports photographs and their often ambiguous messages turns attention to a discussion of the bigger picture, and merits further examination, in particular of the implications of the still under-exploitation of televised images.

Finally, while in France research has mainly focussed on the media reporting of the Paralympic Games in terms of subject and message, research into the production process of the media discourse on the Paralympics and its reception - meaning its impact on the general public in terms of the social representation of disabled persons - has yet to be analysed.

References

Combeau-Mari, E. (Ed.). (2007). *Sport et presse en France (XIXème-XXème siècle)*. Paris: Le Publieur.

Combrouze, D. (2000). L'information sur les personnes handicapées motrices et sensorielles dans les journaux télévisés. *Handicap, Revue de sciences humaines et sociales*, 82, 27-43.

Combrouze, D. (2003). Personnes handicapées et fictions : deux exigences contradictoires. In A. Blanc, & H.J. Stiker (Eds.), *Le handicap en images, les représentations de la déficience dans les œuvres d'art* (pp. 27-41). Paris: Erès.

Génolini, J.P. (1995). L'expression euphémique du handicap mental dans les messages de presse sur le sport. *Revue européenne du handicap mental*, 2/ 8, 54-63.

Giami, A. et al. (1988). *La figure fondamentale du handicap : représentations et figures fantasmatiques*. Rapport de recherche, Mire-Geral.

Gorin V. (2010). De la grande guerre à la guerre d'Irak. Photographies de soldats mutilés, entre corps abandonné et réhabilitation. *Revue ALTER : European journal of disability research*, 4, 3-17.

Kerlan, A. (2007). Exclus et inclus. Le droit à l'image. *Reliance*, 25, 38-44.

Lachal, R.C.(2000). La représentation des personnes handicapées dans les médias :de l'objet au sujet, *Prévenir*, 39, 97-105.

Lachal, R.C., & Combrouze, D. (1998). La représentation des personnes handicapées à travers des émissions documentaires de la télévision française. Analyse thématique de 35 émissions diffusées entre 1986 et 1996. *Cahiers Ethnologiques*, 19, 239-262.

Lebel, E., Marcellini, A., & Pappous, A. (2010). Regards croisés sur une photographie sportive. Photojournalisme sportif et athlètes handicapés : mise en scène du corps et production de sens. *Revue ALTER: European journal of disability research*, 4, 18-33.

Le Goff, J. & Truong, N. (2003). *Une histoire du corps au moyen-âge*. Paris: Liana Levi.

Léséleuc, E. de, Pappous, A., & Marcellini A. (in print). The Media Coverage of Female Athletes with disability. Analysis of the daily press of four European countries during the 2000 Sydney Paralympic Games. *European Journal for Sport and Society*.

Marcellini, A., & Léséleuc, E. de (2002). Les Paralympic Games vus par la presse : analyse différentielle entre l'Espagne, la France et l'Angleterre, *Actes du IVème Forum de la Fondation Olympique de Barcelone / 8 et 9 novembre 2001*, [CD-ROM]. Barcelona: Fondation Barcelona Olimpica.

Marcellini, A. (2006). Des corps atteints valides ou de la déficience au *"firmus"*: Hypothèses autour de la mise en scène sportive du corps handicapé. In G. Boetsch, N. Chapuis-Lucciani, & D. Chevé (Eds.), *Représentations du corps. Le biologique et le vécu : normes et normalité* (pp. 59-68). Nancy: Presses Universitaires de Nancy.

Marcellini, A. (2007). Nouvelles figures du handicap? Catégorisations sociales et dynamique des processus de stigmatisation / déstigmatisation. In G. Boetsch, C. Hervé, & J. Rozenberg (Eds.), *Corps normalisé, corps stigmatisé, corps racialisé* (pp.201-219). Bruxelles: De Boeck.

Marcellini A., Vidal, M., Ferez, S., & Léséleuc, E. de (2010). La chose la plus rapide sans jambes. Oscar Pistorius ou la mise en spectacle des frontières de l'humain. *Revue Politix, 90, 139-165.*

Paillette, S. (2001). *La médiatisation des Jeux Paralympiques : des logiques sportives ou sociales?* Mémoire de DEA en sciences de l'information et de la communication, Université Lille 3.

Paillette, S., Delforce B., & Wille, F. (2002). La médiatisation des Paralymic Games à la télévision française : quelles évolutions? *Les Cahiers du Journalisme*, 11. Retrieved January 10 from : www.cahiersdujournalisme.net/cdj/pdf/11/13_Paillette_Delforce_Wille.pdf

Paillette, S., Delforce B., & Wille, F. (2002). Les différents visages de la médiatisation des Paralymic Games, à travers la PQN et la télévision, de 1988 à 2002, *Actes de la 6ème Conférence de l'Association Européenne de Recherche en Activité Physique Adaptée*, Amiens.

Paillette, S., Wille, F., & Delforce, B. (2005). Quelques résultats de la médiatisation du Handisport; aspects de method. *Reliance, 1, 15,* 68-70.

Paillette, S., Delforce B., & Wille, F. (2003). La médiatisation de la natation aux Paralymic Games, *Actes des 3ème journées spécialisées en Natation*, Lille.

Paillette, S., Delforce B., & Wille, F. (2004). Les championnats du Monde Handisport d'athlétisme, un événement comme les autres? In C. Dorvillé (Ed.), *Sport en Nord*. Lille: Presses Universitaires du Septentrion.

Paillette, S. (2005). La médiatisation des compétitions sportives "Handisport" : entre logiques de la médiatisation sportive et logiques sociales de la médiatisation du handicap. *Actes des Journées Doctorales de la SFSIC (Société française des sciences de l'information et de la communication)*, 15 juin 2005, Nanterre.

Pappous, A., Marcellini, A., & Léséleuc, E. de (in press). From Sydney to Beijing: the evolution of the photographic coverage of Paralympic Games in 5 European Countries, *Sport in Society*.

Pappous, A., Léséleuc de, E., & Marcellini, A. (in press) Current and future directions for research on the media coverage of female Paralympic athletes in the global sport arena: a review, *Sport in Society*.

Schantz, O. & K. Gilbert (2001). An Ideal Misconstrued: Newspaper Coverage of the Atlanta Paralympic Games in France and Germany. *Sociology of Sport Journal*, 18, 69-94.

Schantz, O., & Marty, C. (1995). The French press and sport for people with handicapping conditions. In I. Morisbak, & P.E. Jørgensen (Eds.), *Quality of life through adapted physical activity* (pp.72-79). Oslo: Hamytykk.

Schmitt, J. C. (1981). Gestus-Gesticulatio. Contribution to the study of medieval vocabulary of gestures. In Y. Lefèvre (Ed.). *La lexicographie du latin médiéval et ses rapports avec les recherches actuelles sur la civilisation du Moyen-Age*, (pp. 377-390). Paris: CNRS.

Schmitt, J. C. (1990). *La raison des gestes dans l'Occident médiéval*. Paris: Gallimard.

Stiker, H.J. (2010). Notes sur la photographie de Xavier Torres prise par Bob Martin. *Revue ALTER : European Journal of Disability Research*, 4, 34-37.

Chapter 9
British Media Portrayals of Paralympic and Disability Sport

Ian Brittain

Introduction

With limited exceptions the Paralympic Games is often the only time that disability sport receives any kind of national media coverage in countries around the world. Academic investigation of the media coverage at the summer Paralympic Games, whilst limited in depth, has been occurring in some form after every Games since Seoul in 1988. These include Seoul (Stein, 1989), Atlanta (Schantz & Gilbert, 2001; Schell & Duncan, 1999), Sydney (Thomas & Smith, 2003) and Athens (Quinn, 2007). Pappous (2008) also produced a comparative study of newspaper coverage in five countries of the Sydney and Athens summer Paralympic Games. Thus far there appears to have been little or no academic study of media coverage at the Winter Paralympic Games. This chapter will attempt to give an overview of how media coverage of Paralympic and disability sport has developed within Great Britain and how the coverage in Great Britain compares with coverage elsewhere in the world.

A Short History of British Media Coverage of Paralympic and Disability Sport

Schantz and Gilbert (2001) claim that media coverage of the Paralympic Games is an indicator of public representations of, and attitudes toward, sport for persons with disabilities. Media coverage of Paralympic and disability sport in Great Britain has been going on since competitive disability sport began at Stoke Mandeville hospital on 29th July 1948 with the archery demonstration at the first Stoke Mandeville Games. The next day a brief article appeared in *The Times* newspaper entitled 'Games for the Paralysed: Archery Tournament at Ministry Hospital'. Analysed through the lens of today's understanding of disability the article would be criticised on a large number of grounds. There was no actual coverage of the sport itself except to express surprise that people in wheelchairs should be partaking in such an activity. The major part of the text relates to the presence of the Minister of Pensions, although the final paragraph does describe the role of sport in the rehabilitation of paralysed patients at the hospital and how it enables them to compete successfully with "normal healthy persons". Perhaps unsurprisingly given the focus of the article it appeared in the news section of the paper rather than the sports section. Although the Stoke Mandeville Games received quite good coverage in local papers such as *The Bucks Herald* and the Paralympic Games received intermittent coverage from a variety of national newspapers over the next thirty years the existence of Paralympic and disability sport passed by relatively unnoticed in Great Britain during this period. In fact, Ludwig Guttmann, the founder of the Paralympic Games, in his report of the 1976 Paralympic Games in Toronto, clearly voiced his dissatisfaction at the media coverage the Games had received in Britain:

> "In contrast to the splendid coverage of our Games given by Canadian and other countries' press etc., was the miserable coverage given in Great Britain. In spite of full information before and during the Games given to the press, radio and television, it was BBC TV in particular who has continued its previous policy of giving as little coverage as possible to our disabled athletes".
>
> (Guttmann, 1976, p.11)

However, since then media coverage of the Paralympic Games in Great Britain has slowly improved and increased over the last twenty-five years, although still nowhere near the levels of coverage received by major non-disabled events such as the Olympics or the football World Cup. The earliest television coverage of the Paralympic Games in Great Britain began with the 1980 Games in Arnhem. Bob (in Brittain, 2002), who participated in those Games, claims the coverage in those early days bordered on the offensive to people with disabilities:

Bob '...they were very low key and I know that BBC had a 45 minute programme on them (1984, New York) and it was very... I was going to say derogatory, derisive, but they were just demeaning really'.

Interviewer 'In what sense'?

Bob 'In an oh! Look at these disabled people aren't they marvellous that they're getting out there and doing something and it was the same after Seoul with Cliff Morgan. Patronising I think is probably the best description'.

(Bob in Brittain, 2002. pp.150-151)

By failing to look on the performances of these early Paralympic athletes as athletic, and depicting them as objects of pity, this kind of patronising coverage reinforced the message that athletes with disability and, therefore, people with disabilities in general, were incapable of doing anything worthy of recognition in their own right.

Value of Paralympic and Disability Sport within the British Media

Although this kind of language may no longer be used to portray athletes from the Paralympic Games, or disability sport in general, it should still be noted that the views behind such language use may still be present within the media. This may be indicated, for example, in the differences in time spent covering disability and non-disabled sport. As stated earlier, Schantz and Gilbert (2001) claim that media coverage of the Paralympics is an indicator of public representations of, and attitudes toward, sport for persons with disabilities. If this claim has any validity it should be evident in the coverage and portrayal of athletes with disabilities, and people with disabilities in general, by the media within Great Britain. It is reasonable to suppose that the relative amount of air time given to non-disabled and disability sport events gives some indication as to how these events are differently valued by the programmers. One possible example of this is the amount of airtime that the Paralympic Games receives on television in comparison to the Olympics. According to Richard (in Brittain, 2002) the difference in airtime given by the BBC to the Sydney Olympic and Paralympic Games was indicative of discrimination against disability sport:

> "There was 540 hours available of Olympic showing time on TV and there was ten? Ten or twelve of the Paralympics? That's the sort of discrimination that's going on".

(Richard in Brittain, 2002, p.152)

Media coverage given to an event suggests the 'value' placed on it by programmers and programmers who cover an event for a variety of reasons, be it financial, perceived interest to the viewing public or sponsors or simply newsworthiness. If the BBC provides more airtime to Olympic Sport then it appears that it perceives it to have far greater 'value' than its Paralympic counterpart. Since sport is a creation originally for non-disabled people, which gives priority to certain types of human movement (Barton, 1993) disability sport does not, apparently, provide images that fit within the norms that delineate sporting images within British society. This lack of exposure has numerous knock-on effects. It limits the visibility of disability sport within Great Britain, therefore, lessening the possibility of non-participating people with disabilities becoming aware of it or inspired to take part themselves. Since young people with disabilities, who are interested in sport, have limited role models with a disability to inspire them they may, therefore, be forced to turn to non-disabled sportspersons as role models. There is a possibility, therefore, that they model themselves and their sporting lives on a non-disabled conception of sport based on (masculine, non-disabled) physical strength and performance. Consequently, they may perceive their own performances as inferior.

The lack of media coverage is implicated in the lack of recognition of the capabilities of athletes with a disability. In 1998, the World Disability Athletics Championships were held in Birmingham in Great Britain. Danny (in Brittain, 2002) felt that the media reaction to those championships was less than inspiring:

> "I don't think it was ever shown. I don't think it was ever televised or anything really. It was atrocious".
>
> (Danny in Brittain, 2002, p.153)

By failing completely to give any coverage to these championships the media effectively reinforced the message that disability sport, even at world championship level, is neither interesting nor worthy of attention. One British athlete, Lloyd, became a double world champion at this event, at the age of fifteen, in his very first international event, but according to him even this avoided the attention of all but his local newspaper (Brittain, 2002). It is hard to conceive that if he had achieved this feat at the non-disabled World Championships that he would not have achieved national recognition in the media and as such gives a further indication of the low regard in which the media held disability sport and the performances of athletes with disabilities at that time. Whether the lack of coverage was based on a perceived lack of commercial viability, which really should not have been an issue in a government funded organisation like the BBC, or on prejudice and lack of understanding amongst those in power is difficult to assess. This lack of understanding was clearly highlighted by the embarrassing situation that arose at the BBC Sports Personality of the Year Awards, following the Sydney Olympic and Paralympic Games, when Tanni Grey-Thompson, a wheelchair Paralympic athlete who had won four gold medals in Sydney, won third place and was unable to go up to collect her award as no ramp had been put in place, only steps. Even though it was known that Tanni was in the final five nominees a long time prior to the event, following her superb performances in Sydney, it appears that those responsible for putting on the programme either assumed that there was no way she was going to win anything or just failed to take into consideration the needs of a person with a disability when planning the show. Either way it demonstrates a complete lack of awareness of the needs of people with a disability by those responsible for the show, even though the BBC had been broadcasting the Paralympic Games for twenty years. Incidents such as these are a clear indication and reinforcement of the 'outsider' or marginalised status of people and athletes with disabilities within the non-disabled community. The incident did receive some attention within the national media (for example *The Daily Telegraph*, 11th December 2000) which could potentially help raise awareness of issues such as this. However, it is unlikely that this coverage, which consisted of a small article in the 'Sports Round-Up' section, had anything to do with increasing awareness of the plight of people with disabilities within Great Britain. It is more likely that the fact it got reported at all highlights the sensationalist and often negative nature of the media in that an item is often only newsworthy if it shows someone or something up in a bad light.

Moving up the Learning Curve: Towards Better Quality Coverage

There can be little doubt that the BBC learnt a tough lesson from the events that occurred with Tanni-Grey Thompson and the Sports Personality of the Year Awards. There are also clear signs that a variety of media organisations have worked hard to overcome some of the criticisms they have face regarding their coverage of disability sport in general and people with disabilities in particular. The BBC have increased their coverage of the Paralympic Games every four years in response to public demands for greater coverage and the National Union of Journalists (NUJ) got together with the producers of UK newspaper *Disability Now* to produce a guide for journalists entitled 'Hacked Off: A Journalists Guide to Disability' in order to try and put an end to discriminatory and negative portrayals of people with disabilities as objects of pity within media reporting in Great Britain (NUJ website, 2010). Measures such as this have played an important role in improving the quality of reporting and coverage of disability issues, which has fed into the reporting and coverage of Paralympic and disability sport in Great Britain.

GB gains a new host broadcaster for the London 2012 Paralympic Games

The BBC have been covering the Paralympic Games in Great Britain using various formats (television, radio, online) since 1980, as well as a host of other disability sport events including the annual Paralympic World Cup from Manchester, and they were apparently so confident of being the host broadcaster for the London 2012 Paralympic Games that the BBC sport website was already proclaiming it to be 'the Paralympics Broadcaster' (Guardian website, 2010). However, LOCOG, keen to maximise revenue and apparently fearing a low price from the BBC set up a tender process, which Channel 4 won with a bid worth more than £5 million and a promise to broadcast an unprecedented 130 hours of coverage from the Games on its main channel (insideworldparasport website, 2010a). Although Channel 4 have a good record in bringing disability into the mainstream, they have little or no experience of covering disability sport and this has led to some fearing for the long-term future of the media coverage of disability sport within Great Britain. 'ParalympicsGB' released a statement stating it was saddened by the loss of its long-term broadcast partner and that although they looked forward to working with Channel 4 they feared for the coverage of disability sport post-2012 (insideworldparasport website, 2010a). This fear has possibly been made worse by the fact that Channel 4, as part of its build up to London 2012 has stated that it wishes to bid against the BBC to host the Paralympic World Cup (insideworldparasport website, 2010b). However, as LOCOG Chairman, Sebastian Coe remarked 'the commercial value of this deal has raised the bar financially for the Paralympic movement' and Roger Mosey, BBC Director of Sport has stated 'we will, of course, continue to support the Paralympics too – and our commitment to disability sport in general remains' (BBC website, 2010). It would appear; therefore, that having two large media corporations such as Channel 4 and the BBC competing to broadcast disability sport could potentially be good for disability and Paralympic sport in Great Britain both financially and in terms of the quality and amount of exposure they receive.

British Coverage of Paralympic and disability sport versus the rest of the world

Huang (2005) reports that in Taiwan there was no live media coverage of the Athens 2004 Paralympic Games and the fact that the Games received any coverage at all was largely due to the fact that the Taiwanese President's wife, who is a wheelchair user, led the Taiwanese team in Athens. A group of nearly forty political journalists followed the President's wife to Athens and reports generally appeared as political rather than sporting news. There was only one professional sports journalist from Taiwan with the delegation. Apparently once the President's wife left Athens the reporting of the Games all but ceased. Quinn (2007) reports that the Canadian Broadcasting Corporation had around 200 staff in Sydney to cover the Olympic Games. It asked a team of six to stay on in Sydney to oversee the Paralympic Games, who produced four one hour shows that were shown in Canada after the Games were over. According to Cashman and Tremblay (2008) TV New Zealand also showed four one hour specials after the Sydney 2000 Paralympic Games had ended and in the United States CBS broadcast a two-hour special entitled 'Role Models for the 21st Century: The Sydney 2000 Paralympic Games' in November, nearly two months after the Games had ended. This practice continued in the United States for the both the Athens and Beijing Paralympic Games despite mounting criticism. In response to this there were a number of internet based petitions protesting at the fact that NBC were going to give blanket coverage of the Olympics from Beijing, but no live coverage of the Paralympic Games. It would appear, therefore, that for all the criticisms that might be laid against British media coverage of Paralympic and disability sport the coverage given in Great Britain is far greater than most countries in the rest of the world.

IPC Media Awards

In 2005 the International Paralympic Committee introduced media awards in a variety of categories that are awarded in the year following each Paralympic Games. The aim of these awards is to honour members of the international media in recognition of extraordinary coverage of an athlete or team at the Paralympic Games (Summer or Winter) in the media. The 2009 awards were awarded in four categories (Broadcast, Written 'print and online', Photo and Radio) (IPC website, 2010). Of the eleven awards made since 2005 the BBC has won once in each of the broadcast, written (online) and radio categories and *The Daily Telegraph* and *The Sunday Telegraph* have won the written award once each. This means the British media organisations have won nearly half of all the awards made.

Conclusions

Whilst it would be wrong to claim that media coverage of disability and Paralympic sport in Great Britain is anywhere near perfect, it would be fair to say that compared to most of the rest of the world it receives far greater attention and coverage. This may, in part, be due to the fact that Great Britain is the birthplace of the Paralympic movement and also the place where the social model of disability was first theorised in the mid-seventies as a means of fighting for the rights of people with disabilities within the rest of society. It would appear that the British media, or at least certain parts of it, are leading the way when it comes to raising the profile of disability and Paralympic sport and increasing its profile in a positive and constructive manner. This is not to say that it cannot be improved still further, but in a country where the media is often criticised for its negativity it is good to be able to refer to them for once in a positive light.

References

Barton, L. (1993). Disability, Empowerment and Physical Education. In J. Evans (Ed.), *Equality, Education and Physical Education*, (pp. 43-54). London: The Falmer Press.

BBC Website (2010). Channel 4 lands 2012 Paralympics. Retrieved February 19, 2010 from: http://news.bbc.co.uk/sport1/hi/olympic_games/london_2012/8448236.stm

Brittain, I. (2002). *Elite Athletes with Disabilities: Problems and Possibilities*. Unpublished Ph.D. thesis. Buckinghamshire, Chilterns University College, UK.

Cashman, R. & D. Tremblay (2008). Media. In R. Cashman, & S. Darcy (Eds), *Benchmark Games: The Sydney 2000 Paralympic Games.*, Sydney: Walla Walla Press.

Guardian Website (2010). Paralympics deal fires starting gun for Channel 4's post-Big Brother era. Retrieved February 19, 2010 from: http://www.guardian.co.uk/media/organgrinder/2010/jan/08/paralympics-deal-channel-4

Guttmann, L. (1976). *Report on the Olympiad for the Physically Disabled held in Toronto, Canada, from 3rd – 11th August, 1976*. (IWAS Archives).

Huang, C.J. (2005). *Discourses of Disability Sport: Experiences of Elite Male and Female Athletes in Britain and Taiwan*, Unpublished PhD Thesis, Brunel University, UK.

Insideworldparasport Website, (2010a). *ParalympicsGB fear for coverage post-London 2012 after Channel 4 deal*. Retrieved February 19, 2010 from: http://www.insideworldparasport.biz/index.php?Option=com_content&view=article&id=8371:paralympicsgb-fear-for-coverage-post-london-2012-after-channel-4-deal&catid=145:news&Itemid=303

Insideworldparasport Website (2010b). *Exclusive: Channel 4 target BT Paralympic World Cup*. Retrieved February 19, 2010 from: http://www.insideworldparasport.biz/index.php?option=com_content&view=article&id=8445:exclusive-channel-4-target-bt-paralympic-world-cup &catid =145:news&Itemid=303

IPC Website (2010). *Paralympic Media Awards*. Retrieved February 19, 2010 from: http://www.paralympic.org/IPC/Awards/Paralympic_Media_Awards/

NUJ Website (2010). Hacked Off: A Journalist's Guide to Disability. Retrieved February 19, 2010 from: http://www.nuj.org.uk/get-file.php?id=244

Pappous, A. (2008). *The Photographic Coverage of the Paralympic Games*, paper presented at the Third Annual International Forum on Children with Special Needs "Sport and Ability", Shafallah Centre, Doha, Qatar, 20 – 22 April, 2008.

Quinn, N. (2007). *The Representation of Disability by the Canadian Broadcasting Corporation (CBC) during the 2004 Summer Paralympic Games*, Unpublished Master's Thesis, University of Toronto, Canada.

Schantz, O. J. & Gilbert K. (2001). An Ideal Misconstrued: Newspaper Coverage of the Atlanta Paralympic Games in France and Germany. *Sociology of Sport Journal*, 18, 69-94.

Schell, L. A. B. & Duncan M. C. (1999). A content analysis of CBS's coverage of the 1996 Paralympic Games. *Adapted Physical Activity Quarterly*, 16, 27-47.

Stein, J.U. (1989). U.S. Media – Where Were You During 1988 Paralympics? *Palaestra*, Summer, 45 – 52.

Thomas, N. & A. Smith (2003). Preoccupied with able-bodiedness? An analysis of the British media coverage of the 2000 Paralympic Games. *Adapted Physical Activity Quarterly, 20* (2), 166-181.

Chapter 10
USA vs. Canada

An Analysis of Media Coverage of Paralympic Athletes

Anna Fong & Sid Katz

Introduction

Most sport journalists agree there is not enough coverage of the Paralympic Games and many published newspaper articles are filled with stereotypes regarding athletes with disabilities (Bertling & Schierl, 2008). Stories about female athletes are often focused on their sex appeal, which is a disadvantage for disabled female athletes because according to Bertling and Schierl (2008), "eroticism and pure entertainment do not seem to sit comfortably with the serious nature of disabled sport". An image of an athlete with a disability often appears unattractive to mainstream consumers (Bertling & Schierl, 2008). Schantz and Gilbert (2001) found a majority of German newspapers portrayed women as "athletes first" but there was an article about a female paraplegic athlete who was characterized as an "attractive young lady". It appears that disabled female athletes are starting to receive acknowledgements in the press related to sexual attractiveness but from our viewpoint this in-it-self can be labeled as a form of disability. In reality and more often than not female athletes are marginalized in the beauty stakes and as sexual objects and their athletics skills are also portrayed as secondary. Other researchers who analyzed over two thousand articles related on the coverage of the 2000 Sydney and 2002 Salt Lake City Winter Olympic games (Bertling & Schierl, 2008) discovered that only 82 articles (approximately 2.4%) were written about the Paralympics and, on average, were 33 lines shorter than the articles written about the Olympics. Another study compared French and German daily newspapers with a specific focus on the 1996 Atlanta Summer Paralympic Games coverage; German journalists wrote the majority of the articles (86%) and most of the Paralympic coverage occurred the day after the opening ceremonies (Schantz & Gilbert, 2001). Once the games ended, further media discourse on the Paralympics generated only two articles "published two days after the end of the Paralympics, whereas the centennial Olympics Games were objects of comment up to two weeks after their closing" (Schantz & Gilbert, 2001).

What is this chapter about?

Journalists who cover the Olympic and Paralympics must gain accreditation by the International Olympic Committee (IOC) and the International Paralympic Committee (IPC) before they are allowed to report on the Games. This 'license' to report is meant to ensure fair international coverage. In the Olympic charter it states "....the IOC takes all necessary steps in order to ensure the fullest coverage by the different media and the widest possible audience in the world for the Olympic Games."

However, many articles written about disabled athletes focus on their accomplishments or extraordinary feats, but the same articles mention that the athletes require outside assistance. Conscious or unconscious sympathy is evoked after reading these articles and the athletes themselves would prefer the focus be on their achievements and not their disabilities (Bertling & Schierl, 2008). About 40% of sport journalists said articles on disabled athletes "should centre on the personal history of the individual athlete". This means an "ideal coverage of the Paralympics from the journalists perspective would be considered discriminatory by many of the disabled athletes" (Bertling & Schierl, 2008). What is going on out there? This and other questions came to mind and so we decided to go back to the grass roots in media coverage between the U.S. and Canada to discover elements of the truth regarding our fundamental principle that we believe that disabled athletes want to be "accepted as normal, high-achieving members of society" and stories that evoke pity will further segregate them from societal acceptance (Bertling & Schierl, 2008). In attempting to solve this riddle we designed this current study, where we set out to determine how Canadian coverage of the Paralympics differs from the United States and how Paralympic athletes are actually portrayed in the North America media.

Methods

The Canadian Newsstand database was used to search for *The Globe and Mail* and *Vancouver Sun* articles while the Lexis Nexis (Canadian) database was used to find articles from the *The New York Times* and *Washington Post*. Two different databases were selected because the Lexis Nexis database does not contain articles published by the *Vancouver Sun*. To maintain a degree of validity Canadian articles were obtained using the same database. The search terms used were: "(Paralympic or Paralympics) and (Athens, Beijing or Vancouver)".

To determine whether Canadian and American coverage of the Paralympics differed, each article was counted for words and the articles placed into three different categories to determine whether there was a predominant theme or topic used by each country. The same three categories created by Schantz and Gilbert (2001) were used (i.e. scandals, competitions and reflections/opinions on the Paralympic Games.)

In terms of how Paralympic athletes are portrayed, the content of the articles were analyzed to determine if any of the following stereotypes were present: 1) pitiable and pathetic 2) supercrip 3) sinister, evil and criminal 4) better-off dead 5) maladjusted 6) burden and 7) unable to live a successful life (Schantz & Gilbert, 2001; Nelson, 1994). Interviews were also conducted with sports editors and reporters, in most cases, from the newspapers surveyed.

Results and Analysis of 2004 Athens and 2008 Beijing Paralympics

A total of 307 newspaper articles were analyzed from an initial search that produced 768 stories. Articles were discarded if they were duplicates, unrelated to the Athens or Beijing Paralympic games or, if they were not about the athletes themselves. Canadian papers published more articles on Paralympic athletes as compared to the United States. About 54% more articles were published in Canada (Table 1).

Table 1: Published articles on Paralympians from the Athens and Beijing Games

Newspapers	Articles in initial search	Articles analyzed
Globe and Mail	168	69
Vancouver Sun	418	130
Total Canadian	**586**	**199**
New York Times	100	69
Washington Post	82	39
Total American	**182**	**108**

The average article lengths were similar; stories in United States averaged 700 words and in Canada they were roughly 690 words. The majority of articles were feature stories over 1500 words in length. *The Washington Post* had the least number of articles on Paralympians but the stories were the second longest in length because most were features.

Table 2: Average article word length in Canadian and United States newspapers

	American		Canadian	
	New York Times	Washington Post	Globe & Mail	Vancouver Sun
Average length	687	713	630	749
Total Average length	700		690	

More features, opinion pieces or short biographies about the Paralympic participants were published. Most of the articles were categorized as "Reflections/Opinions" as opposed to "Competitions" or "Scandals" (Table 3). The only exception was in *The Globe and Mail* where more articles on "Competitions" were published than "Reflections/Opinions".

Table 3: Article themes or focus in Canadian and United States newspapers

	Scandals	Competitions	Reflections/Opinions
Globe and Mail	20	28	21
Vancouver Sun	18	50	62
New York Times	17	25	27
Washington Post	10	8	21
Total	**65**	**111**	**131**

The New York Times and *The Globe and Mail* were almost equal in their distribution of articles in all three categories while more articles were published in the Vancouver Sun on stories identified as "Reflections/Opinions".

The most frequently used stereotype in the articles reviewed was "Pitiable and Pathetic" and "Supercrip" (Table 4). The total number of articles analyzed does not equal the total number of articles obtained. This is why a percentage is included in the results because not all of the articles had a stereotype. For example, the *Washington Post* only had 12 articles with the first stereotype "Pitiable and Pathetic" (31%) but a total of 39 articles were analyzed.

"Pitiable and Pathetic" appeared with similar frequency in all papers, ranging from 25% to 31%. The *New York Times* used the second stereotype "Supercrip" more often than the other papers while the *Washington Post* used the sixth stereotype "Burden" more frequently. The fifth stereotype, "Maladjusted" was not used often by any of the newspapers.

Table 4: Number of stereotypes in Canadian and United States newspapers

Label	1	2	3	4	5	6	7
	Pitiable and Pathetic	Supercrip	Sinister, Evil and Criminal	Better-off Dead	Maladjusted	Burden	Unable to Live a Successful Life
Globe and Mail	20 (29%)	10 (14%)	5 (7%)	5 (7%)	2 (3%)	2 (3%)	6 (9%)
Vancouver Sun	33 (25%)	20 (15%)	2 (2%)	1 (1%)	4 (3%)	4 (3%)	4 (3%)
New York Times	21 (30%)	24 (35%)	3 (4%)	4 (6%)	3 (4%)	6 (9%)	10 (14%)
Washington Post	12 (31%)	6 (15%)	3 (8%)	1 (3%)	3 (8%)	7 (18%)	2 (5%)

Results of the Analysis of the Vancouver 2010 Paralympic coverage

It is not a surprise that the host city (Vancouver Sun) produced the most articles. A total of 152 articles were analyzed from an initial search that brought back 715 articles. Duplicates and articles unrelated to the athletes were discarded. The Globe and Mail was second with 31 articles from 158 in the initial search, followed by *The New York Times* with 7 articles (from 18) and the Washington Post with only 2 articles (from 6).

Canadian papers produced a greater number of articles but the smaller number of articles from the United States could be due to a limitation of the search engine which does not include Blogs or online articles; both the Washington Post and New York Times may have provided the majority of their Paralympic coverage online as opposed to in print. Despite the increased coverage by Canadian newspapers, the average word length remained similar.

Table 5: Average article length from a search during September 1st 2009 to April 1st 2012 in Canadian and United States newspapers about Paralympic athletes

	American		Canadian	
	New York Times	Washington Post	Globe & Mail	Vancouver Sun
Average length	555	814	740	632
Total Average length	685		686	

Again, most of the articles were features, opinion pieces or biographies of the athletes. This contributed to the high average word length and similarity in word length between the United States and Canada. Prevalent themes are summarized in Table 6. Again, many articles were reflections or Opinions and not actual reporting on the results of the competitions. The Vancouver Sun produced the most articles related to the competition results and had articles that explained the classification system as well as how medals were awarded based on the level of disability of each athlete.

Table 6: Articles themes or focus in Canadian and United States newspapers

	Scandals	Competitions	Reflections/Opinions
Globe and Mail	1	13	17
Vancouver Sun	12	72	68
New York Times	0	2	5
Washington Post	1	0	1
Total	14	87	91

The frequency of articles published as scandals declined from 21 % for the Athens and Beijing Games to only 7% for the 2010 Paralympic Games. "Supercrip" was the stereotype used most often by Canadian newspapers, while *The New York Times* used "pitable and pathetic" (Table 7). Admittedly, it is difficult to compare with the results of the Athens and Beijing Games due to the low number of articles returned for analysis but it is worth noting that the overall number of stereotypes declined and the "better-off dead" or "maladjusted" stereotypes were never used.

Table 7: Seven stereotypes used in Canadian and United States newspapers

	New York Times	Washington Post	Vancouver Sun	Globe and Mail	*Total*
Pitiable and Pathetic	3	0	11	3	17
Supercrip	1	0	24	6	31
Sinister, evil and criminal	0	0	2	0	2
Better-off dead	0	0	0	0	0
Maladjusted	0	0	0	0	0
Burden	1	0	1	1	3
Unable to live a successful life	0	0	2	0	2

Unfortunately, it still appears that Paralympic athletes do not receive a fair amount of media coverage as compared to their Olympic counterparts. Yet, the tone of the articles appears to have improved.

Discussion and Conclusive statements

Our analysis showed that American newspapers had less coverage of Paralympic athletes but did not have fewer stereotypes than Canadian newspapers. It appears that the existence of the American for Disabilities Act does not influence the language used in news articles. In fact, according to reporter Alan Schwartz of *The New York Times*, this legislation is not something news editors keep in mind when they edit a story.

The majority of stories from the United States and Canada were features but *The New York Times* and *The Globe and Mail* stood out as papers that published almost an equal number of stories on the "Competitions" and "Scandals" of the Games. The reason this occurred is unclear but editors interviewed said the most engaging story is often written as a feature because it details the life and accomplishments of an athlete. Therefore it is not a surprise that the majority of articles about Paralympians are framed as features. Both athletes and journalists admit sad stories are what the public enjoys reading but athletes think this focus should be reduced. Instead they prefer the focus be on their hard work and training.

American and Canadian journalists both expressed efforts to be sensitive to the language they used but stereotypes such as 'Pitable and Pathetic" still exist. For example, a *Globe and Mail* article about Neroli Fairhall a Paralympic athlete from New Zealand who used a wheelchair stated, "She lay on the ground for 21 hours before she was found, her legs useless. Determined to make the most of what she had left, Fairhall took up archery" (Christie, 2006).

Canadian and American reporters admitted they knew the Paralympics had less coverage but said the reasons were not personal. They were a result of budget restrictions and the limited space allocated for each section. American editor, Jason Stallman from *The New York Times* said it was also due to a lack of public interest. He said they have tracked hits on their websites for popular articles and often the ones about the Paralympics did not receive as many hits. Yet, one wonders how many people were unable to access them. For example, a visually impaired person cannot read a story on a website.

Other research has looked at the types of disability coverage as either traditional or progressive. Traditional coverage focuses on stories which discuss the individual differences between the disabled person and society. Often stories discuss how the person thrives "despite their disability" or frames the athlete as a "supercrip". Progressive coverage focuses on how society deals with people who have disabilities. Often they view the dysfunction as lying not with the individual with a disability but in "society's inability or willingness to adapt" (Clogston, 1994). Research in the early 90's discovered 55% of stories focused on the stereotype 'supercrip'. A lower prevalence of this stereotype was found in this study but it was still one of the most popular stereotypes. Clogston (1994) labels *The New York Times* as progressive in their coverage of disabilities but said that many of the "reporters had progressive attitudes towards those with physical disabilities but their attitudes had no connection with how they wrote about disability". In this study, the prevalence of traditional stories was still abundant although reduced in the 2010 Vancouver Paralympic Games coverage compared to the Athens or Beijing Games. Clogston (1994) also suggested two ways to improve disability coverage: First, he said newsroom style guides should explicitly state examples of what is meant by traditional and progressive stories. Second, disabled reporters should be hired in newsrooms but not be used as 'token experts'. Instead, they should be integrated into the system, similar to what has been done with racial minority groups (Clogston, 1994).

Elizabeth Walker-Young is a retired Paralympic swimmer who won silver and bronze in Athens and worked as a Paralympic Classification Specialist at the Vancouver 2010 Paralympics. In her experience with journalists, Walker said there were times when she was asked personal questions that made her feel uncomfortable. Fortunately, she says there has been an improvement in the coverage of Paralympic sport. She especially enjoyed the blog written about the Beijing Paralympics by the Canadian Broadcasting Corporation's Scott Russell as he focused on the fitness and level of athleticism of the athletes as opposed to their disabilities.

The role of the International Paralympic Committee in the framing of stories is important. Journalists said they relied upon press releases or wire reports for stories on the Paralympics. Sandra Keenan a *New York Times* reporter said they always research their stories and speak with athletes on the telephone despite not physically being there. Still this would mean the story ideas are influenced by the information initially provided from press releases. The choice to focus on athletes like Oscar Pistorius may be due to the lack of awareness about other athletes. In other words, the IPC is partially responsible for the proliferation of stories with an overwhelmingly positive frame but also with specific stereotypes.

References

Bertling, C. & T. Schierl (2008). Disabled sport and its relation to contemporary cultures of presence and Aesthetics. *Sport in History,* 28 (1), 39-50.

Christie, J. (2006, June 13). Corruption Scandal Hits Beijing. *The Globe and Mail,* p. S4.

Clogston, J.S. (1994). Disability coverage in American newspapers. In J.A. Nelson (Ed.), *The disabled, the media and info age* (pp. 45-53). Westport CN: Greenwood Press.

Nelson, J.A. (1994). Broken Images: Portrayals of those with disabilities in American media. In J.A. Nelson (Ed.), *The disabled, the media and the info age* (pp. 1-17). Westport, CN: Greenwood Press.

Schantz, O.J. & K. Gilbert (2001) An Ideal Misconstrued: Newspaper Coverage of the Atlanta Paralympic Games in France and Germany. *Sociology of Sport Journal,* 18(1), 69-94.

Chapter 11
A Way Forward

Researching International Perspectives on Media and the Paralympics

Eric de Léséleuc

Introduction

How do the media discuss athletes with disabilities in general and those who participate in the Paralympic Games in particular? What stereotypes, social representations, ideologies or common sense ideas are they conveying through their discourse and images? Which way do they broadcast their unspoken comments and silences or uncomfortable facial expressions regarding Paralympic athletes? The purpose of this chapter is to indicate how researchers of different countries have attempted to answer the previous questions.

A quick synthesis of the most well-known works will be promulgated, on the one hand to put an emphasis on the knowledge they are putting at societies disposal, and on the other hand to underline how it is difficult, in the present state of world media affairs, to share this knowledge at an international level. As a matter of fact, most of the time the data corpus, and the concepts and methods involved invite us to compare the results of the answers, but the lack of definitions and other indicators make such comparisons across nations almost impossible.

State of the question: similar approaches that invite comparison[1]

First of all, it is clearly noticeable that there is little scientific literature in the social sciences relating directly to the analysis of the 'mediatisation of disabled athletes'.

This explains the importance of the writings of authors, like O. Schantz and K. Gilbert who were pioneers in Europe and internationally, and who based their work on analysing the 'mediatisation' of athletes in general across differing cultures. Other works, maybe because they mainly come from the USA, rose up from the academic area commonly called 'gender studies'. The main purpose of the academics who write in the area of gender studies is the analysis of the discrimination of sportswomen in the media, with the will to highlight masculine hegemony in both sport and media. In a certain way, it marked the beginning of research regarding the 'mediatization' of disabled athletes because, as we shall see, we can find similar structures in disability and media research as in the context of gender research papers.

Identical legitimations

From a general point of view, research on sport, media, woman and the persons with disabilities (whatever the crossings or articulations between those terms) legitimate themselves by the necessity to demonstrate the different kinds of discrimination that affects athletic women, athletes with disabilities or female athletes with disabilities. To do so, researchers often evoke the principles of equality of opportunity and treatment or by quoting the laws forbidding discrimination between sexes or towards disabled persons. Two theoretical approaches are generally used to support research and these are; on the one hand, the role of social representations as the determining factor of the behaviours, and on the other hand, the role of the media as a vehicle for transmission of stereotypes, of values and of various dominant ideologies in contemporary societies. Therefore, if these researches have a legitimacy, it is because they propose to shine an academic light on media (whatever they are: television, written press, radio, books, internet, etc.) as a source of production or reproduction of social representations, and if they participate or not in the process of discrimination of those specific populations by transmitting non-egalitarian messages. This double "inscription" in the

---

1. See Notes after conclusive statements for further details.

gender and disability studies, associated with the socio-anthropological approach of discrimination has led different researchers to formulate quite similar questions.

a. Similarity of basic questions and research objectives.

In general, as mentioned above, the main framework for researching the disability arena as utilized in this chapter is the analysis of gender inequalities. It is specified by questions which can be summarized as follows: Are sports women receiving media coverage equal to that received by men? For example, Buysse and Duncan, included this question in their research from an historical approach because the authors want to know if the increase in women's sport generated transformations in their mediatisation (Did it increase? Did it change in a qualitative way? Did it approach parity with males? etc.) Also, some authors attempted to understand if female athletes are more mediated when they practice sports i.e. do they appear "feminine" or not?

However, the problem remains, as Duncan (2006) succinctly questions: How do media and sports join together to present messages about sport and gender? It is hoped that the answers to the above question will help to explain why researchers that were analysing the relationship between sport and disability began to wonder about the role of the media in the integration process of persons with disabilities.

The objectives of this research were to provide an analysis of gender stereotypes and gendered sport stereotypes, including an analysis from a historical perspective over a period from approximately 1980 to 2010. Throughout, other questions arose concerning the different kinds of disabilities (for example, do some disabilities have a higher profile than others in the press?), or when concerning the comparisons between athletes with disabilities and athletes without disabilities (are athletes with disabilities more or less evoked than able bodied athletes? How? etc.)

b. Corpus of data from the written press and its conceptual similarity.

Mainly, corpuses or genre are constituted within individual newspapers[2], and mostly divided into two categories: [1] general-interest press (daily newspapers, national newspapers) and [2] sports press, which is produced either by publishing companies or sports institutions[3] themselves.

---

2. M. Messner seems to be one of the only academics specializing in the analysis of the television media (although other collaborations with authors analysing the written press have been found). Interestingly, the internet remains, at the moment, barely utilized for research in this area.

3. The sports press which is produced by large publishing companies; for example, *Sports Illustrated for Kids* analysed by M.C. Duncan et A. Sayaovong (1990). And the sports press produced by sports institutions; For example, newspapers produced by the *National Collegiate Athletic Association* as analysed by J.M. Buysse et M.S. Embser-Herbert (2004).

Whatever the corpus are and due to the proximity of the questions, only some concepts are used to categorize data. Indeed, five of them appear in a recurrent manner. These are: trivialization, infantilization, feminization (sexualism), sportivisation, and marginalization. Trivialization is used to categorize the elements of the articles or illustrations that do not present the actors in a sporting situation. For example, it is the case when one's talking about the athletes evoking their children, lovers, husband or wife, etc. This means that athletes are considered as trivialized when the characteristics of sport like performance, record, training and so on, are not presented. Infantilization is used to categorize the elements that refer to situations of athletes' childhood (for example to cry, to be called by their first name in spite of their name, to be protected in their parents' arms, etc.). Feminization or sexualisation (depending on the authors preference) research is used to categorize the elements referring to features of the feminine stereotype (e.g. the use of make-up, feminine dress, focalization on parts of the body with sexual connotation like breast or buttocks). It is to be noticed that features of masculine sexualisation are rarely mentioned. The concept of sportivisation[4] is also rarely formulated in this manner, but we define it as the gathering of data that refers to an individual's attitude to sports. It is the case in research studies that try to understand if the written press provides an image of "real" athletes when the images present athletes in the place of the event, with sportswear or during the sportive action[5]. At last, the concept of marginalization (or discrimination or stigmatization) is used when a certain number of processes are underscored and lead to unegalitarian treatment and a discretization of the individual, whether of women or persons with disabilities.

This conceptual similarity has been underlined and mildly denounced by Duncan (2006) who recommends the use of new processes to renew the framework of analysis concerning these research objects. Nevertheless, for now, the model is still in place.

c. Similar and comparable results

Whether they are qualitative or quantitative, research results mostly argue that there is a form of marginalization or discrimination concerning sports for women vs. men or sports for athletes with disabilities vs. ablebodied athletes. Results demonstrate that women and persons with disabilities are, in general, under-represented[6] in the media. Furthermore, results also show that when they are presented, they are more trivialized, more infantilized and less sport oriented, than for the able bodied individuals.

---

4. This concept is rarely evoked directly this way.
5. For example, J. Vincent et al (2002) or Pappous et al. (2011)
6. This under-representation was called into doubt by Léséleuc et al. (2010)

A comparison appears impossible

The unanimity of the results, based on similar processes, gives the image of a very strong coherence that leads the reader to believe that these results can be compared to each other. The similarity of the procedures, of the theoretical corpus of references, of questions, of objectives, of concepts, etc., makes this comparison possible. Furthermore, the recognized quality of the authors and of the international reviews in which those results are published and the actual context of internationalization of the development of the researches in contemporary social sciences, points to the fact that they are similar. We are conditioned to believe that if authors can publish their results, and if they write that X% of the press articles trivialize sportswomen, and that another author may write that Y% sportswomen are trivialized, that those results can be compared. But is it really true?

As we will see, with an example of categorization of grounded data used in this kind of research, the conditions of this comparison are not, for the moment, established at an international level. For example if we look at the case of one of the most used concepts: infantilisation and try to categorize an article extract[7] from the media coverage of the Beijing Paralympic Games to demonstrate the above point.

The following article was published in a Thai newspaper:

> "After the competition, a female athlete from Chaiyapum, Somkuan spoke with her teary eye that this is the happiest moment in her life because she came to this competition to bring a medal for her mother. [...] Somkuan will use her 5 hundred thousand baht money reward for her mother. Doctor expects to restore her mother's left eye after she got hit by hammer [...] which she already spent about 30000 baht for curing. Another part of the money will go to refine her mother's home [...]"

The question is to know how searchers, isolated from each other, but working with the same concepts, and using the same categories of variables, can end up with the same categorization (necessary condition to compare the results) when analysing the above extract for the article?

The first stage of this work, the cutting in analysis units, allows us to evoke the first problem. The scientific articles (of which it is all about) are never precise as to what exactly we call "units of cutting" or "units of analysis". In other words we do not know what exactly is the number of occurrences counted by the different groups of researchers across the world. In the case of the article, for example, we could count whether the words, the sentences, the grammatical structures (subject, verb, complement[8]), or even

---

7. Article: Thai Paralympic athletes gain another three bronze medals, in *Matichon*, 11 Sept 2008, p. 31

8. Concerning our research team "SantESiH", we choose the grammatical clause (subject, verb, complement) because within the evoked problematic, it is the actor/subject and its gender (male or female) that is at the centre of the analysis. Each action or situation presented will then be characterized by a verb and a complement, then counted for each actor.

the paragraphs. The differences in the 'cutting in analysis units' have obvious consequences because they suppose possible differences in terms of the results. The lack of precision on this subject in the scientific articles leaves us without clue of what the authors count, and so makes the results, by principle not comparable between each other.

However, this is only one part of the problem, let's assume that the cutting unit has been defined. Let's take, for example, a cutting in grammatical stuctures (subject, verb, complement). Then the text would be cut like this:

1. After the competition, female athlete from Chaiyapum, Somkuan spoke with her teary eye that this is the happiest moment in her life
2. because she came to this competition to bring a medal for her mother
3. Somkuan will use her 5 hundred thousand money reward for her mother
4. Doctor expends to restore her mother's left eye
5. after she got hit by hammer [...]
6. which she already spent about 30000 baht for curing.
7. Another part of the money will go to refine her mother home [...]

From this cutting, each unit must integrate one, and only one analysis category.

In the proposal n°1, there is "clearly" an infantilizing dimension because the athlete (Somkuan) is presented with tears in her eyes. This is linked to the dimension of the child crying, and is part of the definition of infantilization as depicted by Duncan (2006). In the same way, the proposition n°2 has an infantilisation dimension because it presents the "daughter" bringing back a medal to her "mother". These two propositions are not difficult to categorize. What about the propositions n°3, 6 and 7? Can we put them in the "infantilization" category because the subject of the action is considered as "the daughter of..."? Or should we put them out of this category because she acts as an adult by taking care of her mother, and that does not refer to an image of the childhood? If we undertake this form of analysis and according to the qualitative answers provided by the researchers, the results would be different.

Considering the difficulty in answering this question, without going back to the reference of scientific literature and without legitimating these choices in relation to the construction of the object of research, it is certain that researchers, separated from each other are going to answer in different ways. In this instance then, we can be sure that we couldn't compare the obtained results.

In a certain way, we are facing the classical problem of the building of an analysis grid of discourse content. This is often solved locally with an elaboration procedure within the research team[9], working together on the same data to the precise definition of each category. This step of exploratory elaboration respects a principle of saturation which is often validated

---

9. This is what we do in our research team.

statistically to verify that all the categorization problems are eliminated in the same way by all the researchers working on the same project[10]. Then, the elaborated grid is used as the common work basis for all researchers of this reference group, even if they work together while living in different countries[11]. The problem is that this work is at present done by each groups working in an autonomous way and that it cannot lead to the elaboration of an international standard across the research. This means that, even if they make publications in the same international scientific reviews, each group remains isolated and works with its own analysis grid. As we already mentioned this prevents researchers from comparing results that at first sight seemed comparable.

The remedy would be the common elaboration of analysis grids with the researchers who are considered all over the world as individual references in that kind of research and to put it at the international scientific community's disposal. What would be interesting would be the development of the publication of a methodological manual. However, that would be far larger than any scientific article and difficult to develop. This implies that a stage of negotiation and collaboration should be organized between research teams, so that a procedure of sharing the problems leads to the elaboration of a common definition of the analysis of the categories of press articles. The results of this joint international work should have very large built in communication and international validation procedures so that, finally, the principles of reproducibility and comparability which are the foundation stones of the production of quality scientific knowledge be respected and indicated in the research concerning the medias analysis of sports people, whether they are disabled or not.

The point here is to provide a remedy for one of the more recurrent problems which is widely denounced, and is also one that partly discredits sociology; that is, the lack of unity in the conceptual definition and what goes with the research process and the lack of unity in terms of methodological procedures across borders. We can argue that all science works on the basis of the sharing of research objects and on the way to define and analyse them. As previously mentioned this allows the reproducibility and the comparability of results which are obtained globally by different teams. However, this is barely the case in sports sociology. Indeed, the problems encountered with this research program already illustrate this phenomenon. The epistemological specificities of sociology and the necessary contextualization of its processes do not always make possible the sharing of results or ideas at an international level. Nevertheless, in the case presented herein, the small number of teams working on disability research (and the related tasks) all over the world, find that the concepts we are working with

---

10. For example with the method of: *Intercoder Reliability Method* (or Interrater agreement)

11. It is the same in our case when we collaborate with foreign researchers (Thailand, Spain, Canada and Argentina)

do not pose specific problems of definition (as would concepts of identity or of individualization) and the possibilities of international collaborations. This works well for the elaboration of a common analysis tool. It is important now to find financial means so that some researchers get involved in this procedure and develop a pilot group of researchers working at a cross cultural and international level.

References and Bibliography

Andrews, D.L. (1998). Feminizing Olympic Reality. *International Review of the Sociology of Sport*, 31(1), 5-18.

Altheide, D.L. (1984). Media hegemony: A failure of perspective. *Public Opinion Quarterly*, 48, 476-490.

Asch, A., & Fine, M. (1992). Beyond portrayals: Revisiting the lives of women with disabilities. In M. Fine (Ed.), *Disrupting voices* (pp.139-174). Ann Arbor: The University of Michigan Press.

Auslander, G.K., & Gold, N. (1999). Media reports on disability: A binational comparison of types and causes of disability as reported in major newspapers. *Disability and Rehabilitation*, 21 (9), 420-431.

Baroffio-Bota, D., & Banet-Weiser, S. (2006). Women, Team Sports, and the WNBA: Playing Like a Girl. In A. A. Raney & J. Braynt (Eds.), *Handbook of Sports and Media* (pp. 485-500). Mahwah, NJ: Lawrence Erlbaum Associates.

Barnes, C., Mercer, G., & Shakespeare, T. (1999). *Exploring Disability: a Sociological Introduction*. Cambridge: Policy Press.

Bogdan, R., & Taylor S. (1989). Relationships with Severely Disabled People: The Social Construction of Humanness. *Social Problems*, 36 (2), 135-148.

Clogston, J.S. (1990). *Disability Coverage in 16 Newspapers*. Louisville: Advocado Press.

Eastman, S.T., & Billings, A. (2000). Sports casting and sports reporting. The power of the gender bias. *Journal of Sport & Social Issues*, 24(2), 192-213.

Buysse, J. A., & Embser-Herbert, M. S. (2004). Constructions of gender in sport: An analysis of intercollegiate media guide cover photographs. *Gender Society*, 1, 66-81.

Crolley, L., & Teso, E. (2007). Gender narratives in Spain. The representation of female athletes in Marca and El Pais. *International Review for the Sociology of Sport*, 42, 149-166.

Crossman, J., Vincent, J., & Speed, H. (2007). The times they are a-changing: Gender comparisons in three national newspapers of the 2004 Wimbledon championships. *International Review for the Sociology of Sport*, 42, 27-41.

Dellinger, K., & Williams, C. L. (1997). Makeup at work: Negotiating appearance rules in the workplace. *Gender and Society*, 11, 151-177.

DePauw, K. (1997). The (in)visibility of (dis)ability: cultural contexts and "sporting bodies". *Quest*, 49, 416-430.
DePauw, K. P., & Doll-Tepper, G. (2000). Toward progressive inclusion and acceptance: Myth or reality? The inclusion debate and bandwagon discourse. *Adapted Physical Activity Quarterly*, 17(2), 135-143.
Douglas, D. (2002). To Be Young, Gifted, Black and Female, *Sociology of Sport On-line*, 5 (2). Retrieved April 2nd from: http://physed.otago.ac.nz/sosol/v5i2/v5i2html
Dumitrescu, A. (2006). *Representation of female athletes in Western and Romanian Media.* Master's thesis, Florida State University, USA.
Duncan, M. C., & Brummet, B. (1987). The mediation of spectator sport. *Research Quarterly for Exercise and Sport*, 58, 168-177.
Duncan, M. C. (1990). Sports photographs and sexual differences: Images of women and men in the 1984 and 1988 Olympic Games. *Sociology of Sport Journal*, 7, 22-42.
Duncan, M. C., & Messner, M. A. (1998). The media image of sport and gender. In L. A. Wenner (Ed.), *Media Sport* (pp. 170-195). New York: Routledge.
Duncan, M. C. (2006). Gender warriors in sport: women and the media, in A. Raney & J. Bryant (Eds.), *Handbook of sports and media* (pp. 231-252). New York: Routledge.
Elliot, D. (2003). Moral responsibilities and the power of pictures. In P.M. Lester & S.D. Ross (Eds.), *Images that Injure* (pp. 7-21). London: Praeger.
Farnall, O., & Smith, K. A. (1999). Reactions to people with disabilities: personal contact versus viewing of specific media portrayals. *Journalism and mass communication quarterly*, 76(4), 659-672.
Ferri, B., & Gregg, N. (1998). Woman with disabilities: Missing voices. *Women's Studies International Forum*, 21, 429-439.
Frank, G. (1988). On Embodiment: A Case Study of Congenital Limb Deficiency in American Culture. In M, Fine & A. Asch (Eds.), *Women with Disabilities: Essays in Psychology, Culture, and Politics* (pp. 41-71). Philadelphia: Temple University Press.
Frith, T., Cheng, H., & Shaw, P. (2004). Race and Beauty: A Comparison of Asian and Western Models in Women's Magazine Advertisements. *Sex Roles*, 50, 53-61.
Früh, W., (1994), *Realitätsvermittlung durch Massenmedien: die permanente Transformation der Wirklichkeit*: Opladen.
Fullerton, R. (2007). Not Playing Fair: Coverage of Women & Minorities in the Sports Pages. *Studies In Media & Information Literacy Education*, 6, 1-13.
Génolini, J.P., & Rodriguez, L. (2008). Les représentations sociales des jeux paralympiques dans la presse française. In J.M. Hoc & Y. Corson (Eds.), *Actes du Congrès National de la Société Française de Psychologie, Nantes septembre 2007* (pp. 189-198). Nantes.

Hardin, M., Chance J., Dodd, J. E., & Hardin, B. (2002). Olympic Photo Coverage Fair to Female Athletes. *Newspaper Research Journal*, 23, 64-78

Hardin, B., & Hardin, M. (2003). Conformity and conflict: Wheelchair athletes discuss sport media. *Adapted Physical Activity Quarterly*, 20(3), 246-259.

Hardin, M., Lynn, S., & Walsdorf, K. (2005). Challenge and conformity on "contested terrain": Images of women in four women's sport/fitness magazines. *Sex Roles*, 53, 105-117.

Hargreaves, J. (2000). *Heroines of sport: The politics of difference and identity*. London: Routledge.

Hartmann-Tews, I. & Rulofs, B. (2001). International Media Coverage of Women's Sports. In K. Christensen, A. Guttmann, & G. Pfister (Eds.). *International Encyclopedia of Women and Sport*. New York: Macmillan.

Higgs, C. T., Weiller, K. H., & Martin, S. B. (2003). Gender bias in the 1996 Olympic Games: A comparative analysis. *Journal of Sport and Social Issues*, 27, 52-64.

Holtzman, L. (2000). *Media Messages*. New York: Armonk M.E. Sharpe.

Hooper, S. (2002). Fading starlet. Lack of success tarnishes Kournikova's marketability. Retrieved December 05, 2007, from: http://sportsillustrated.cnn.com/tennis/2002/us_open/news/2002/08/27/kournikova_tennis/

Hoover-Dempsey, K. V., Plas, J. M., & Wallston, B. S. (1986). Tears and weeping among professional women: In search of new understanding. *Psychology of Women Quarterly*, 10, 19–34.

Jones, R., Murrell, A. J., & Jackson, J. (1999). Pretty versus powerful in the sports pages: Print media coverage of U.S. women's Olympic gold medal winning teams. *Journal of Sport and Social Issues*, 23, 183-192.

Kafer A. (2000). Amputated Desire, Resistant Desire: Female Amputees in the Devotee Community Disability World. Retrieved April 1, 2008 from: http://www.disabilityworld.org/June-July2000/Women/SDS.htm

Kane, M. J. (1989). Media coverage of the female athlete before, during, and after Title IX: Sports Illustrated revisited. *Journal of Sport Management*, 2, 87–99.

Kane, M. J., & Parks, J. B. (1992). The social construction of gender difference and hierarchy in sport journalism: Few new twists on very old themes. *Women in Sport and Physical Activity Journal*, 1, 49-83.

Kilbourne, J. (1999). *Can't buy my love: How advertising changes the way we think and feel*. New York: Touchstone.

King, K. (2007). Media Portrayals of Male and Female Athletes. A Text and Picture Analysis of British National Newspaper Coverage of the Olympic Games since 1948. *International Review for the Sociology of Sport*, 42, 187-199.

Klein, M.-L. (1988). Women in the discourse of sports reports. *International Review for the Sociology of Sport*, 123, 139-151.

Lachal, R.C. & Combrouze, D. (1997). La représentation des personnes handicapées à travers des émissions documentaires de la télévision française. *Cahiers Ethnologiques*, 19, 239-262.

Lachal R.C. (2000). La représentation des personnes handicapées dans les médias : de l'objet au sujet. *Revue Prévenir*, 39(2), 97-105.

Lee, J. (1992). Media portrayals of male and female Olympic athletes: Analyses of newspaper accounts of the 1984 and the 1988 Summer Games. *International Review for the Sociology of Sport*, 27, 197-219.

Léséleuc, E. de (2009). Internacionalizar los estudios sobre la discapacidad: un punto de metodologia. *IIX Congreso Argentino y III Congreso Latinoamericano de Educacion Fisica y Ciencias*. Universidad de La Plata, Argentina, 12 mai 2009.

Léséleuc E. de, Pappous, A. & Marcellini, A., (in print). The mediatisation of sports women with disability. Newspapers analysis from four European countries during the Sydney's 2000 Paralympics Games. *European Journal for Sport and Society*.

Louveau, C. (2000). Au-delà des Jeux Paralympiques de Sydney. Femmes sportives, corps désirables. *Le Monde Diplomatique*, 25.

Maas, K. W., & Hasbrook, C. A. (2001). Media promotion of the paradigm Citizen/Golfer: An analysis of Golf Magazines' representations of disability, gender, and age. *Sociology of Sport Journal*, 18(1), 21-36.

Malec, M.A. (1994). Gender (In)equity in the NCAA News? *Journal of Sport and Social Issues*, 18, 376-378.

Marcellini, A., Léséleuc de, E. & Gleyse, J. (2003). L'intégration sociale par le sport des personnes handicapées. *Revue Internationale de Psychosociologie*, 20, 59-72.

Marcellini, A. (2006). Des corps atteints valides ou de la déficience au «°*firmus*°» : Hypothèses autour de la mise en scène sportive du corps handicapé In G. Boetsch, N. G., Chapuis-Lucciani, & D. N., Chevé D., (Eds.), *Représentations du corps. Le biologique et le vécu : normes et normalité* (pp. 59-68). Nancy : Presses Universitaires de Nancy.

Marcellini, A. (2007). Nouvelles figures du handicap ? Catégorisations sociales et dynamique des processus de stigmatisation / déstigmatisation, In G. Boetsch, C. Hervé, & J. Rozenberg, (Eds.), *Corps normalisé, corps stigmatisé, corps racialisé* (pp. 201-219). Bruxelles: De Boeck.

Messner, M. A., Duncan, M. C., & Cooky, C. (2003). Silence, sports bras, and wrestling porn: Women in televised sports news and highlights shows. *Journal of Sport and Social Issues*, 27, 38-51.

Messner, M.A., Duncan, M.C., & Jensen, K. (1993). Separating the men from the girls: The gendered language of televised sports. *Gender and Society*, 7, 121-137.

Mikosza, J. M. & Phillips, M. G. (1999). Gender, sport and the body politic: Framing femininity in the golden girls of sport calendar and the Atlanta dream. *International Review for the Sociology of Sport*, 34, 5-16.

Moragas, Spa M. de (2000). Olimpismo, comunicacion y cultura, Retrieved December 05, 2007, from: http://olympicstudies.uab.es/pdf/wp095_spa.pdf

Nelson, J. (Ed.). (1994). *The Disabled, the Media, and the Information Age*. Westport: Greenwood.

Nelson, J. (1996). The invisible cultural group: Images of Disability. In P. Martin (Ed.), *Images that injure. Pictorial stereotypes in the media* (pp. 75-185). Westport, CN: Praeger.

Nixon, H. (2007). Constructing Diverse Sports Opportunities for People with Disabilities. *Journal of Sport & Social Issues*, 31, 417-433.

Jones, R., Murrell, A. J., & Jackson, J. (1999). Pretty versus powerful in the sports pages: Print media coverage of the US Women's Olympic gold medal winning teams. *Journal of Sport and Social Issues, 23,* 183-192.

Oliver, M. Y. (1990). *The politics of disablement*. Basingstoke: MacMillan.

Oliver, M.Y. & Barnes, C. (1998). *Social Policy and Disabled People: From Exclusion to Inclusion*. London: Longman.

Pappous, A., Marcellini, A. & Léséleuc E. de (in print). Current and future directions for research on the media coverage of female paralympic athletes in the global sport arena: A review. *Sport in Society*.

Pappous, A., Marcellini, A. & Léséleuc E. de (in print). From Sydney to Beijing: The evolution of the photographic coverage of Paralympics Games in 5 European countries. *Sport in Society, Special Issue Sport and Disability*.

Reichert, T. (2003). *The erotic history of advertising*. New York: Prometheus books.

Reichert, T., Lambiase, J., Morgan, S., Carstarphen, M., & Zavoina, S. (1999). Beefcake and cheesecake: No matter how you slice it, sexual explicitness in advertising continues to increase. *Journalism & Mass Communication Quarterly*, 76, 7–20.

Robinson, L. (2002). *Black tights: Women, sport and sexuality*. Toronto: Harper.

Rose, G. (2001). *Visual Methodologies*. London: Sage

Rowe, D. (2006) Media sport culture: An education in the politics of acquisition. Retrieved January 26, 2008, from: http://www.playthegame.org/News/Up_To_Date/Sports_journalists_spinners_or_spun_08020001.aspx#

Ruiz, J. (2005). La discapacidad como estigma: un análisis psicosocial del afrontamiento del desempleo de las personas con discapacidad física. *RedSi: revista especializada en formación y empleo de los colectivos con riesgo de exclusión*, 6.

Shildrick, M. (2002). *Embodying the monster. Encounters with the vulnerable self*. London: Sage.

Smith, A. & Thomas, N. (2005). The 'inclusion' of elite athletes with disabilities in the 2002 Manchester Commonwealth Games: An exploratory analysis of British newspaper coverage. *Sport, Education and Society*, 10, 49-67.

Salwen, M. B., & Woods, N. (1994). Depictions of female athletes on Sports Illustrated covers, 1957-89. *Journal of Sport Behavior*, 17, 98-107.

Schantz O.J., & Gilbert K. (2001). An Ideal Misconstrued: Newspaper Coverage of the Atlanta Paralympic Games in France and Germany. *Sociology of Sport Journal*, 18, 69-94.

Schantz, O. J. & Marty, C. (1995). The French press and sport for people with handicapping conditions. In I. Morisbak, & P.E. Jørgensen (Eds.), *Quality of life through adapted physical activity* (pp.72-79). Oslo: Hamytykk.

Schell, B., & Rodriguez, S. (2001). Subverting bodies/ambivalent representations: Media analysis of Paralympian, Hope Lewellen. *Sociology of Sport Journal*, 18, 127-135.

Schell, L.A.., & Duncan, M.C. (1999). A content analysis of CBS's coverage of the 1996 Paralympic Games. *Adapted Physical Activity Quarterly*. 16, 27-47.

Sherrill, C. (1993). *Adapted physical activity, recreation and sport: Crossdisciplinary and lifespan*. Boston: McGraw-Hill.

Shifflett, B., & Revelle, R. (1994). Gender Equity in Sports Media Coverage: A Review of the NCAA News. *Journal of Sport and Social Issues*. 18, 144–150.

Shugart, H. (2003). She shoots, she scores: Mediated constructions of contemporary female athletes in coverage of the 1999 U.S. women's soccer team. *Western Journal of Communication*, 67, 1-31.

Taub, D.E., Blinde, E.M. & Greer, K.R. (1999). Stigma management through participation in sport and physical activity: experiences of male college students with physical disabilities. *Human Relations*. 52, 1469-1483.

Trowler, P. (1996). *Investigating the mass media*. London: Collins Educational.

Thomas, N., & Smith, A. (2003). Preoccupied with able-bodiedness? An analysis of the British media coverage of the 2000 Paralympic Games. *Adapted Physical Activity Quarterly*, 20, 166-181.

Urquhart, J., & Crossman, J. (1999). The Globe and Mail coverage of the winter Olympic games: A cold place for women athletes. *Journal of Sport & Social Issues*, 23 (2), 193-202.

Van Dijk, T. A. (1985). *Handbook of discourse analysis*. London: Academic Press.

Vincent, J., Imwold, C., Masemann, V., & Johnson T. J. (2002). A comparison of selected «serious» and «popular» British, Canadian and United States newspaper coverage of female and male athletes competing in the centennial Olympic Games. *International Review for the Sociology of Sport*, 37(3-4), 319-335.

Vincent, J., Pedersen, P. M., Whisenant, W. A., & Assey D. (2007). Analyzing the print media coverage of professional tennis players: British newspaper narratives about female competitors in the Wimbledon Championships. *International Journal of Sport Management and Marketing Issue*, 2, 281 - 300.

Wenner, L. A. (Ed.), *MediaSport*. London: Routledge.

Zola, I.K. (1991). Communication barriers between "the able bodied" and "the handicapped". *The psychological and social impact of disability*. New York: Springer, 157-164.

Part II
Visibility of Disability

Chapter 12
Analyzing Disabled Athletes' Photographs

The Case of the 2008 Beijing Paralympic Games

Capucine Germain & Julie Grall

Introduction

There is little doubt that the first recorded physical activities for disabled people had a medical objective which concentrated on supporting physical therapy. Progressively and more recently however, a stronger sport perspective has appeared to support physical therapy activities (Marcellini, 2005a). The Paralympic Games which represent a gathering place between 'sport and disability', make those two distinct worlds compatible, which in many ways seems contradictory because they are an "unexpected and apparently paradoxical meeting between the world of excellence, performance and the world of .....inability" (Marcellini, 2007, p.202). There is then simultaneous staging of 'sport and disability', and mixed understandings as to which status is attributed to those disabled athletes? How are they designated by the audience? In this case the media? Are they recorded as athletes, disabled athletes, disabled people, athletes with disabilities? These and other questions regarding the relationship between the media and the

Paralympics need to be answered. In short, this chapter questions how the new identification may support the image of sporting status for disabled persons.

In Beijing, French television, which provided around fifteen hours of live broadcasting each day for the Olympic Games, only offered two daily off-line schedules of seven minutes for the Paralympic Games (Deffontaines, 2008). This unequal media coverage shows a real distinction between these two events. The media, which collectively are some of the only links to the Games and the outside world, seem to play "a major part in the production and the reproduction of the social representations" (De Léséleuc, Marcellini & Pappous, 2005, p.45). As such they influence the readers in their social representations towards disability, particularly through sport, and they are a tool enabling the "understanding of the continuity and transformation logic at work in the collective conceptions about disability" (De Léséleuc et al., op. cit.).

Indeed, in the world of sport, and particularly the Olympic Games "the staging of this efficient 'perfect' body is at the basis of the sport show, and of the recognition signals which act on the narcissistic imagination of the viewers" (Raufast & Raufast, 2006, p. 6). In this way the media play an important role in the social representations of the readers towards the athlete. However, how do they present the disabled athlete and which influences do they have on those athlete representations for the readers? It is clear that the visibility in the media of the athlete termed and classed as 'disabled' has a symbolic function as argued by Defrance (2006, p. 78) "the representation of ability figures within dominated groups [...] plays a part in the symbolic struggles aiming at smashing the negative stereotypes linked to those groups". Yet, in sport, the media almost always present 'perfect' bodies. If truth be told, "Everything which is not standard must be hidden, concealed, erased, and above all steamrolled by standardization" (Meynaud, 2005, p. 29). This sifting and blatant sorting of the broadcast information (Kientz, 1971) has overtime become normal behavior. Indeed, the mass media tend to select the topics, and sometimes transform the pictures thereby following the consumers' perceived desires.

In summary disability just like other features become almost invisible except when underlining a loss, a deficiency, or a potential danger. It is as if the disabled athlete has no acknowledged social life apart from this supposed and/or real physical deficit portrayed by the media. Keller et al. argue in their work that; "When articles mentioned the impact of the disability on the person's life, they often portrayed the negative impact of the disability" (Keller, Hallahan, McShane, Crowley, & Blandford, 1990, p. 271). With these thoughts in mind we need to question ourselves about the media and consequent readers' representations towards disabled athletes and in completing this task we studied the collective conceptions built by the media towards disabled athletes at the Beijing Paralympic Games.

Disability and sport

If we take into consideration the visibility impact of disability in social interactions then we must heed the words of Stiker (2006) who comments of disabled individuals as those who have "damaged bodies" or even as Goffman (1975) recalls disabled individuals as the "bodies monstrosities" are some of the different words used by the scientific world to report about physical disabilities within interactions. This physical difference, when visible, directly interferes in social interactions, as well as in everyone's representations. The subject carrying this "mark" is then "discredited" (Goffman, op. cit.), he suffers from a phenomenon of "labeling" (Becker, 1963). "This unfortunate difference with what we [the "normals"] were expecting" thus destroys "the rights he has towards us because of his other attributes" (Goffman, 1975, p. 15). The physical disability appears here as one of the subject's master status traits, and not as an auxiliary status trait, according to Hughes (1945). It prevails over the other signals that can inform us on the identity of the person. "The disablement acts on the sense of who we are, of what we are, a much stronger hold than any social role, even the key roles such as age, profession, and ethnic belonging" (Murphy, 1990, p. 150).

Everything occurs as if the disabled person had no acknowledged social life apart from this inadequacy. Taking up again the distinction between the master and the subordinate statuses (Hughes, 1945), the subject carrying a visible disability would then be first and foremost "a disabled person". Yet, it seems that in the sport world, the disabled athlete appears to get a more favorable status.

Secondly, let's see if the impact of the disability visibility has proceeded in the same way in the interactions particular to the world of disabled sport. Sport is acknowledged as a sphere which favours the "distigmatization process" for the disabled subjects, making their visibility more accepted (Marcellini, 2005b). Indeed, high-level disabled athletes mention a "greater body welfare" when they practice sport, which then is experienced as a "remedy for the disability injury" (Lachheb & Moualla, 2009, pp. 388-389). From then on, according to the disabled athlete, within the interactions "the disabled or abnormal body, until then condemned to concealing, invisibility, or fair exhibitions sees its meaning changing as soon as it becomes athletic" (Marcellini, 2006, p.63). But what about the public or the viewers' point of view? It seems that even in the world of sport, the disabled person's status is first seen by the viewers. High-level disabled athletes explain that their circle see them at first as athletes, whereas the "others" are centered on their deficiency which "imposes itself" to the eye (Lachheb & Moualla, 2009) and whatever the situation "the disabled or deviant people always remain like this in reference to a body pointed out as deficient" (Raufast & Raufast, 2006, p.6). In that case, can't we assess that sport activities, in which the body is specially displayed, risks to sharpen that difference, to reinforce the stigmatization?

Indeed, sport activities may bare the body. On the athletes' point of view, it could correspond to a "reversal of the stigma" (Wieviorka, 2005) in which the actor assesses his difference and becomes relieved of it. The broadcasting of pictures of the Paralympic Games through the media seems to participate in this process providing the visibility of the deficiency. Yet, can we not figure out the opposite effect, that is a reinforcement of the stigma through the media? Thus, if we adopt a more global vision, which representations of disabled athletes and the non-disabled readers will they build? So we will make the assumption that the media participate in the creation of a negative stigmatization process is important and that which contributes to viewing the disabled athletes as inability carriers and not as athletes.

Disability and performance

Since the development of the "performance worship", athletic champions have been symbols of social excellence. "All of them can, on the face of it, challenge any of them" (Ehrenberg, 1991, p. 39). Athletic challenge seems then to solve a tension between men's equality of principles and their real social inequality. Besides, the performance is enhanced "to such an extent that it sometimes obscures the other possible meanings that the subject may invest in his activity" (Garel, 2005, p. 39). Will it possibly be borne out during the Paralympic Games? Will this performance message be conveyed, going beyond the body "deformities"?

Through this performance worship, excellence, progress, surpassing are enhanced (Heilbrunn, 2004; Queval, 2004). The body is thus at the center of the performances production, its abilities being constantly assessed. Challenge displays the body impossibilities and inabilities. The subject then seems to break the social rules related to the dominating beauty standards or with profitability, production. "The features of the athletic body and of the disabled body prove antinomic" (Lachheb & Moualla, 2009, p. 382). When publishing the Olympic Games and Paralympic Games records, the media emphasize this opposition.

Performance being at the center of any athletic challenge, and because of this of the Olympic Games and Paralympic Games, assessing the Paralympic records estimate[1] may account for an indicator of the media readers' representations. Estimating a Paralympic record going by the Olympic record may reveal the questioned person's representation about the disabled athlete. We can suppose that by the apparent deficiencies of the disabled body emphasized by the challenge, the reader will underestimate the

---

1. By estimating, we mean "determining the approximative value" of the paralympic record, basing on the value of the same olympic record. We have measured those estimates through a questionnaire, first without pictures, and second in support with pictures of athletes achieving those records.

Paralympic records. Because of this, if we observe an important and systematic depreciation, that would underlie the idea that the disabled athlete's status distorts the athlete's.

If we consider that it is indeed the athlete's body who is at the center of this stigmatization process, its picture displayed by the media may account for a new object of analysis. Through those pictures, let's try to understand how the visibility of those deficiencies is received by the reader. This discrepancy between the features of the athletic body and the disabled body is enhanced by the pictures of the Paralympics. Here, we receive those pictures as "messages about disabled athletes" which are part of social speeches (Lebel, Marcellini & Pappous, 2010, p. 20). Thus, assessing the estimate of Paralympic records[2] drawing on pictures of disabled athletes may account for an indicator of the media readers' representations[3].

Disability and compassion

The pictures account for an interesting analysis and objective to debrief media readers representations towards disabled athletes, since they are attributed "a special power in terms of influence on the collective conceptions" (Lebel et al., 2010, p.20). They differ from articles in the sense that "the main feature of visual material is its faculty to enkindle emotions" (Joffe, 2001, p.102). Which feelings do those pictures conjure up to readers? Which messages could they evoke towards non-disabled or disabled athletes?

The performance logic being valued both for the Olympics and the Paralympic Games are those media pictures of non-disabled and disabled athletes thus referring to readers' feelings of power and speed. Therefore, the media display of non-disabled or disabled body carrying out a performance points at "the attributes of movement, autonomy, stability, order" (Lebel et al., 2010, p.23). But the media pictures of the Olympic Games and the Paralympic Games also seem to reinforce the stigmatization process of disabled athletes. The active and efficient disabled body, staging in sport arena is unexpected in comparison with the received idea of still and deficient body. "As such, some pictures on the disabled people's sport seem to bring one closer to a show close to the circus show" (Marcellini, 2006, p.65). Furthermore, this media picture display of deficiency brings readers to feel compassion, towards the disabled athlete. A "miserabilism", according to Grignon and Passeron (1989, p.260) leads to see the disabled people only in terms of lack (Eideliman et al., 2008).

---

2. Beijing PG have been chosen for their recentness as well as for the spatial and temporal proximity with OG. The selected pictures are those first appearing on Google, thus, corresponding to the most mediated pictures.

3. The questionnaire has been submitted to STAPS (Sciences and Techniques of Physical and Sport Activities) students, experts in the sport world. Our study is thus restricted to that particular kind of population.

Those different observations on the picture display of the athletic disabled body bring us to suppose that the media readers will interpret differently the pictures of the Olympic and the Paralympic athletes. The status of a disabled person would show up first, before the athlete's. In itself, "the picture would emphasize the disability and the prosthesis as much, or more than the physical effort and the feat" (Lebel et al., 2010, p.31). Thus, we have questioned the media readers concerning their feelings 'enkindled' by media pictures[4].

Disability and unconscious resistances

First, the assessment of Paralympic records is overestimated. This overestimate is all the more significant when there is a confrontation with pictures.

O. Pistorius record at 100m: 10.91 seconds				
	Estimates WITHOUT picture		Estimates WITH picture	
Average	11.17 (+/- 2,21)	2.38%*	10.83 (+/- 1.57)	0.74%*
Measurement of estimates				
	Number	Percentage	Number	Percentage
10.59 <N< 11.23**	20	26.32	18	23.08
N < 10.59	37	48.68	46	58.97***
N > 11.23	19	25	14	17.95
* Discrepancy in percentage compared with the exact value of the record. ** We have considered the right estimate at 3% within the exact value of the record. *** The polled overestimate of about 48.68 % the performance without picture, and of about 58.97 % with athlete picture. This ten point difference, even if it is not significant, deserves a particular attention.				

Table 1: Example of Paralympic record results related to Oscar Pistorius

---

4. To measure the difference of feelings enkindled by pictures of non disabled and disabled athletes (which constitutes the second part of the questionnaire), we chose "similar" pictures, that is to say media pictures displaying of olympic and paralympic athletes in similar positions and transmitting close feelings or meanings. The items associated to those pictures show notions of performance and compassion: *"femininity, masculinity, aestheticism, joy, focusing, speed, performance, fighting spirit, technique, the spectacular aspect, bravery, effort, other (specify)"*.

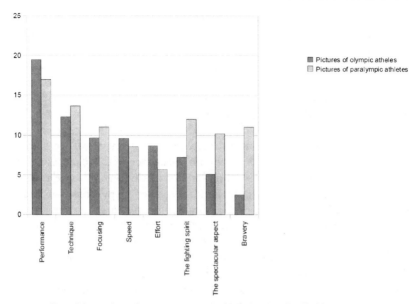

Fig 1: Main selected items concerning the feelings enkindled by pictures

Thus, if the subjects tend to overestimate Paralympic performances, it seems as if they first consider the athlete's qualities, their capacities, and their performance, before their deficiency. As a consequence, the athlete status prevails upon the disabled person status. This invalidates our assumption. The impact of the media pictures increases that phenomenon. The staging of the athletic deficient body seems not to participate in this process of Paralympic athlete stigmatization, quite the contrary, it points to their attributes and their physical capacities. "The bracing and the profiling of the athlete's disabled body are in line with the athlete body, and invalidate the stigma of the first anomaly in the mimesis of an organized and built body with the aim of a supra-normal efficiency" (Marcellini, 2006, p. 66). Secondly, when we questioned the students about their feelings concerning those pictures, the first selected items are those linked to performance. But after that, some differences appear: for the pictures of disabled athletes, the items expressing compassion show through, namely "the fighting spirit", "bravery", and "the spectacular aspect".

This distinct handling between those two kinds of media pictures shows that readers don't have the same representations towards those athletes. The disabled status seems to prevail over the athlete status, which validates our assumption. The media pictures display of the disabled athlete body seems here to participate in the negative stigmatization process. Thus, the disabled athletes are seen as carriers of incapacity and not as athletes. This contradicts the previous results about the measurement of records estimates[5].

People are trained to live in the respect of societal norms not to be pointed out as deviant by the society. But, as actors, they can have a behavior reproved by the moral, and are thus obliged to pretend that they are following norms (Goffman, 1973). The respondents, to follow norms, will then want to show that they consider disabled athletes as athletes "like the others". Thus, they would have overestimated the performances. Yet, they let their feelings show a kind of compassion. In the face of those pictures, "the stigmatized people suffer from the same lot as the one we have towards our controversial issues: the repression [...] Against many 'conscious' statements advocating the integration of disabled people, on the contrary, the daily reality gives us many examples of "unconscious' resistances" (Simon, 1991, pp. 219-220). Indeed, the subjects would have overestimated the performances to show they first consider the athlete, but in reality, it is the disability which gains the upper hand. Sport students would then want to regard the disabled athlete differently, yet some "unconscious resistances" seem to remain (Simon, 1991, p. 220).

Conclusions

The media pictures and display of disabled athletes have a significant influence on collective conceptions. They contribute to the setting up of a negative stigmatization process which leads those people to be seen as incapacities carriers, and not as athletes. "For some people, sport challenges of disabled persons are, at the best, only pretenses of the "real" sport which would be given value with some compassion" (Marcellini, 2005a, pp. 48-49).

Yet, according to Berger and Luckmann (1966), the social reality is built by social categories. Sport and Disability are categories, each of them being defined, but not essentially (each subject has his own conception of categories, according to his social reality). Those authors use the term polemology, which consists in building a social reality by the meeting between those categories. It would no longer be, as written here, a question of a prevailed status, but of a re-definition of those categories between them, by their interaction. Thus, from that point of view, we could approach those social categories to throw light on a social reality, and to unravel this tension between those two worlds which are apparently "antinomic".

---

5. Would the individuals polled have responded by overestimating to be "politically correct"? Indeed, this "political correctness" could constitute a hindrance to our study. If we have chosen a questionnaire, favoring anonymity, it was to control this pitfall.

Finally, this study concerned a special population of students, who were expert in physical and sport activities, and we wish to broaden our work in the future to a wider population in order to make comparisons and draw definitive conclusions regarding the images of disability in life settings.

References

Becker, H.S. (1963). *Outsiders.* Paris: Editions A.M. Métailié.
Berger, P., & Luckmann, T. (1966). *La construction sociale de la réalité.* Paris: Armand Colin.
Deffontaines, N. (2008). Les JP s'ouvrent dans l'indifférence. *Le Monde*, 28.
Defrance, J. (2006). *Sociologie du sport.* Paris: La Découverte.
Ehrenberg, A. (1991). *Le culte de la performance.* Calmann-Lévy.
Eideliman, J.S., & S. Gojard (2008). La vie à domicile des personnes handicapées ou dépendantes: du besoin d'aide aux arrangements pratiques. *Retraite et société*, 53, 89-111.
Garel, J.P. (2005). Sport d'élite et sport pour tous au regard du handicap. *Reliance*, 15, 33-44.
Goffman, E. (1973). *La mise en scène de la vie quotidienne.* Paris: Seuil.
Goffman, E. (1975). *Stigmate, les usages sociaux des handicaps.* Paris: Editions de Minuit.
Grignon, C., & J.C. Passeron (1989). *Le Savant et le populaire. Misérabilisme et populisme en sociologie et en littérature.* Paris: Le Seuil.
Heilbrunn, B. (2004). *La performance, une nouvelle idéologie.* Paris: La Découverte.
Hughes, E.C. (1945). Dilemmas and contradictions of status. *American Journal of Sociology*, 50(3), 353-359.
Joffe, H., (2001). Le pouvoir de l'image: persuasion, émotion et identification. *Diogène*, 217, 102-115.
Keller, C.E., Hallahan, D.P., McShane, E.A., Crowley, E.P., & Blandford, J. (1990). The coverage of persons with disabilities in American Newspapers. *The Journal of Special Education*, 24 (3), 271-282.
Kientz, A. (1971). *Pour analyser les médias.* Montréal: HMH.
Lachheb, M., & Moualla, N. (2009). Un corps sportif et handicapé. Regard sur l'expérience du corps d'athlètes handicapés physiques tunisiens. *ALTER, European Journal of Disability Research*, 3, 378-393.
Lebel, E., Marcellini, A., & Pappous, A. (2010). Regards croisés sur une photographie sportive. Photojournalisme sportif et athlètes handicapés: mise en scène du corps et production de sens. *ALTER, European Journal of Disability Research*, 4, 18-33.
Léséleuc, E. de, Marcellini, A., & Pappous, A. (2005). Femmes/hommes: la mise en scène des différences dans la couverture médiatique des Jeux Paralympiques. *Sciences de l'Homme et Sociétés*, 73, 45-47.
Marcellini, A., (2005a). Un sport de HN accessible ? Jeux séparés, jeux parallèles et jeux à handicap. *Reliance*, 15, pp. 48-54.

Marcellini, A. (2005b). *Des vies en fauteuil. Usages du sport dans les processus de déstigmatisation et d'intégration sociale*. Paris: CTNERHI.

Marcellini, A. (2006), Des corps atteints valides ou de la déficience au «°firmus°»: hypothèses autour de la mise en scène sportive du corps handicapé. In G. Boetsch, N. Chapuis-Lucciani, & D. Chevé (Eds.), *Représentations du corps. Le biologique et le vécu: normes et normalités* (pp. 59-68). Nancy: Presses Universitaires de Nancy.

Marcellini, A. (2007). Nouvelles figures du handicap? Catégorisations sociales et dynamique des processus de stigmatisation / destigmatisation. In G. Boetsch, C. Hervé, & J. Rozenberg (Eds.), *Corps normalisé, corps stigmatisé, corps racialisé* (pp. 199-219). Bruxelles: De Boeck.

Meynaud, F. (2005). Comment favoriser l'accès de tous à une pratique sportive? *Reliance*, 15, 28-32.

Murphy, R.F. (1990). *Vivre à corps perdus*. Paris: Plon.

Queval, I. (2004). *S'accomplir ou se dépasser : essai sur le sport contemporain*. Paris: Gallimard.

Raufast, A., & Raufast, L. (2006). Sémiologies sportives, handicaps, et stratégies éducatives. *Recherches & éducations*, 11. Retrieved September 12, 2010 from : http://rechercheseducations.revues.org/index390.html

Simon, J.L. (1991). Conclusion. In C. Gardou (Ed.), *Le regard interrogé: handicap, handicapés* (pp. 253-254). Paris: Erès.

Sticker, H.J. (2006). *Les fables peintes du corps abîmé. Les images de l'infirmité du XVIe au XXe siècle*. Paris: Editions du Cerf.

Wieviorka, M. (2005). *La différence: Identités culturelles: enjeux, débats et politiques*. Paris: Edition de l'Aube.

Chapter 13
Disabled Heroes in the Media

Louise Charbonnier & Cristina Popescu

Introduction

The traditional French media tend to present people with disabilities in a stereotypical and Manichean manner (Lachal, 1990) that's if they bother to mention them at all. Paralympic athletes are classed in the French press as either pitiable individuals, or super-cripples (Combrouze, 2000). Indeed, the Vancouver Paralympic Games which took place from March 12th to March 21st 2010 were sparsely covered by French newspapers and only the daily national newspaper *La Croix*, catholic in tradition[1], distinguished itself

---

[1] Contemporary French catholic print media appears to be concerned by the topic of disability and makes a vow of reflection and thoughtfulness (Giddens, 1994). It tries to keep its distance from an excessively condescending attitude, full of good feelings (charity, pity, compassion), which spills into a tearful pathos. Disability sport and Paralympic Games, then, are crucial moments within which one may think about media representation of disability (Etre, 2003).

by presenting several portraits of disabled athletes. All six of them[2] were analysed in the paper according to the 'looking glass of storytelling' (Salmon, 2007), and through the narration of their athletic performances. Within these portraits, the codification of athlete as hero is part of the classic narrative pattern (Lits, 2008) which structures each article. For example the initial state of non-disability, accident/fall, and athletic performances, were highlighted in the Paralympic Games of Vancouver. Interestingly, after the disabling accident, the media reports the discovery of sport reveals itself as a crucial element which brings a new meaning into the life of the disabled athlete.

The stories in *La Croix* focused less on describing impairment than on contemporary meanings of disabilities understood as social issues. This is excellent and impairments are indeed mentioned, but only when they can be linked directly to the identity of the athlete. Physical impairment is the most frequently mentioned (more precisely, the motor impairment) and comments such as the following are widespread in the newspaper: Jean-Yves Le Meur is an "amputee of the lower limbs", Marie Bochet is "born without a left arm", Vincent Gauthier-Manuel is "born without a left forearm", Yannick Bourseaux has a "partially paralized arm", Romain Riboud is "an athlete with hemiplegia". One sole article - concerning Nathalie Morin, partially sighted because of retinitis pigmentosa - deals with sensory impairment. Above all, two important categories are to be distinguished in the portraits, influencing the narrative pattern. These are: born with a disability and acquired disability (Devenney, 2005). In the case of congenital disability, the sport gives new meaning to the life of the disabled person. In the case of the accident victim disability sport brings the main character closer to the norms of non-disabled society through the medium of sport. There are two ways to access sports: the athlete who suffered an accident discovers the sport through his/her own initiative (in this case, his/her relationship with the activity and athletic performance becomes an intimate matter); while it is the family, peers and medical fraternity who reveals the way to follow in the case of a congenitally born disabled person. For instance, Vincent was "detected" by the Federation when he was eleven years old, "as he was running with the able-bodied"[3]. After having met these secondary characters (in this case his friends who had accepted him into their society) who play the role of adjuvants, the athlete (Vincent) decides later to compete with those who, according to the norms of the able-bodied, are like

---

2. "Romain Riboud, porte-drapeau français des Jeux paralympiques", *La Croix*, 12/03/2010
"Jean-Yves Le Meur, l'ingénieur chercheur d'or", *La Croix*, 15/03/2010
"Marie Bochet, l'or n'attend point le nombre des années", *La Croix*, 16/03/2010
"Nathalie Morin, sa victoire personnelle", *La Croix*, 17/03/2010
"Vincent Gauthier-Manuel, le Jura derrière lui", *La Croix*, 18/03/2010
"Yannick Bourseaux, militant handisport", *La Croix*, 19/03/2010

3. "alors qu'il courait avec les valides"

him. Indeed, he doesn't initially feel or perceive himself to be disabled. It's only when he becomes ensconced in disability sport that he views himself as different from the norm. Disability sport is thus empowering and disempowering at the same time, leading to split motives, personalities and different meanings of what it means to be disabled in the sporting context.

The Figure of the Multiple Hero

The life story of the disabled athlete hence includes main and secondary characters (as mentioned previously adjuvants). According to Marc Lits (2008), the main character is an emblematic figure that mobilises the attention of the reader (phenomena of hero identification, empathy). Moreover, the figure of a multiple hero seems to emerge here. A multiple hero is not a collective hero; rather, he/she is an association of distinctive characters[4]. Every main character has his or her moment of glory, but his or her story is never independent, autonomous, or auto-sufficient. All athletes form a team which represents France in the Paralympic Games. They have common goals which are to participate in the competition, in order to keep France among the ten main nations, but also to present themselves as athletes with disabilities rather than as "people with disabilities who practice sports". This discursive comment was used by the team's flag holder, Romain[5] arguing that it has the advantage of transforming norms, as well as the social imaginary representations of "normality" and "disability". By recruiting the athletes, the French Federation unifies all these athlete life stories and in this network, other kinds of links are woven between characters: a main character can become a secondary one within the story of another athlete. Hence, Jean Yves helps Vincent by showing him the way towards developing in disability sport. Vincent in his turn stands as model for Yannick[6] and so on. In this manner the French team becomes a series of narratives which if reported correctly can only be utilised to promote the athlete as an athlete rather than a disabled person who plays sport at a high level.

---

4. In the view of Sarah Sepulche (2009), "the multiple hero can be actualized through different forms: the duos, the trios, the families, the professional teams, the communities, etc. However, they are not different actualizations of the main figure" (pp. 50-51; our translation). We often find this kind of hero in motion pictures or television shows, but it can be interesting to use this notion within the analytical field which interests us here. This framework allows one to better understand indeed how the journalist displays the world of heroes with disabilities.

5. "We transformed from people with disabilities that practice sport into athletes with disabilities" ("Nous sommes passés du statut de handicapés qui font du sport à celui de sportifs de haut niveau qui ont un handicap").

6. "Like Vincent Gauthier-Manuel, who obtained bronze yesterday in the Giant Slalom, Yannick would have liked to give to France its very first podium." ("Yannick aurait voulu, comme Vincent Gauthier-Manuel, médaillé de bronze hier en slalom géant, offrir à la France son tout premier podium").

A sentimental community

Some other decisive secondary characters also revolve around the hero. For example, the family, the spouse, the other disabled athletes, the Federation, the local community, associations, and fan club. The family takes a fundamental place among all of these secondary characters; not surprising for a newspaper of catholic tradition and the father or mother are the main witnesses and accompanying persons within the athlete's life. This is achieved by allowing the reader to take part in their enthusiastic and loving perception of the hero, and in their emotions, these parental figures represent authentic connectors to the reader's empathy but are rarely utilised in newspaper reporting of the Paralympics.

The sporting staff could well be considered as a secondary character. Trainer, guide, colleagues, and Federation all encourage the hero or heroine and motivate them for the competition. Likewise, the local community often appears to be an important support to the disabled sportsperson. For example: the inhabitants of Arêche-Beaufort "are behind" stated Marie, while Vincent is surrounded by his fan club members and by an association. The medical team constitutes another type of adjuvant. For instance, a kinesiotherapist facilitates Romain's encounter with the sporting competition. There is not only one character that helps the hero in his/her discovery, but the combined action of many. Long before the kinesiotherapist's advice, when Romain was only three years old, his parents initiated him to skiing "like every child of the ski station". However, above all, the will and determination of the hero or heroine remain decisive. Ultimately, all of these characters who help the disabled athlete invite the reader to join a community of sentimentality.

A Pathos-based Discourse

It is no wonder that storytelling media strategy appeals to the reader's affective empathy by playing on pathos and emotions. The journalist doesn't need to summon heavy sentimental weaponry; he/she needs only report the parents' own words e.g., *"'Marie always astounds us even more'*, Yvan exults at the idea of seeing his daughter rush down an Olympic run. *'Even if I tell myself it's true, I have to pinch myself to know if I'm dreaming or not*, he enthuses. *Just imagine: her main competitors are 21-22 years old at least!"*[7]. A good deal of joy adorned with an exclamation mark, an indirect address to the reader (*"Just imagine"*) wrapped up in appreciative verbs (*"exult"*, *"enthuse"*)... The journalist uses the same recipe every time to appeal to the reader's compassion and engage the identification process with the positive hero figure.

---

7. "'*Marie nous bluffe chaque fois davantage*', exulte Yvan Bochet à l'idée de voir sa fille s'élancer sur une piste olympique. '*J'ai beau me dire que c'est vrai, je me pince pour savoir si je rêve ou pas*, s'enthousiasme-t-il. *Imaginez : ses principales concurrentes ont 21-22 ans au minimum !*'".

The construction of emotional closeness between the hero and the reader may also be obtained thanks to converging iconic strategy. Indeed, some of the articles are accompanied with a photo portrait of the disabled athlete posing with a smile on his/her face. In those posed portraits, the close-up framing focuses the viewer's attention on the facial expression, and the gaze makes it possible to simulate a communication situation with the viewer. This type of photographic discourse adequately upholds the mostly affective type of storytelling used by *La Croix*. However, what is at stake in those pictures goes far beyond the frame of rhetoric playing on pathos.

To Be or Not To Be Visible?

The arrival, more or less recently, of pictures of disabled athletes in newspapers raises the problem of the visibility (or invisibility) of disability and of its representation in the media and society. In the case of *La Croix*, the Federation for disabled athletes is the source of the pictures and these pertain to an educational discourse destined to inform a broad public. The stakes of referential photography are, on the one hand, to show and make known the different sports of the Winter Paralympic Games. On the other hand, this communication strategy, which in turn is adopted by this newspaper, is consistent in telling the spectators: "see, we are all alike." This photographic discourse on the recognition of the people with disabilities, is where resemblance (analogy, mimesis) overrules difference, while simultaneously appearing to elude the visibility of the disability. This is a dangerous ambivalence?

The avoidance of disability in photography appears to rest on two tactics. In the case of the posed pictures, where the body is static, offering itself to observation, exposed, exhibited (and hence vulnerability?); the face-centred framing rejects the disabled body out of shot. The choice made here is to keep quiet about difference, which has no reason to be included in the shot or concerned about by the photographer. In the case of the disabled body photographed in movement, in the heart of action, the disability erases itself before the beauty of the athletic gesture, dramatised by the photographic instant. The disability does not in this case, lend itself to dissection and to an inquisitive attitude, as in the case of the immobile body; rather, it blends into the athletic performance, where the entire body is engaged in a meaningful dynamism (within a flow).

When Mind Controls Body

Yannick Bourseaux visits schools and sports students in particular to teach them about what he himself found out thanks to his accident. '*My body was wrecked, but I was still the same inside*[8]: this discourse about Yannick, an athlete who is now a sports teacher in charge of the promotion and development of disability sport, tells a lot about the social role the disabled athlete has to embody nowadays. Put forth as a model for the others (disabled as well as able-bodied) he has to act as a paragon of the mind's mastery over the body (pushing one's physical limits by sheer will). He therefore appears like the stigma of a postmodern western society under crisis, where the end of great narratives has left the individual to his own devices. Perhaps a prey to the endless quest for meaning? In these media portraits, the disabled athlete is thus taken in a classic narrative pattern, which infuses meaning into the social body. It is striking to note that the post-human hero is an athlete who is able to control the 'Flesh' according to three principles in which the 'Mind', the 'Word', and the 'Technology' transform these bodies which are becoming more than ever prosthetic. In that perspective it evokes the image of the cyborg as well as that which Christ resurrected.

Let us consider this three-fold principle of control of the 'Flesh' by the 'Mind', the 'Word' and by 'Technology'. First the 'Mind'. In these tales reported by the media, the willpower of the disabled heroes enables them to triumph over a physically weakened body. With "vital strength" deep inside, they demonstrate "endless resolve", remaining true to the pledge they made to themselves of overcoming this disability thanks to their mental sweat-stained stamina (indeed Nathalie "fulfilled the pledge she had set to herself"[9]). In this instance the 'Mind' takes revenge over bad luck, over the fortune buffets that have affected the body deeply. It comes then as no surprise to read that the disabled heroes become endowed with numerous moral values, in which courage ranks first. They exude extraordinary fighting spirit (this moral quality is endlessly illustrated). Such is the case with Yannick who "has already proved he could take up the challenge"[10]. The media discourse shows them as perfectionist, like Vincent who had certainly "wanted to surpass himself". Another moral quality is brought to the forefront: that of humility ("Vincent is not the pestering type. He prefers staying in the background"[11]). Finally *La Croix* lays the stress on another moral quality, namely concern for one's fellow human being. For instance the disabled hero is grateful to those who have helped him (Romain "never forgets to thank his father and his mother for their never flagging support of his projects"[12]). He also shows empathy, like Yannick who after a defeat in

---

8. "Yannick Bourseaux intervient dans les écoles et auprès des étudiants en Staps, notamment pour leur transmettre la leçon qu'il a lui-même tirée de son accident. *'Mon corps était abîmé, mais au fond de moi j'étais resté le même'*".
9. "a rempli le contrat qu'elle s'était elle-même fixé".
10. "a déjà montré qu'il savait relever la tête après une déroute".
11. "Vincent n'est pas du genre à demander quoi que ce soit. Il aime rester discret".
12. "ne manque jamais de remercier son père et sa mère qui l'ont toujours soutenu dans ses projets".

competition placates and comforts his mother ("*I told him we mustn't look back at the past, and we mustn't lose heart,* mentions Brigitte. *But he felt I wasn't feeling fine myself. He was the one who eventually cheered up my spirits*"[13]).

The second principle of the control of the Body is the 'Word'. "In the beginning was the Word...and the Word was made Flesh" these famous lines from the Bible (Jean, 1, 1-18) seem to fit perfectly with these heroes for whom saying (they will overcome their disability) is already doing it. This incantation is the first step towards success. Words are meant to supersede disability so that the athlete can transcend himself "when skiing, you fight first against yourself. You have to excel or outdo yourself. This is how I managed to overcome my disability"[14], "I'll go on training, I have to improve my records"[15]. The power of speech assumes a biblical meaning when the journalist writes: "Jean-Yves uttered this completely unexpected sentence when he left the emergency unit: *'I'll do as if I had legs'.* Acknowledged. After a 9 month fight, the young man was able to stand up on his prosthesis and walk, with the desire to go on walking up to his own limits"[16]. "Arise [...] and go thy way" said by Jesus to the sick of the palsy (Marc, 2, 1-12) turned into a self-fulfilling and self-centred promise that the hyper modern individual (Lipovetsky 2004) addresses himself.

What is being built here from a rhetorical viewpoint is the image of the disabled athlete – a complex representation at the crossroads of the portrait depicted by the media and the ethos which the sportsman tries to convey[17]. Romain, indeed, declares that he aims at showing the way to the next generation: "I'm trying to act as a link. I also do my best to surround the young who come and see me. I share my experience with them."[18] And yet it is hard to make out what corresponds to the effort to act like the hero label that society now seems to impose on the disabled athlete. Social pressure, which is dealt with and expanded by the media, seems to demand that these athletes become models for the disabled as well as the able-bodied. "For the time being, Marie ski's first and foremost out of sheer pleasure and she doesn't aim at solving problems in relation with the perception of disability.

---

13. "*Je lui ai dit qu'il fallait aller de l'avant, ne pas perdre courage,* raconte Brigitte. *Mais il a senti que je n'étais pas très bien moi-même. Au final, c'est presque lui qui m'a remonté le moral!*".

14. "En ski, on se bat plus d'abord contre soi-même. Il faut se dépasser. C'est aussi de cette manière que j'ai surmonté mon handicap".

15. "Je vais continuer à m'entraîner, je dois améliorer mes performances".

16. "Jean-Yves eut cette phrase que personne n'attendait à la sortie de la salle de réanimation : *'Je ferai comme si j'avais mes jambes'.* Dont acte. A l'issue d'un combat de 9 mois, le jeune homme avait appris à se dresser sur ses prothèses et à marcher, avec la volonté de continuer à avancer encore jusqu'à trouver ses propres limites".

17. the image he wants to give of himself.

18. "J'essaye de faire le lien. Je fais tout aussi, pour entourer les jeunes qui viennent me voir. Je leur fais partager mon expérience".

Now she has become a well-known person in her region, she is starting to realise though that her results can have an impact"[19]: the discourse of *La Croix* lends further credence to this social imaginary representation.

The third principle of the control of the Flesh: 'Technology' turns the prosthetic body of the disabled athlete into a post-human cyborg, thus illustrating the old body-machine analogy. The 'New Flesh' which was anticipated by the visions of movie-maker David Cronenberg (a New Flesh which was likewise suffused with references to Christ) seems nowadays embodied in these images of athletes whose performances are increased by technology. The superhuman capabilities of the disabled heroes foreshadow man's future increased and synaesthesia-like reality thanks to a body endowed with unheard-of sensory capabilities.

The analogical contamination of the body by technology brings to an end its imaginary transformation into a machine whose mechanism can be improved, correcting the "flaws": And "the uproar of the opening ceremony could have impaired her hearing capacity, which is of paramount importance to a visually impaired or visually handicapped biathlete who adjusts her shot with the sounds emitted by headphones, the closer the aim, the sharper the sound."[20] Technological breakthroughs may well shape the imaginary world of the disabled body by taking advantage of a currently stigmatising abnormality in order to create a redeeming post-normality. They may well manage to nullify the discriminatory social representation of a flawed disabled body and give rise to the more positive image of a superhuman, resurrected, and transfigured body. As we can see, the technological imaginary world can easily transcend its prosthetic bodies into prophetic bodies.

Beyond the Discursive Frame

Today, the discourse of *La Croix* calls the disabled athlete to accomplish a social contract where he/she is supposed to play the role of hero, as much for the able bodied as for people with disabilities, re-enacting in this way the victory of 'Mind over Body'. In this case, media storytelling wants to give meaning to the world by reactivating founding narrative schemes as well as common encyclopaedic references. Furthermore, by showing the athlete in search of a lost able-bodyness, the media excludes any questioning of pre-discourses (Paveau 2005) about normality, able-bodiedness, disability. One may also wonder if changing normality does not implicate the implosion of

---

19. "Pour le moment, Marie skie avant tout pour le plaisir, et ne se donne pas pour mission de résoudre les problèmes liés à la perception du handicap. Maintenant qu'elle est devenue une figure publique de sa région, elle commence toutefois à prendre conscience de l'effet de ses résultats".

20. "le tumulte de la fête inaugurale aurait pu dérégler ses facultés auditives, très précieuses, puisque tout biathlète malvoyant ou non-voyant guide son tir à l'aide de sons émis par un casque qu'il place sur ses oreilles, et qui deviennent de plus en plus aigus à mesure qu'il se rapproche de la cible".

this narrative structure within which the initial state of not being disabled implicitly corresponds to the idea of a happy normality. In one word, *going beyond* this discursive frame.

References

Combrouze, D. (2000). L'information sur les personnes handicapées motrices et sensorielles dans les journaux télévisés. *Handicap – Revue de Sciences Humaines et Sociales*, 85, 27-45.

Debord, G. (1967). *La Société du spectacle*. Paris: Buchet-Chastel.

Devenney, M. (2005). *The Social Representations of Disability. Fears, Fantasies and Facts*. Doctoral dissertation. University of Leeds, Leeds. Retrieved June 2nd, 2011 from: http://www.leeds.ac.uk/disability-studies/archiveuk/devenney/

Etre. Handicap information (2003). 68/69. Paris: Etre et Connaître SARL.

Giddens, A. (1994). *Les Conséquences de la modernité*. Paris: L'Harmattan.

Gilbert, K., & Schantz, O.J. (2008). (Eds.). *The Paralympic Games. Empowerment or Side Show?* Maidenhead, UK: Meyer & Meyer.

Goggin, G., & Newell, C. (2005). *Disability in Australia: Exposing a Social Apartheid*, Sydney: UNSW press.

Lachal, R-C. (1990). Les personnes handicapées vues par la presse régionale française. Constantes et évolutions de 1977 à 1988. *Handicaps et inadaptation. Les cahiers du CTNERHI*, 51/52, 1-29.

Lits, M. (2008). *Du récit au récit médiatique*. Bruxelles: De Boeck.

Lipovetsky, G. (2004). *Les Temps hypermodernes*. Paris: Grasset.

Paveau, M-A. (2006). *Les Prédiscours*. Paris: Presses de la Sorbonne Nouvelle.

Salmon, C. (2007). *Storytelling: la machine à fabriquer des histoires et à formater les esprits*. Paris: La Découverte.

Sepulche, S. (2007). *Le héros multiple dans les fictions télévisuelles à épisodes* Unpublished doctoral dissertation. Université catholique de Louvain, Louvain.

Chapter 14
Media Coverage of Pistorius

What are the Angles? What is Missing?

Gregor Wolbring

Introduction

Disabled people are under-represented in sports on various levels from participants (Brittain, 2004; Kew, 1997; Collins, & Kay, 2003) to leadership positions in the *sport* industry (Masteralexis, Barr, & Hums, 2008). Although 12.4% of Canadians have disabilities related to activity and functional limitations, they represent only 1% of the memberships of National Sport Organizations (Canadian Heritage, 2008). The non inclusion of disabled people in mainstream sport is seen as one reason for 'separate' sports opportunities for disabled people (Nixon II, 2007). How media deal with the Paralympics plays a big role in the participation of disabled people in sport. According to Brittain who interviewed various Paralympic athletes from the UK, "....the lack of media coverage is implicated in the lack of recognition of the capabilities of athletes with a disability. According to most of the participants in this research, the interest from the media is very fleeting and dies away completely within 2 to 3 weeks of the Paralympic closing ceremony" (Brittain, 2004). Colin Grannell, executive vice president of Visa Europe acknowledged this attention gap between the Paralympics and

Olympics "Of course, the question at the beginning was to know whether we would get a good return for our business investment by doing it, because the media attention for the Paralympics is a lot less than for the Olympics. However, we decided to do this over the long term and I think that in the future we'll see the Paralympics become much bigger" (EurActiv.com, 2006).

New challenges are appearing for sport in general and also the Paralympics that among others are triggered by advances in new and emerging science and technology products. Advances in science and technology allow for the internal and external modification of athletes and the creation of external tools athletes can use, both of which influence the athlete's ability to perform (Wolbring, 2008). Furthermore, the time is near where so called 'therapeutic assistive devices,' generated to mimic species-typical body structures and expected body functioning will outperform in numerous functions the species-typical bodies giving rise to 'therapeutic' enhancements (Wolbring, 2009). Science and technology all the time enables the generation of new sport disciplines. Now advances in therapeutic assistive devices allow them to also generate new sport disciplines. The story of the Paralympic athlete Pistorius whose artificial legs were labelled as 'techno doping' is only the first of many to come where a therapeutic assistive device is seen to outperform the species-typical body function it was developed to mimic. As Pistorius stated; "For me, prosthetic technology is ...Life enabling. Without it I would be pretty stranded. Everyday legs are more comfortable these days, but there is always more they can do. I help out with research and development for something called the Proprio foot. It has a USB slot to charge and reprogram it. I've discovered that you can charge your iPod off it too, but the scientists get angry when you do that!" (BBC Ouch Team, 2009). As the media play such a big role in the perception of the Paralympics and the situation of Paralympic athletes how did the media portray Pistorius and the consequence of his techno-leg advances to the date of writing this chapter?

The Pistorius story up to late 2010

Pistorius is a South African below the knee amputee Paralympic athlete. According to the write up on the webpage of Ossur the company that produces the Cheetah legs of Pistorius "the Pistorius story really started in January 2004 when he shattered his right knee on the rugby field and doctors recommended he switch to track. At age 17, he ran the 100m in an open competition at the Pilditch stadium in his hometown of Pretoria after training for only two months. He ran it in 11.51 seconds; the world record was 12.20." (Ossur, 2010) He is the world record holder in the 100, 200 and 400 metres track and field events of Paralympic athletes in the moment. Pistorius was regarded as being fast enough to earn a spot for the 200 and 400 meter sprints on South Africa's 2008 Olympic team (Josh McHugh, 2007). Pistorius asked to be allowed to run in the 2008 Olympics if he would qualify for his country's Olympic team. The world governing body for track and field (IAAF) ruled on 14th of January 2008, invoking its rule 144.2 which deals with technical aids: "that double-amputee sprinter Oscar Pistorius is ineligible to compete in the Beijing Olympics because his prosthetic racing legs give him a clear competitive advantage" (IAAF, 2008; Raf Casert, 2008). Athletics South Africa stated that it would immediately apply the decision, making it impossible for Pistorius to qualify for the South African Olympic team (Casert, 2008). Pistorius appealed to the Court of Arbitration for Sport (CAS) questioning the judgment that his prosthetic racing legs give him a clear competitive advantage and that his so called Cheetah legs are a case of techno doping. He did not pursue an argument that he should be allowed to run against Olympic athletes even if the legs give him an unfair advantage. In April 2008 the CAS ruled in his favour stating that not enough evidence exists to claim that his Cheetah legs give an unfair advantage (The Courts of Arbitration for Sport [the "CAS"] 2008). At the same time the CAS made clear that if data would prove that the legs lead to an unfair advantage he could not compete against the 'normal' leg Olympic athletes.

How did the media portray the Pistorius story so far?

The Pistorius story was and still is covered extensively in the public domain and with the expectation that Pistorius will try out for the 2012 London Olympics the media interest very likely will not wane. Google generates 191,000 hits with the search term "Oscar Pistorius". How have the media dealt with the case of Pistorius? What questions did they raise? What were their angles? What conclusions did they generate? To answer these questions the author reviewed all the articles in the New York Times, Times.com, Sport Illustrated and ESPN that covered the Pistorius story. Forty articles were identified as eligible from the New York Times archives, six from Time.com, thirteen from Sport Illustrated and eight from ESPN (that had ESPN as author and were not associate press feeds).

There are four important time frames for the Pistorius story so far. One covers the Pistorius story until the IAAF Ruling 14th of January 2008. The second covers the time from the IAAF ruling to the CAS Ruling 16 May, 2008. The third covers the time after the CAS ruling until it was clear that Pistorius would not qualify for the Beijing 2008 Olympics and the fourth covers the time after it was clear that Pistorius would not qualify for the Beijing Olympics until today.

Two main themes crystallized out of the media coverage of Pistorius today. One theme concerns itself with his Cheetah legs, and whether his therapeutic assistive devices give him an unfair advantage in competing against 'normal' athletes. Linked to this theme is the subtheme of whether the tests performed to ascertain whether the legs lead to an advantage were and are appropriate. The second theme is about whether Pistorius should be allowed to compete if his legs indeed give him a performance advantage (Longman, 2007; Mark Sutcliffe, 2008; Associated Press, 2008; Casert, 2008).

Dissecting the media coverage in the different time frames the author found that before the IAAF Ruling 14th of January 2008 the media themes were mostly about whether it was fair that Pistorius participates in the Olympics and that he tried to qualify. Between the IAAF Ruling 14th of January 2008 and before the CAS Ruling 16 May, 2008 the theme of whether it was fair that he competes in the Olympics was joined by the theme of whether the tests relied on for deciding whether his legs are giving him an advantage or not give reliable and usable results. After CAS and until it was clear that Pistorius would not qualify for the Beijing Olympics the themes were a) is it fair? b) can he qualify? c) is it safe for Olympic athletes if Pistorius competes against them? and d) is the test correct? Finally after it was clear that Pistorius would not qualify for the Beijing Olympics the themes were still whether is it fair that he wanted to compete in the Olympics and whether the test used on his legs was correct? These two themes were joined by an interest into whether Pistorius will try to qualify for London 2012 and how he performed at the Beijing 2008 Paralympics. The following themes where raised at different times of the Pistorius coverage; a) fear the non disabled have of the disabled; b) sport has to re-examine its core principles and c) that there will be more like Pistorius.

Some interesting information from the public coverage of Pistorius

The first story which looked at the issue of whether Pistorius has an advantage was not concerned with the Olympics. In 2005 long before the media picked up on Pistorius and his run for the Olympics and debated whether the Cheetah legs give an unfair advantage against Olympic athletes a story titled "The Archrival" from May 2005 in Sport Illustrated highlighted that the legs Pistorius were using were also seen as giving him an unfair advantage in the Paralympic sport. At that time the issue was about the proper length of the legs. The article stated "International Paralympic Committee is trying to determine the proper length of prostheses and expects to have an "Oscar Rule" in place for the 2008 Paralympics in Beijing." This statement could be seen as an attempt to standardize the 'Cheetah' legs. In the same article it was highlighted that Pistorius was running the sixth-fastest 400 by a South African, abled or disabled and that "neither the IOC nor track's governing body, the IAAF, has rules prohibiting a disabled runner from competing against able-bodied runners; in fact the IAAF has invited °Pistorius° to run in the 400 at a Grand Prix event in Helsinki in July". The article predicted legal challenges and quoted Olympic 100-meter champ Justin Gatlin predicting that the Paralympic runners will be as fast as the Olympic runners soon and he did not have any problems of running against Pistorius or Marlon if they can qualify (Sport illustrated, 2005). Indeed, over the time of the Pistorius story various 'abled-bodied' athletes were asked to comment on Pistorius. A 2007 BBC story (Austin, 2007) for example highlighted the view of British 400m runner Tim Benjamin who stated that he does not think the South African should be depriving others of a place (talking about the 2007 British Grand Prix in Sheffield). However, the negative opinion was not linked to the discourse of unfair advantage of the cheetah legs but that he felt that Pistorius was not fast enough and should not run in Sheffield as he did not meet the qualifying criteria in play for 'abled-bodied' athletes.

What is missing from the media coverage?

Many angles and possible consequences of the Pistorius story have not been and are not covered by the media and were and are not part of the public discourse. For example little analysis exists of the CAS decision beside the obvious that the CAS did not feel evidence existed that showed his legs would give an unfair advantage and that the CAS concluded that if data will be generated in the future that show an advantage that Pistorius could not run against abled-bodied athletes. Very little analysis exists in regards to the reaction of athletes towards the CAS decision. One 2008 New York Times Story (Robinson & Schwartz, 2010) had some reactions of Paralympic athletes to the CAS ruling.

> "I am extremely shocked that the CAS has made that decision," said Marlon Shirley, a single amputee who holds world records in the 100 meters, the 200 meters and the long jump in his Paralympic class. "It's a very brave decision and one that's definitely going to revolutionize sports."

Ann Cody, a seven-time Paralympic medalist for the United States in basketball and track and field who sits on the governing board of the International Paralympic Committee, added: "It sends a message. People with disabilities can see people like them compete, and they'll connect. They'll say, maybe I can do that, too".

No analysis exists as to why the IAAF was trying, so rashly it seems, to deal with Pistorius. Pistorius is by no means the first disabled athlete who has competed in the Olympics. There were quite a few others from George Eyser in 1904 (wooden leg) to Natalie Du Toit, whose left leg was amputated above the knee and who competed without an artificial leg. Pistorius was in no position to outrun the Olympic winner in Beijing so it's curious that the IAAF did not wait for the data around the Cheetah legs to be made available.

Another angle not covered is whether there are any regulatory hurdles for Olympic sport disciplines that are based on therapeutic assistive devices. On www.Olympic.org one reads "To make it onto the Olympic programme, a sport first has to be recognised: it must be administered by an International Federation which ensures that the sport's activities follow the Olympic Charter. If it is widely practised around the world and meets a number of criteria established by the IOC session, a recognised sport may be added to the Olympic programme on the recommendation of the IOC's Olympic Programme Commission." (see www.olympic.org).

That leads to the question whether one could not have Cheetah leg sport disciplines in the Olympics (if they lead to an unfair advantage) if they are administered by an International Federation, follow the Olympic Charter and are 'widely' practised around the world. As mentioned above the International Paralympic Committee looked into standardizing therapeutic assistive devices such as the Cheetah legs, although not with the thought of them being used in Olympic events, which would be one step to have a consistent playing field for athletes who want to compete with artificial legs.

The Pistorius CAS ruling did not close off the possibility that Paralympic athletes who use therapeutic assistive devices such as Cheetah legs or wheelchairs could obtain their own event within the Olympics. This scenario would be similar to the case of other external tools such as a pole used in pole vaulting by species-typical body-normative athletes (Wolbring, 2008). Pole vaulting athletes do not compete against the high jumper but they have their own event. Some might say that not everyone can use Cheetah legs and set as a prerequisite for a Olympic sport that everyone has access to the tools. That would mean that events based on Cheetah legs could not be in the Olympics as they cannot be worn by able bodied athletes. However, even if one looks at the tools used by abled-bodied athletes not everyone can afford the tools like bobsleighs…. today. Furthermore, taking the same logic, if it is a prerequisite for an Olympic sport discipline to be accessible to all (ignoring economic factors) it seems that this rule could also be employed to mean that a sport can only be in the Olympics if it can be performed by so called disabled and non disabled athletes alike. Indeed, the UN Convention on the rights of persons with disabilities (CRPD) (article 30) could be used to justify this reasoning.

Another angle, barely covered, is what will/might/should happen if therapeutic assistive devices increasingly outperform the equivalent functions within the normative body. Article 4g-i and article 20, 25 and 26 of the CRPD provide strong language for disabled people to make a strong case for the production, development of and access to therapeutic devices even if they enhance performance (Wolbring, 2009). What will we do if performances in the Paralympics outshine the Olympic counterparts? What will the future relationship between the Olympics and Paralympics be? What would be the impact on recreational sport?

Conclusions

It seems that the media did not understand or did not want to cover various angles posed by the Pistorius story. Advances in therapeutic assistive devices might; a) lead to new sport disciplines based on therapeutic assistive devices enable ability enhancement; b) impact the self understanding of all athletes but in particular Paralympic and Olympic athletes; c) blur the line between Olympic and Paralympics athlete; d) raise expectations of Paralympic athletes and their role in sport in general; e) trigger research and development in new products and processes that can be used to improve the bodily functioning of all athletes Paralympic and Olympic; high performance and recreational and their external equipment to ever higher levels of performance impacting in turn the expectations athletes, officials, spectators and governments will have on sports and athletes (Wolbring, 2008). It seems the public discourse has to be broadened from where it is so far.

References

Associated Press. (2008, July 17). World champ says race against Pistorius wouldn't bother him. *USA Today on-line* Retrieved January 15 2011 from: http://www.usatoday.com/sports/olympics/2008-01-17-564544338_x.htm

Austin, S. (2007). Blade Runner's ongoing battle. *BBC News [On-line]*. Retrieved January 15 2011 from: http://news.bbc.co.uk/sport2/hi/athletics/6292786.stm

BBC Ouch Team 13 Questions: Oscar Pistorius. (2009). *BBC [On-line]*. Retrieved January 15 2011 from: http://www.bbc.co.uk/ouch/interviews/13_questions_oscar_pistorius.shtml

Brittain, I. (2004). Perception of disability and their impact upon involvement in sports for people with disabilities at all levels. *28, Journal of Sports & Social Issues, 4*, 429-452.

Casert R. (2008, January 14). IAAF rules sprinter Pistorius ineligible. Associated Press [On-line]. Retrieved January 11, 2012 from: http://news.yahoo.com/s/ap/20080114/ap_on_sp_ol/oly_run_iaaf_ pistorius

Collins, M. F., Collins Mike, & T. Kay (2003). *Sport and Social Exclusion*, London, New York: Routledge.

EurActiv.com 'Disabled access to sport must be improved'. (2006). *EurActiv.com [On-line]*. Retrieved January 15 2011 from: http://www.euractiv.com/en/sports/disabled-access-sport-improved/article-160198

Government of Canada. Department of Canadian Heritage (2008).Canadian Heritage, S. C. B. Sport Participation Strategy 2008 - 2012 . Retrieved January 10, 2012 from: http://www.pch.gc.ca/pgm/sc/pubs/part/part-eng.pdf

How does a sport become Olympic? (2010). International Olympic Committee [On-line]. Retrieved December 11, 2010 from: http://www.olympic.org/en/content/Sports/

IAAF Oscar Pistorius - Independent Scientific study concludes that cheetah prosthetics offer clear mechanical advantages. (2008). IAAF [On-line]. Retrieved January 15 2011 from: http://www.iaaf.org/news/newsId=42896,printer.html

Kew, F. (1997). *Sport: Social problems and issues*, Oxford, UK: Butterworth, Heinemann.

Longman, J. (2007, May 15). An Amputee Sprinter: Is He Disabled or Too-Abled? *New York Times [On-line]*. Retrieved January 15 2011 from: http://www.nytimes.com/2007/05/15/sports/othersports/15runner.html?pagewanted=all 10.

Masteralexis P. L., Barr, C., & Hums, M. (2008). *Principles and Practice of Sport Management* (3rd ed.). Sudbury, MA: Jones & Bartlett.

McHugh J. (2007). Blade Runner. *Wired Magazine* [On-line]. Retrieved January 15 2011 from: http://www.wired.com/wired/archive/15.03/blade.html

Nixon II, H. L. (2007). Constructing Diverse Sports Opportunities for People With Disabilities. *Journal of Sport & Social Issues, 31(4)*, 417-433.

Ossur Oscar Pistorius - Special feature. (2010). Ossur [On-line]. Retrieved July 11, 2010 from: http://www.ossur.com/?PageID=13008

Robinson, J. & A. Schwartz (2010, May 17). Olympic Dream Stays Alive, on Synthetic Legs *New York Times* [On-line]. Retrieved Januar 11, 2012 from: http://www.nytimes.com/2008/05/17/sports/olympics/17runner.html?pagewanted=print

Sutcliffe M.(2008, Januar 13). Amputee sprinter treads uneven track. *The Ottawa Citizen*. Retrieved January 11, 2012 from: http://www.canada.com/ottawacitizen/columnists/story.html?id=51d55c3d-72fd-4261-b138-35a0f1709b1f&p=2

The Archrival. (2005, May 23). *Sport Illustrated* [On-line]. Retrieved Januar 11, 2012 from: http://sportsillustrated.cnn.com/vault/article/magazine/MAG1111353/index.htm

The Courts of Arbitration for Sport (CAS) (2008). Pistorius vs IAAF arbitral award. Retrieved August 10, 2010 from: http://www.tas-cas.org/d2wfiles/document/1085/5048/0/Pistorius+award+(scanned+published+on+CAS+website).pdf"

Wolbring, G. (2008). Oscar Pistorius and the Future Nature of Olympic, Paralympic and Other Sports. *5, SCRIPTed - A Journal of Law, Technology & Society*, 5(1),139-160. Retrieved Januar 11, 2012 from: http://www.law.ed.ac.uk/ahrc/script-ed/vol5-1/wolbring.pdf

Wolbring, G. (2009). 'Therapeutic', enhancement enabling, assistive devices and the UN Convention on the Rights of Persons with Disabilities: A missing lens in the enhancement regulation discourse. *6, Journal of International Biotechnology Law*, 6(5), 193-206.

Chapter 15
Post-modern Perspectives of the Media and Disability

Emily Coutant

Introduction

Currently, the analyses of the media treatment of disabled athlete's remains anchored in a modern vision of the world with its myths of high performance, ecstasy of movement and the courage required by the athletes to perform. At first glance one can observe that the major part of the iconographies found in the press or on the internet generally focus on the disability (missing limb or a prosthesis) or on facial expressions showing an effort, a fighting spirit or the surpassing of one's self while under difficult circumstances. As a matter of fact the 'mediatisation' of disabled people is still based on stereotypes of social representations prevalent among the general public and the body of a disabled athlete remains a body perceived through its limits, its incapacities and its shortcomings. In consequence the media treats disabled sports as a semblance of regular sports.

The modern perspectives of the relationship between media and disability reveal nothing either of the imaginary encased in these images, or on the symbolic and mythical forms which are present in the images of disabled sports or on the prospects that these athletes generate for humanity. However, the current sports imaginary appears thoroughly shaken by the growing 'mediatisation' of disabled athletes. Indeed, the visibility of the achievements of the disabled athletes in the media and elsewhere has a symbolic feature underlined by Jacques Defrance, who comments '....the representation of the competency figures within groups dominated under various connections plays a role in the symbolic struggles that aim at shattering the negative stereotypes linked to these groups' (Defrance, 2006, p. 77[1]). Beyond the influence of this 'mediatisation' on the perception of the disabled by the non-disabled, it highlights new and even hybrid representations of corporeity by staging an obvious, mutilated body, which highlights the fantasy of a split body. The sports phenomenon and disabled sports in particular contributes to the moulding of the individual and collective imaginaries in contemporary societies. Therefore the rational interpretation of the sports hubris has to give way to emotional processes and to the aesthetics of the sensation. The proliferation of the disabled sports images in the media is in line with the disruption of society's standards and values: the passage of Modernity to Post-modernity becomes sociality characterized by a new baroque[2] type of sensibility. The post-modern prospect of how the media treats people with disabilities requires an approach which is simultaneously comprehensive, phenomenological and "formist" (Simmel) and to register this approach is tantamount to the development of a sociology of the imaginary to better seize the myths and the archetypes that liven up the figures of the sportsmen in Paralympics.

What is the meaning and the function of the media images of disabled athletes? What myths and fantasies surround the visibility of such figures? How does the hybridism of these physical forms lead us on the way to an unforeseen experience of humanity? By adopting an intuitive and innovative point of view to answer these questions we shall reveal the anthropological importance of the Paralympics.

The spiritual function of images: Or the ethics of aesthetics

As alluded to previously the post-modern society is characterized by the saturation of the former modern values and the institution of new forms such as sensual pleasures, importance of affects, logic of the "will-being" (vouloir-être), pluralisation of the person, hedonism, and so forth. In such a societal configuration, we witness the (re)birth of an imaginary world which means a way of being and thinking imbibed by the image, the imaginary, the symbolic and the material. This imaginary becomes a constitutive element of a fun-

---

1. Translation by the author.

2. Eugenio d'Ors underlines that the baroque is an 'eon°'. We could say a state of mind that is a sensibility which we are going to find transversally, in many historical periods. A state of mind where reliance outweighs on separation, where the complementarity replaces the exclusion, where the relativism takes the place of the universal, where the plural person, finally, substitutes for the individual in the "indivisible" identity. The baroque prefigures the vitalist swarm of post-modernity/postmodernism (Ors, 1985 [1935]).

damental belong-together or belonging ("l'être-ensemble"). The renewal of the perspectives and the methodologies appears as a necessity to fully comprehend the mutations which take place within this social configuration. Hence adopting a triple approach to the problem (phenomenological, comprehensive and formist) seems innovative. The phenomenological approach is a kind of return to the perception of the sensitive and to the manifestations of the appearance. The image operates towards passage of the sensitive impression - a perception of the visible - to the representations' world, livened up by the symbolic activity. The prevalence of the image and the appearance in the post-modern paradigm, indeed, indicates the saturation of the essential for the benefit of an effervescence of the form. According to Michel Maffesoli, following Georg Simmel, "the shape is the matrix which gives birth to all the aesthetic phenomena restricting the post-modern culture" (Maffesolie, 2005, p. 107). The form is formant which means that it constructs the society. While valorising the body, the images, and the appearances, it forms the social body. The form aggregates, gathers and shapes a unit. In actuality, "These forming forms are going be expressed under the figure of a musical or sports star in a empirical way (...).These figures are as so many magic caricatures in which everyone (...) recognize oneself" (Maffesolie, 2005, p.111)".

It is this process that is used in the media images of the disabled athletes. The images have a spiritual function - they are at the same time the sources, the medium and the product of social representations, with the properties of representation, emotion and ambiguity. The post-modern sociality is based on these ethics of the aesthetics in the real sense of 'aïsthesis: the fact of having common feelings'. It is an ethic which aggregates and creates links favouring the attraction and the aversion. The emphasized, epiphanised body is built to be seen. It is a 'socialization: to integrate into a set and to transcend the individual' (Maffesolie 2007, p. 34).

In the imagined world of the Paralympics, the sport creates an emotion by introducing an extraordinary aspect. The media contribute to transforming these athletes into heroes and their adventure into an epic by portraying the struggles, the new developments, and the moments of suffering. What we have here is a body feast, collective enthusiasm that can be compared to the religious rites of exotic societies with the introduction of the sacred into the sports shows that are considered religious rites with plot twists.

Furthermore, the fact of focusing e.g. on the prosthesis or the disability shows a will to display the underestimated essence of the human condition. One can say that the mutilated body, or a body equipped with a prosthesis, represents the darker side in each of us, a zone in every one that is mutilated and equipped with prosthesis. This injured and incomplete body testifies to a particular subjectivity and enlightens certain underestimated, dark and disturbing aspects of mankind. The disability or the disease constitutes a figure among multiple, heterogeneous and fluctuating figures that are displayed to the contemporary individual for defining an identity which is more and more diverse and plural.

In this sense the iconographies of the disabled athletes take part in the revelation of the identity's plurality, and fit it into the ethics of the aesthetics, and an ethos which compels a renewal of the perception of things different. These ambiguous images create as much fascination as aversion, but they are also factors of identification in the sense of an emotional identification by an affective analogy. In this dramatization and epiphanization of the bodies, one can distinguish a kind of collective narcissism that is both cause and effect of a world of life (Nietzschean Lebenswelt). Sport appears as a big social link and weaver of people's lives and perhaps a substitute for religion in society. It obliges the subject to conform to others and thus becomes vector of identification for the individual and society. Two identification processes are possible through the imaging of the disabled athletes: an identification to the 'disabled person' and an identification to the 'regular athlete' seen as a hero and a model of the athlete with a perfect body. The essential is the being-together and galvanized by the identification. It is about a real communicational atmosphere where the entertaining body is the cause and effect of communication. One observes in this projection towards the other a desire of fusion the purpose of which is to exist in the eyes of the other. The identity asserted by the disabled athlete is far from being perceived as inviolable reality - it is on the contrary excessively pluralized. There exists a construction of a multiple body where the opening of the person widens until integrating daïmonic (the guardian angel representative of the divine) or inhuman (animal or hybrid) qualities are displayed.

The Disabled Athlete: Prototype of tomorrow's human

The display of the deviant body is a possible analyzer of the relations that society maintains with the infirmity and its evolutions, conceptions, and treatment. It is also an analyzer of the relations that society maintains with bodies by reminding of the fragility of the human condition. It also seems to reactivate in everyone the inhuman part of our being. The disability confers to an originality and thereby gives rise to an emotion which can go as far as eroticisation. An example would be 'Venus de Milo', the arms of which are left amputated, whereas the nose, the lip and the big toe have been repaired. This amputation is at the source of the emotion that it rouses. The disabled individual reminds people of the unbearable fragility of the being. The image projection of this fragility makes us modify our intimate relation with this disturbing otherness inside us and wakes in each of us the native fantasy of the split body.

As mentioned before, the presenters and the sports correspondents put forward in the choice of their wording the will and the courage which tend to render the produced performance exemplary. However, it is necessary to note in addition that this performance is not only valued because it is surprising and rouses admiration, but that it is also valued because it opens the way to an unforeseen human experience which is especially forbidden for a regular human body. The disabled people are not disabled when they have prosthesis: they renew the perception and the social representations of the capacities of a body. This hybridization installs a new integration with the world, the object or the others by the installation of medicine, techniques and/or machines within the body. These fixed human beings showing their prosthesis, to which spare parts have been added, implicit in the essence of the man of the future. We could even say that they are real prototypes of the man of tomorrow. The difference between them and us, the regular men and women, is this: most of us live with organs that were given to us in birth by nature, and languish under the natural effect of aging. To put it in other words, our bodily unity is still natural, whereas the athletes with disabilities like Oscar Pistorius, a fascinating sprinter with two half-artificial legs, already lives in a future time of what some call 'patched men' whose bodies no longer have the unity of a regular body. Disabled people are already numerous. Their bodily unity is already artificial to a large extent. Biotechnologies foresee in the near future the possibility of rather easily replacing parts of the human body, just as the world of stem cells promises the possibility of regenerating certain parts of the human body. These two methods (prosthesis and regeneration) will be the weapons in the combat against aging and against disability. Therefore we can identify a disabled athlete as an indication of a sort of a man to come. The organic unity received at birth that most humans have in common at present, will then be only a memory of bygone days.

In this sporting context the disabled body appears as a hybrid body that not only renews the standards, but also remodels the forms by the prosthesis and the genetic manufacturing of new species and new individuals. For example, the insertion of a prosthetic knee or a hip is going to replace the weakened organ by restoring the articulatory function. The foreign body hybridizes with the muscular mass of the natural body in a biosubjective reorganization of the body schema. The flesh will reorganize itself around the implant. The hybridization therefore appears as a process of biological adaptation which transforms the material system of the body. The hybrid becomes a modality of the future of reality as the hybridization incorporates the world of the others into us, transforms the human into a being of the future and allows us the chance to discover, in the living, the passing of time. All this leads to the creation of the contemporary cyborg myth, an entity half-man, half-machine whose admitted purpose is a transcendence of humanity, a post-human mutation supposed to be free from the physical and moral constraints which are regarded as laws in our societies. In a way, the cyborg or the hybrid is the ultimate embodiment of post-modernity, if one agrees to define the latter as an organic mixture of some archaic and more contemporary elements, of which the technological development is part. The cyborg is the prototype of the model fighter that contains all the possibilities of the human potential, and suggests an exit from the maze of the dualisms in which we inscribe bodies.

From then on, we notice that the tiresome chorus about effort, values and courage, which has replaced the real attention on Paralympics in the media, the political sphere and in the public opinion, has been based on the ideological mode of concealing the truth. On the one hand it testifies to an impoverishment of the way man is perceived in the sense of ignoring that disability can place us on the path of a new experience of the human being. One should not underestimate this ignorance as far as it reflects an insidious way of rejecting disability by assuming that adage - the world of the strong is the only possible world. On the other hand it prevents one from making the following observation: *'the Paralympics have a greater anthropological importance than the Olympics, the disabled champions being pioneers'.* In the near future the reconstructed, repaired and regenerated body will be the norm, whereas the regular bodies of today will be regarded as disabled. They will be numbed with artefacts. *The real reach of the Paralympics has not yet been perceived.* Even though Pistorius, the winner of the 100 meters for disabled, tells a lot more about humanity than Bolt, the winner of the 100 meters in regular athlete category. This post-modern perspective of the relationship between disabled athletes and the media reveals well the obsolescence of the current discourse and analyses surrounding the image of disability. By highlighting the aesthetic function of iconographies, the imaginary surrounding such figures, and the discovery of new (hybrid) forms that surpass the human, the phenomenological approach registered within the framework of the sociology of the imaginary allows to seize in more detail the mythical aspects of disabled athletes. The dominant discourse that depicts the disabled model as heroic and hides the darker side of that disability is actually a negation of disability and its specificity. And yet disability and disease are also human experiences endowed with value in itself. They indicate a possible way towards another type of humanity, which is hybridized. The disabled athlete seems closer to the divine, or at least to the man of future, as he holds a form of power which is not accessible to the regular athletes. It all comes down to another idea according to which the sports imaginary and the sport for people with disabilities have this capacity to imagine the future. From there onwards, the disabled athlete is the hero of the post-modern, a hero who by essence would offer the possibility of believing in the impossible, would allow to imagine that we can always push farther, higher and stronger the limits of the human's organic potential, thanks to courage and the exercise of the will.

References

Defrance, J. (2006). *Sociologie du sport*. Paris: La Découverte.
D'Ors, E. (1985 [1935]). Du Baroque (A. Rouardt-Valéry, Trans.). Paris: Gallimard.
Maffesoli, M. (2005 [1996]). *Eloge de la raison sensible*. Paris : La Table Ronde. (1990).
Maffesoli, M. (2007 [1990]). *Au creux des apparences. Pour une éthique de l'esthétique*. Paris : La Table Ronde.

Chapter 16
Rehabilitating Heteromasculinity

The Sexual Politics of Murderball

Cynthia Barounis

Introduction

To suggest that *Murderball* (2005), a documentary chronicling the lives of a set of quadriplegic wheelchair rugby athletes, focuses on and is immersed in hetero-masculinity more than likely states the obvious to anyone who has seen the film. The key players featured throughout appear rugged, athletic, occasionally tattooed, and are often 'trash-talking' whose ultimate goal is to crush the competition and come home from the Paralympics with a gold medal. The documentary eschews sentimentality in favour of a more hard-edged realism that foregrounds its subjects as ordinary specimens of a male sports world. It appears throughout as though when they're not giving (or getting) a beating on the court, they're drinking and having sex with women, or bragging about drinking and having sex with women. Indeed, the film's emphasis on the heterosexual potency of quadriplegic men is one of its most provocative features, and one that has received widespread praise and criticism from reviewers.[1]

On a basic level, the film's popularity can be considered a success for disability cultural activism. It is an authentic portrayal of a disabled subculture that avoids the traditional narrative traps of many mainstream disability films.[2] The viewer is immediately directed to check his or her well-intentioned sympathies at the door, along with any preconceived notions about the fragility of the disabled body. And disabled sexuality, a taboo and uncomfortable territory for many non-disabled viewers, is reclaimed with a vengeance.[3] Indeed, one of the difficulties in analyzing *Murderball* is that its most radical features are simultaneously its most conventional. Thus, while non-disabled viewers may find their assumptions and stereotypes challenged by the masculine sexual bravado of *Murderball*'s quadriplegic rugby players, there may be a simultaneous sense of relief at ironclad endurance of male heterosexual privilege. It can be argued therefore that heterosexuality no longer functions as evidence that a disabled masculinity has finally been artificially "cured"; instead, it's the masculinization of disability that holds the power to rehabilitate heteronormativity from its own isolated gender troubles.

Far from the typical narrative arc of a heteromasculinity lost through injury and reclaimed through rehabilitation, the documentary figures disability as not only reflecting but, in fact, amplifying a deeply constant heterosexual masculine selfhood. Revisiting the night of his injury, for example, Mark Zupan explains doing "shots with the girls" at a local bar to celebrate a soccer win before passing out in the back of his best friend's truck; his friend, unaware of Zupan's presence in the vehicle, drove home drunk and

---

1. Matthew Leyland, for example, offers the following praise in *Sight and Sound*: "Dispelling misconceptions in an unfussy fashion, Shapiro and Rubin... venture into taboo territory with an X-rated debate about quad sex. As well as answering questions most disability movies are afraid to ask, the sequence is very funny. 'The more pitiful I am, the more [women] like me,' one wheelchair user chirps unapologetically" (Leyland, 2005 p. 70).

2. In *The Cinema of Isolation*, Martin Norden identifies one such narrative trap as the tendency for Hollywood to put well-known, able-bodied actors in disabled roles. Like a straight-identified actor playing a gay role, the casting of able-bodied stars in disabled roles become an opportunity for the able-bodied actor to demonstrate superior Oscar-quality acting skills by successfully impersonating what the public would view as extreme difference or otherness (Norden, 1994, p. 2).

3. In his comparative reading of the armless Venus de Milo and a quadriplegic woman, Pam Herbert, Lennard Davis draws our attention to the able-bodied assumptions underlying Western standards of physical beauty. Thus Davis explores "how people with disabilities are seen and why, by and large, they are de-eroticized" (Davis, 1995, p.128). The film's intense eroticisation of quadriplegic men can then be read as a radical reclaiming of that which has long been denied to disabled people; that this is accomplished through heteronormative masculinization and at the expense of the disabled whom are further "queered" by the logic of the film, however, is a tension that this section explores in greater detail.

had an accident in which Zupan was thrown into nearby canal where he held onto a branch for fourteen hours before anyone discovered him. It's a story that mixes ordinary masculinity with extraordinary toughness and endurance. Explaining the origins of their disabilities, the rugby players relate similar tales of risky behavior associated with masculinity. Scott Hogsett was thrown off of a balcony during a fistfight; Keith Cavill was injured while attempting a set of dangerous motorcycle stunts; and while Bob Lubjano explains that his amputated limbs are the effect of a "rare blood disease," the back of the DVD release puts on a slightly different spin, characterizing his impairment as the result of an encounter with "rogue bacteria." These acts of anthropomorphosis endows the simple act of injury or sickness with a quality of combat, aggressivity, and risk taking

But if honorable combat is positioned as that which put the players in the wheelchair, then it's the chair itself that opens up greater opportunities to accumulate more battle scars.[4] One reviewer admires the fact that the rugby chairs resemble "chariots of war", a point that is in no subtle way driven home by an interviewee who explains how the chairs are made: "What we do is we take these wheelchairs and turn them into a gladiator, a battling machine, a *Mad Max* wheelchair that can stand knocking the living daylights out of each other." In this respect, the film's opening sequence, characterized by Zupan himself as "preparing for battle," is worth examining. In the beginning we hear and see the rip of duct tape, the whirring of the wheel, and the clanging of metal. Later, we will watch an animated clip in which metal screws are incorporated into the skeletal drawing of a spine; the image gradually fades into a shot of the actual scars that mark one players neck. Thus both man and chair are visually constructed as the product of custom-built state-of-the-art manufacturing. If, according to the logic of the film, it was the amplification of ordinary masculinity that led to Zupan's injury, then this extraordinarily refashioned machinstic masculinity is nothing less than mythical in its origins.

In a recent issue of *Narrative*, Rosemarie Garland-Thomson has described the players featured in *Murderball* as "[c]yborgs composed of steel fused with flesh," arguing that, in the documentary, "[d]isability provides an unanticipated opportunity for boys to come into themselves as athletes and men" (Garland-Thomson, 2007: 115).[5] Garland-Thomson generously concludes however, that rather than reconstructing heteronormative masculinity, *Murderball* provides us with "what Judith Halberstam calls an alternative masculinity," one which is essentially "non-phallic" (Garland-Thomson, 2007 p.116). However, to redefine disability through masculinity, as the documentary certainly does, is not necessarily to redefine masculinity itself. Al-

---

4. This is not the first time images of masculine combat have framed narratives of rehabilitation. See Daniel Wilson's "Fighting Polio Like a Man," for a compelling analysis of how narratives of polio rehabilitation during the Cold War drew parallels between military combat and the act of fighting the disease.

5. My thanks to Megan V. Davis for this reference.

though the film does present us with multiple images of the male cyborg, these images seem to fall short of approximating Haraway's feminist technoscience or Halberstam's technotopic body.[6] Indeed, Haraway's cyborg myth contests both the legitimacy of the masculinist cyborg and the overall male monopoly on technoculture. Repudiating narratives of origin, cyborgs and technotopic bodies are not aimed at helping "boys to come into themselves as athletes and as men" but, rather, at creating alternative queer temporalities in which boys sometimes become something other than men, and girls sometimes become something other than women. Additionally, Garland-Thomson's claim that *Murderball* creates an "innovative, non-phallic, alternative sexuality," (Garland-Thomson, 2007 p.116) focuses on a single reference to cunnilingus while overlooking the dynamic staging that privileges heterosexual phallic penetration as the measurement of the players' masculinity[7]

---

6. Examining the work of three different visual artists, Halberstam defines this technotopic body as "a body situated in an immediate and visceral relation to technologies—guns, scalpel, cars, paintbrushes—that have marked, hurt, changed, imprinted, and brutally reconstructed it" and notes that "in all three instances, the impact of technological intervention is to disrupt gender stability... [suggesting that] we should locate femaleness not as the material with which we begin nor as the end product of medical engineering but as a stage and indeed as fleshly place of production" (Halberstam, 2005, pp.116-117). The men of *Murderball* are certainly "situated in an immediate and visceral relation to technologies that have marked" each of them. But while for Halberstam the technotopic body "disrupts gender stability" and showcases anatomical sex as neither the "material with which we begin nor as the end product of medical engineering," the technologized masculinity of the quad rugby athletes is visually framed within a narrative of continuity that privileges the anatomical origin of maleness and the technologically-enhanced final product of heteronormative masculinity. What might have become a radical celebration of technology's roles in producing alternative or queer modes of embodiment here collapses into a reification of gender difference.

7. While Mark Zupan certainly mentions that most wheelchair athletes "like to eat pussy," it is important to point out that this comment is embedded within a sentence that begins with Zupan gesturing downwards and reassuring the viewer: "that still works". In another scene, the ability to have an erection is somewhat taken for granted as an essential feature of quadriplegia. After reassuring an attractive ablebodied woman that the three players sitting at the table are all fully functional, Scott Hogsett relates the following story:

    "When I first got injured, I was in intensive care, and, uh, everyone was curious how I was gonna be, how much function I was gonna have when I came out of my coma that I was in, and I was about ready to wake up, and the nurses decided to give me a bed-bath in the bed, and the one nurse got so excited that I got a woody, she ran outside and got my mom and showed her my, uh, erection".

    What is significant about this exchange is the swiftness with which the image of the impotent quadriplegic is replaced by the image of the quadriplegic whose erection is being celebrated by the community of women surrounding him. While the woman's question might well have opened up a conversation about alternative sexual practices that don't privilege phallic potency, the response ultimately ends up both creating a heteronormatively functional elite among the disabled while simultaneously generalizing the situation of that elite to the entire quadriplegic community.

Towards an Alternative Masculinity

There is, however, at least one representation of an "alternative masculinity" present in the film *Murderball*. Following an exchange in which an American player accuses former U.S. Coach Joe Soares of "betray[ing] his country" by leaving to coach team Canada, the camera cuts to an evening scene in the hotel room where all four of the featured U.S. players, along with two or three others, play a game of modified poker. Within the confusion of a lively dialogue, we witness a lanky, long-haired teammate named Sam defend Soares's decision:

> **Sam:** On a professional level, I don't think there's anything wrong with it.
> **Andy:** That's number two on the list of most stupid things I've ever heard at this camp. I heard Sam say that he doesn't like big tits and he'd dump a girl with big tits, if everything was perfect – but, if she has big tits, [imitating Sam] "it's over, they get in the way".
> **Sam:** I like athletic girls. That's what I said all along that night when they asked me.
> **Zupan:** You knew you weren't going to live that one down.
> **Sam:** I'm okay with my sexuality. I can say that. I don't like big tits.
> **Zupan:** You like shoes though.
> **Sam:** I do like shoes.

Following this exchange, everyone laughs and the camera pans to the mechanical card shuffler that happens to be in motion. On the one hand, this scene solidifies the link between heteromasculinity and patriotism as Sam's moral defense of a known "traitor" leads the players to move abruptly into an interrogation of Sam's heteronormativity. Though there's nothing homosexual about a man who "likes[s] athletic girls," there is something queer, according to the film's logic, about a man who lacks desire for the appropriate object choice—in this case, "a girl with big tits."[8] Sam's interest in "athletic girls" thus feminizes (and arguably queers) him to the extent that it's framed as a desire for masculinity (albeit a masculinity that is attached to a

---

8. "Big tits" are, of course, functioning here as a metonym of idealized femininity, with all of its attendant associations of passivity, nurturance and non-athleticism. In The Gender of Desire, Michael Kimmel has argued that hegemonic masculinity is fundamentally rooted in a homophobic impulse to simultaneously deny and desire the feminine. If a boy is to access patriarchy, his successful identification with his father must be accompanied by a disavowal of the feminine within himself, a punishment of effeminacy in other men, and a willingness to turn his mother into an object of desire. (Kimmel, 2005, p. 34) If *Murderball* follows the traditional narrative of masculinity that Kimmel has outlined, the players' masculinity ultimately depends on the sexual acquisition of the girl whose "big tits" prove that she's everything that he's not.

female body).⁹ While this sequence opens up some fascinating tensions, the soft roar of the mechanical card shuffler has the last word, and Sam along with his anti-normative desires are silenced for the remainder of the film.

Because the film has polarized disability as a property of athletic heteromasculinity and able-bodiedness as a property of heterosexual, non-athletic femininity, it leaves no space for the physically disabled athletic woman; her body is not only rendered unintelligible but becomes a palpable threat to the narrative glue that holds masculinity, disability, and heteronormativity firmly together.¹⁰ The few images of disabled women that the documentary presents appear as a set of fleeting and brief snapshots. These images haunt the film's perimeter, a subtle threat to the coherence of a narrative that celebrates quadriplegia as the natural outcome of the hypermasculine

---

9. Interestingly, the player commentary not only conflates Sam's queer object choice with feminization but also with a lack of sexual potency, and a general inability to engage in phallocentric penetrative sex. While watching the poker scene with the commentary function turned on, one hears the players add: "We tried to get Sammy laid the whole year, but he's just not a closer. He's had some opportunities but Sammy cuddles." Sam's decision to not be a "closer" simultaneously resists the narrative *closure* that protectively bounds heteromasculine sexuality in the film.

10. Wendy Seymour has suggested that the same logic that masculinizes the quadriplegic or paraplegic man also functions to both masculinize and desexualize the quadriplegic or paraplegic woman (Seymour, 1998 p. 120). This brings up a set of thorny issues involving whether or not disabled women's exclusion from the structures of conventional heterosexual femininity can open up other liberatory possibilities, even as such exclusions simultaneously police and regulate their sexuality. While a thorough negotiation of these issues is beyond the scope of this chapter, the fact remains that *Murderball* explores neither side of the debate. Disabled women, and particularly disabled female athletes, are not celebrated as having been liberated from oppressive conventions of gender. Nor are they given access to normative femininity; visually, they are never made into objects of the voyeuristic male gaze that, after Laura Mulvey's classic 1975 article, has become common currency in discussions of cinematic spectatorship. Neither, interestingly, are they victims of "the stare," a visual dynamic coined by Garland-Thomson to encapsulate the revulsion of the able-bodied viewer whose lengthy hostile gaze at a "freakishly" embodied other is emptied of sexual desire (Garland-Thomson, 1998 p. 26).

male body.[11] We would do well, however, to take these moments as opportunities to reflect on and draw out the gender trouble that complicates not only the film, but also the cultural past that has inflated the notion of queerness and disability.

References

Bennett, R. (2000). Rugby. *WeMedia*, 4(5), p. 60.

Davis, L. J. (1995). *Enforcing Normalcy: Disability, Deafness, and the Body*. New York: Verso Books.

Garland-Thomson, R. (1997). *Extraordinary Bodies: Figuring Physical Disability in American Culture and Literature*. New York: Columbia University Press.

Garland-Thomson, R. (2004). Integrating Disability, Transforming Feminist Theory. In B. G. Smith and B. Hutchison (Eds.), *Gendering Disability* (pp. 73-104). New Brunswick, N.J.: Rutgers University Press.

Garland-Thomson, R. (2007). Shape Structures Story: Fresh and Feisty Stories about Disability. *Narrative*, 15(1), 113-123.

Halbestam, J. (2005). *In a Queer Time and Place: Transgender Bodies, Subcultural Lives*. New York: New York University Press.

Haller, M.D. (2005). Seat of Power. *Cincinnati Magazine*, October, 39(1), 20-22.

Haraway, D. (1991). *Simians, Cyborgs and Women: The Reinvention of Nature*. New York: Routledge.

---

11. Indeed, even the most attentive viewer might, on a first viewing, miss the few glimpses that are to be had of disabled female athletics. The first opportunity isn't until just before the final dramatic showdown between the U.S. and Canada at the 2004 Paralympics. In a brief montage that showcases a variety of Paralympic sports, there is a two-second clip of female leg amputees playing volleyball. Significantly, they are all low to the ground, and filmed (perhaps unavoidably) from above. Not only does the angle diminish their size and power, but also they are absent of any type of prosthesis or equipment and none of them are using wheelchairs. Given that prosthetics and wheelchair technology have earlier in the film been powerfully deployed to signify and naturalize disabled masculinity, and given that this clip is sandwiched between clips of Paralympic male sports (all of them requiring varying levels of prosthesis), it may be plausible to argue that the framing of these female athletes functions to neutralize any threat to disabled masculinity that their presence might pose. The only other scene in which disabled women are presented in an athletic capacity is during the documentary's final scene, as the players teach a group of newly disabled Iraq War veterans how to play the game. Between clips, we see two young women, though very briefly and in a limited context. While most of the documentary features women only in conventional, able-bodied roles that reify masculinity by performing its opposite, these brief moments confront the viewer with an unapologetic assertion of another type of "alternative masculinity," one that is attached to a female body.

Kimmel, M. S. (2005). *The Gender of Desire: Essays on Male Sexuality*. New York: State University of New York Press.
Leyland, M. (2005). Murderball. *Sight and Sound*, 15(11), 70-71.
Mulvey, L. (2004). Visual Pleasure and Narrative Cinema. *Screen*, 16(3), 6-18.
Norden, M. F. (1994). *The Cinema of Isolation: A History of Physical Disability in the Movies*. New Brunswick, N.J.: Rutgers University Press.
Seymour, W. (1998). *Remaking the Body: Rehabilitation and Change*. London: Routledge.
Shapiro, D.A., Mandel, J. & Rubin, H.A. (2005). *Murderball*, THINKFilm and MTV Films.
Wilson, D.J. (2004). Fighting Polio Like a Man: Intersections of Masculinity, Disability and Aging. In B.G. Smith and B. Hutchison (Eds.) *Gendering Disability* (pp. 119–133). New Brunswick, NJ: Rutgers University Press.

Part III
Reconceptualizing Paralympic Sport, Disability and the Media

Chapter 17
Paralympic Athletes' Perspectives of Media Coverage

Whose Story is it?

Donna de Haan

Introduction

Research on the subject of media coverage of athletes with disabilities is an emerging field which remains the interest of a relatively small pool of academics. Although we can now refer to some seminal pieces of work on the subject, which can help further engage and inform discussion, as with any new area of research, we are often left with more questions than answers.

The majority of studies report on the content of media coverage, and subsequent analysis of terminology, column inches and pictorial presentation. Even though the studies vary in their focus, in all the literature there is a common thread of discontent, which is perfectly portrayed in the following quote from Hardin & Hardin (2003 p. 247)

> 'Of course, the media's disregard for athletics involving disability is not surprising, when considered in the larger context of media and disability. The media's record of ignoring and marginalizing people with disabilities in every respect stretches back as far as studies have explored the topic.'

Whilst I am not purporting to offer a different perspective, I found that the more I read the literature on the topic of media and disability sport, the more questions were recurring to me and I was left asking the following:

If the current media coverage of athletes with disabilities is inappropriate, or offensive or archaic or simply not good enough, what would the ideal coverage look like? And whose ideal would this be? Indeed, can we continue to simply berate the media for their coverage of disability sport if we are unable to offer realistic alternatives?

One could reason that stripped down to its purest form, what is highlighted in the media fundamentally reflects the athletes stories and therefore it is their opinion on the content of coverage that holds relevance to the reporting of disability sport in the media within the Paralympic context. Whilst I am not naive enough to disregard the power and politics of the media, after all what we are presented with in the media is a result of societal, economic and political influence. I am however, surprised by how many studies discuss the negative effect poor media coverage can have on the emancipation of individuals with disabilities (Golden, 2003; Thomas & Smith, 2003; Buysse & Borcherding, 2010), without actually asking or presenting the athletes opinion. It could be argued that sport media is, or at least should, be fundamentally concerned with reporting quantitative facts, i.e. simply presenting the 'results'. Schantz and Gilbert (2001) however, outlined that based on the theoretical concept of news factors, sport-specific news coverage should focus on issues considered news worthy and whilst these include 'quantitative' facts relating to size action, records, and elite performances, they also include issues pertaining to aggression, heroic actions, drama, emotions and celebrities which are all qualitatively accessed. In other words, by moving beyond the simple presentation of sport statistics we begin to address the human experience of sport and as Chari (1975 p. 169) outlines this perspective of 'human element cannot be reduced to a scientific norm'. Indeed, if you pick up any print based media or tune into any TV coverage of sport there is no getting away from the fact that the results are couched in a broader narrative or story, but the question ultimately remains, 'who are the owners of the stories'?

Although not yet evident in studies pertaining to media coverage of athletes with disabilities, narrative forms of inquiry have become increasingly visible within disability studies in general. Smith and Sparkes (2008) suggest that narrative inquiry can provide a different outline regarding disability that refuses and displaces the tragedy story by challenging and resisting social oppression, thereby allowing different body-self relationships to emerge. Narrative analysis has therefore, the potential to provide an alternative map, a different lens through which we can view the medias' coverage of disability sport.

What follows is an attempt to readdress the balance and present the opinion of athletes with regards to the media coverage of disability sport. The content of the discussion presented in this chapter came about following conversations with visually impaired elite Paralympic footballers Keryn

Seal and Will Norman, who between them have over 70 international caps and experience of European and World Championships and Paralympic competition. Hopefully in the following pages you will hear their voices as we discuss the topic of 'sport specific media coverage' and finally address the question of 'whose story is it?'

Playing football with your eyes shut

Ten Summer Paralympic sports currently have a category for Visually Impaired (VI) athletes these include, athletics, cycling, equestrian, football 5-a-side, goal ball, judo, rowing, sailing, powerlifting and swimming. The majority of these sports are open to several different categories of disability and their governance reflects this. Football 5-a-side, goal ball and judo however, are only open to VI athletes and are all governed by The International Blind Sport Association (IBSA) which is recognised as a full member of the International Paralympic Committee (IPC).

Blind football is played with a ball containing ball bearings so that it makes a noise when it moves, it is played on a solid surface surrounded by a rebound wall, and there are no throw-ins and no off-side rule. There are five players in each team, the goalkeeper is sighted but cannot leave the area, and the outfield players must wear eye-patches and blindfolds to take account of differing degrees of eyesight. The goalkeeper provides coaching instruction to his defence and there is a sighted coach behind the goal to direct players' shots on goal, with an additional coach on the halfway line.

The first major football competitions developed by the IBSA were the American Championships and European Championships both held for the first time in 1997, a year later the first World Championships were held, followed in 2005 by the first Asian Championships, each of these tournaments are subsequently held every two years. Football 5-a-side is however, a relatively young Paralympic sport, appearing for the first time in Athens 2004.

Initial Conversations

During our first conversations, the players felt that the 'newness' of their sport influenced media coverage and attention. They also referred to the 'novelty' aspect of their sport, explaining that most people are intrigued by the practicalities of how you play football with your eyes shut. For example Keryn commented:

> "With blind football being a relatively young sport in terms of Paralympic involvement, journalists and broadcasters have sometimes leaned towards the novelty factor of the sport, and forgotten to report on the actual merits of the players or the sport as a whole. I could probably describe it better by saying that I feel some journalists write or broadcast about the sport in a kind of hey look at these guys! They are blind and they play football. Isn't that weird?"

And Will adds,

> "In some ways I think it's only natural that the media should focus on the disability when covering a Paralympic event. After all, my sport is Blind Football. Without the "blindness", what is a game of blind football, just another average Futsal match, and who would tune in for that? What captures the imagination is the thought that players are achieving these standards, executing their skills, and finding the back of the net, all with their eyes shut".

Not only is blind football a relatively new Paralympic sport it is also a relatively new branch of football in the UK, only registering on the radar of the Football Association within the last decade. The Football Association currently run the England Blind football team and provide technical advisors, clothing and equipment and financial assistance to help squads travel to championships. However, the game in England still lags behind other countries with VI football still seen as an amateur minority and marginalised sport. In Argentina, France, Spain and China players are full-time, as they are in Brazil where government funding means there are approximately 80 blind football teams compared to approximately six teams in the UK.

The 'newness' of the sport is not only reflected in the practical development of VI football but also in relation to scholarly interest, with research to date limited solely to the contributions made by Jessica Macbeth and Jonathan Magee (Macbeth, 2009; Macbeth, 2008; Macbeth and Magee, 2006). As we will discuss in the final sections of this chapter, the 'newness' of VI football also influences the development of the 'story'.

Sport Specific Coverage

As previously mentioned, the purpose of this chapter is to give a voice to the athletes, to differentiate their story from the generalised assumptions which are sometimes presented by academics and the media alike. 'Different' is a term we often shy away from when referring to disability, yet the risk at the other end of the spectrum is to homogenise the discourse, are we really saying that all sport for disabled athletes is the same, all media coverage is the same and everyone has the same experience?

One area where 'different' is at the forefront of the discussion is in the general comparison between media coverage of mainstream able-bodied sport and disability sport. Indeed, when analysing media coverage of Paralympic sport it appears that the default position is always to draw comparisons with Olympic coverage, for example:

> 'While NBC paid hundreds of millions of dollars for rights to air the Olympics in prime time each night during the Games, the Paralympic Games garnered one hour of coverage by NBC' (Hardin and Hardin, 2003 p. 246).

Brittain (2010) argues that the disproportionate amount of time the media spends covering the Olympic and Paralympic Games, (as shown in the Hardin and Hardin (2003) quote) is an indicator of societal attitudes towards disabled and non-disabled sport. But there are many reasons why the coverage is 'different'.

Fundamentally commercial sport is a commodity, as such the reflected 'value' media may afford any given event is representative of this perception. However, this does not mean there is a standard equation which will neatly calculate the 'worth' of sport-to-media coverage. The commercial viability of a sport in relation to media attractiveness is based on a combination of social, economic and even political factors. Currently, in the UK, nothing compares to the media powerhouse of male able-bodied football, it would certainly be redundant therefore to try to draw comparisons between this and any other strand of football such as women's football or disability football. In a similar vein, research has indicated that there are differences within disability sport, relating to the amount and type of media coverage each sport receives.

Within the disability sport and media literature, Schantz and Gilbert (2001) explain that print media appears to privilege some specific types of disability. Several studies have identified that female athletes with disabilities are afforded proportionally less coverage than their male counterparts, mirroring the type of gendered media coverage in able-bodied sport, whilst athletes with cerebral palsy and athletes with learning difficulties are afforded less coverage than athletes with other impairments (Sherril, 1997; Schell & Duncan, 1999; Schantz & Gilbert, 2001; Thomas & Smith, 2003).

Several scholars have also reported that the main group of athletes focussed upon are individuals with physical disability, the most overrepresented group being male athletes in wheelchairs (Haller, 2000; Schantz & Gilbert, 2001; Hardin & Hardin, 2003). Hardin and Hardin (2003) refer to this as a media-constructed hierarchy of disability, with males in wheelchairs at the top because they are the 'closest' to the ideal competitor among athletes with disabilities. DePauw (1997) however, argues that this is because the wheelchair can be viewed as a substitute for the lower body function, while the athletes upper body offers 'acceptable' and 'normal looking' physique. Schantz and Gilbert (2001) suggest that the visual image of this group of athletes is so strong that it allows the subject to be labelled as having a disability without it being stated.

The disproportionate representation of media coverage of wheelchair athletes is something Keryn reflected upon and from his perspective as both a spectator of sport programming and as a Paralympian he noted:

> "My strongest memories of the Paralympics I witnessed as a sports fan were images of men and women in wheelchairs competing in athletics events. I would say that 80 to 90% of the newspaper and television coverage I saw of these games, were of athletes competing in wheelchair events. From my own experience of being inside the Paralympic village as a competitor, I know that 80 to 90% of the athletes are not wheelchair users".

At this point I feel it is important to address the issue of 'ownership' and 'power' in the sport/media dichotomy, which begs another question! Do the media predominantly cover male wheelchair sports because these are the most popular or are these sports popular because of the media coverage? In other words who is controlling supply and demand? i.e. who is controlling whom?

Modern day sport is championed by role models. Role models, who ultimately emerge from, and influence media attention. Unfortunately in our current western celebrity obsessed culture this often results in sports personalities appearing on the front pages more often than the back pages of print media. Nevertheless, individual household names promote specific sports, but as Brittain (2010) argues, these role models are decidedly missing from disability sport.

However, one female athlete who has emerged as a role model is ex British Paralympic athlete Tanni Grey-Thompson. Tanni has 16 Paralympic (wheelchair racing) medals, 6 London marathon wins and 30 world records, and is often referred to as Britain's greatest Paralympian. Whilst her sporting record is impeccable, Tanni has also received numerous accolades and awards including an MBE awarded in 1992, becoming BBC Sports Personality of the Year (Helen Rollason Award) in 2000, and being voted 'UK Sporting Hero' by Sport UK in 2001. Since her retirement from competition, Tanni has continued to be involved in sport and is a regular commentator for BBC sport. She is currently a director of UK Athletics and a member of the board of the London Marathon and in 2010 she was appointed to the House of Lords, where she serves as a non-party political crossbench peer. This combination of sporting achievement and political influence means that Tanni's story is out there. She is a role model and a household name, but she is no longer solely championing her own sport. We hear her voice as she expresses her opinion on a variety of issues through various media outlets. For example, in a recent report for BBC sport, Tanni discussed the evolution of the Paralympic programme. She expressed her concerns that events for higher impairment groups would drop off the events programme, 'we have to be careful we are not in danger of discriminating within disability sport by picking those events which appear to be most aesthetically pleasing and least likely to make the public feel uncomfortable watching' (Grey-Thompson, 2011). Whilst I am not refuting Tanni's opinion in any way, this is her opinion. It is great that she is afforded a voice to express her view but it is only one voice. The statement above is not devoid of discrimination. What about the athletes who compete in aesthetically pleasing events (however this may be defined) are they not 'disabled' enough to be worthy of Paralympic status or media attention?

Hardin and Hardin (2003) discussed media coverage with 10 male wheelchair athletes and reported that many of the athletes they interviewed felt that the media did not actively 'build audiences' for disability sport due to the lack of adequate coverage of their sport. Reflecting on Hardin and Hardin's (2003) comment about the media-constructed hierarchy of disability, and Grey-Thompson's (2011) comment on the selection of aesthetically pleasing events, we could perhaps argue that male, visually impaired athletes who participate in a version of the nation's favourite game, have it easy? In that they are less pressured to perform by media led reporting of their events. Indeed, are they more satisfied with the type of media coverage they receive than those at the top of the media-constructed hierarchy of disability?

In the extract below, Will talks about a potentially unique issue relating to his sport, what he refers to as 'comedy coverage'. It would appear that the familiarity of 'football' overshadows the disability aspect of the sport. Placing the sport in this case 'football' ahead of reference to disability could be seen as a positive reflection of the media's engagement with the sport. Yet whilst this focus may place VI football closer to the mainstream version of the game, 'it's just football with your eyes closed', this point perhaps instantly detracts from the unique skills and abilities blind footballers have. As Will argues:

> "Much of the current coverage only ever scratches the surface. It focuses on the game, how it's played, and then usually features the comedy capers of a well-meaning presenter in a blind-fold falling over his own feet and waddling around with his hands out like a drunk Charlie Chaplin. I actually don't mind this kind of coverage myself, if it's the hook to then interest the viewing public in further coverage that will drill down deeper in to the layers of the sport, and the athletes who excel at it. It's this layering that's missing, the serious pieces to follow up the initial headline hilarity".

By simply wearing a blindfold the presenter can to all intense and purpose appear to step into the shoes of the athlete but they cannot walk in their shoes. Reporters report on what they see and hear, they hear a bell and see a ball, but do they see a group of people wearing blindfolds running around after the ball or do they see highly skilled footballers? Do they see a fun children's party game or an entertaining sports match? Schantz and Gilbert chapter 1 (in this text) state that 'people with disabilities have always been sensitive to being stared at rather than embraced and disabled athletes are no exception to this rule'. But does our fear of starring prevent us from looking? Our senses are inextricably linked to our sense making ability. As Bull and Black (2003, p.1) explain 'scopic metaphors are routinely invoked when thinking about how and what it is we know'. Metaphorically speaking, by placing the blindfold on the commentator - does that enable him to see what the athletes see/perceive? The answer to this question can only ever be 'to some extent'. As the following quote from Will demonstrates:

> "You can't unpack the complexity of each disability and undertake a complex social analysis whilst broadcasting a blind football match. Personally though I would like to see more programming that drills down beyond this, and supplements the basic coverage with more in depth features and documentary coverage to try to transmit a sense of what it is to balance these competing pressures in your life with your eyes shut".

Although the sport before disability approach may seem the ideal lens through which to view Paralympic sport, these athletes don't leave their disability behind on the playing field, unlike the commentator, they don't have the luxury of removing the blindfold. We can argue here then that VI footballers do not have it easier with regards to media coverage because they participate in what could be considered an 'aesthetically pleasing sport', they simply face different and complex issues.

Whose story is it?

The players each approached the question of 'whose story is it' from slightly different perspectives. Keryn portrayed a sense of responsibility with regards to promoting and representing his sport. In the following two quotes from Keryn, the 'story' he refers to is that of his sport.

> "The media has done some excellent work in terms of helping us raise the profile of blind football as a sport in the UK".

And,

> "I believe the increase in [media] interest our team generated by qualifying for Beijing 2008, was directly responsible for the increase in participation we see today in blind football... Suddenly parents of blind children and young blind people themselves were contacting the Football Association to find out how they could get involved in blind football".

Keryn's emphasis on the narrative of his sport, may to some extent be a reflection of the fact that his sport is a team game, thereby negating the individual story, or it could be due to the 'newness' of the sport. In the narrative it comes across that Keryn feels responsible for promoting the sport and thereby widening the opportunities for others to participate and also assist in the team's improvement. This sense of individual responsibility for stimulating media attention is mirrored in Hardin and Hardin's (2003) interviews with male wheelchair athletes, as articulated in the following quote:

> '.....athletes with disabilities don't "work hard enough" at the sport or at getting publicity for themselves... It's not their job to further our cause. It's our job to make the game interesting enough and appealing enough to warrant that type of coverage...' (Hardin & Hardin, 2003, p. 255)

Media attention with regards to athletes with disabilities is in the main, restricted to competition performance. The fact that these athletes are not visible in the media outside of completion limits their media exposure and restricts the coverage of their story. We could therefore link these athletes sense of personal responsibility back to the notion of role models. Maybe if more athletes were willing to step up from only participating in their sport to actually championing their sport they may become more visible outside of the parameters of competition. Increased media exposure would foster the sense of familiarity we need to identify and relate to role models. However, we need to remember VI athletes are often juggling training, competition, personal commitments and work and also developing and maintaining relationships with the media is a commitment in itself.

Interestingly, what emerged from the conversations with both players, although not directly alluded to, was a sense that the players as individuals were simply finding their way with regards to media relations. Will comments:

> "As disabled athletes in a minority amateur sport, I think we are all sometimes complicit in grabbing at the attention the media offer us... Perhaps we ourselves, as athletes, are therefore guilty of vanity and naivety in welcoming with open arms the slightest glimmer of a media spotlight when it seems it might fall on us".

This highlighted media innocence is refreshing but also somewhat dangerous as the athletes leave themselves open to media scrutiny which places them in a quandary and raises another question relating to the ownership of the story. If we support Keryn's notion that the 'story' belongs to the sport, combined with Will's admission of media naivety, shouldn't the sport itself (this case the Football Association) take responsibility with regards to the narrative that is presented? The un-policed relationship the VI footballers currently have with the media, offers a refreshing change to the orchestrated and often gagged narratives presented in mainstream sport media, there are negative consequence for such 'freedom' as outlined in the following example from Keryn.

> "....there was one incident involving media and our sport that has left me very cynical and wary of which media engagements I choose to take up. The infamous Paddy Power advert in 2010 was one piece of media work I was very disappointed in... I felt lied to, let down, and even exploited by the production company. It has left a sour taste in my mouth with regards certain media work, and I'm more than happy to pass on certain media opportunities since then. Which in itself isn't a great thing leading in to 2012 as we want to build an even stronger relationship with the media going in to the biggest competition the Great Britain team has been building towards".

Keryn's honest account eloquently summarises the naivety of the athlete's media experience. Whilst I believe the ownership of the story should remain with the athlete, I do believe there is a sense of responsibility from the sport itself to offer media training to help the athletes become media savvy.

Conclusion

As mentioned at the start of this chapter, there is a limited amount of research relating to sport, media and individuals with disabilities, and more especially from the athletes perspective's, thus leaving us with many unanswered questions. Whilst I hope the discourse presented here goes some way to presenting a different perspective on the subject, by providing the voice of athletes, I appreciate that there is simply not the space here to fully engage with the questions raised in this chapter. I hope however, the brief narratives presented have evoked further questions and by doing so will stimulate further research. There is so much opportunity to engage with this subject, that it seems pointless to narrow the potential by suggesting particular areas of future research. Until we as consumers of sport, spectators, scholars, athletes, media representatives and those involved in sport governance are all happy with the media coverage of athletes with disabilities, we should continue to ask questions and attempt to answer them. However, I would like to conclude with this thought... I do not believe that we can group all disabled sports together and homogenise the media coverage into one off the shelf formulaic package. I feel that we have to embrace the differences and acknowledge that each sport and each group of athletes face their own unique issues with regards to media coverage. And in keeping with the intention of this chapter, to provide an opportunity for athletes to voice their own opinion, I leave the last words to the athletes, firstly Will:

> "You can't herd disabled people together according to the nature of their disability, even though this is arbitrarily necessary for sport to occur. I often hear other blind people, other blind sports people, talking on the radio or being interviewed on TV, and I squirm, 'that's not how I feel', I think 'that's not at all how it is for me'. It's an uncomfortable experience, not least because I am worried that others will take this subjective experience as a general truism that applies universally to all those with visual impairments... Perhaps this tension is at the heart of the problem of media coverage. You can't reduce the heterogeneous nuances of every athlete's life and times in to one homogeneous package. Yet this is exactly what's required in order to reduce the complexity to a level that is broadcastable as media".

At the core of this chapter was my desire to ask athletes what their ideal sport media coverage would look like. In the final quote from Keryn I end this chapter on an optimistic note.

> "In my opinion the decision to award the broadcast rights for the 2012 Paralympics to Channel 4, is possibly the best thing that could have happened for Paralympic sports... Their website is exceptional in terms of already building profiles and public awareness of GB teams and their athletes. They seem to have hit the nail on the head in terms of the way they have covered the sports, with the focus being more on the abilities of the athletes, as opposed to their disabilities. Getting really in depth sometimes. Going as far to explore the biological and physiological makeup of certain disabled athletes. Which in my opinion, goes further than any other broadcast media has done in terms of covering disability sport. And they are purely featuring sportsmen and athletes in their own right. Rather than just disabled people who happen to play sport".

If we sit back and reflect on the voices of the athletes we might come to understand that maybe we are moving closer to an ideal type of coverage for athletes with a disability than previously thought?

References

Brittain, I. (2010). *The Paralympic Games Explained*. London: Routledge.
Bull, M. & Black, L. (2003). Introduction: into sound. In: M. Bull, & L. Black (Eds.), *The auditory culture reader* (pp. 1-18). Oxford: Berg.
Buysse, J.A.M. & Borcherding, B. (2010). Framing gender and disability: A cross-cultural analysis of photographs from the 2008 Paralympic Games. *International Journal of Sport Communication, 3*, 308-321.
Chiari, J. (1975). *Twentieth Century French Thought*. London: Elek.
DePauw, K. (1997). The (In)visibility of (Dis)ability: Cultural contexts and "Sporting Bodies." *Quest, 49*, 416-430.
Golden, A. V. (2003). An analysis of the dissimilar coverage of the 2000 Olympics and Paralympics: Frenzied pack journalism versus the empty press room. *Disability Studies Quarterly, 23* (3/4).

Grey-Thompson, T. (2011) Tanni Grey-Thomson asks, is Paralympic sport loosing focus? Retrieved June 16, 2011 from: http://News.bbc.co.uk/sport

Haller, B. (2000). If they limp they lead? News representations and the hierarchy of disability images. In D. Braithwaite & T. Thompson (Eds.), *Handbook of communication and people with disabilities* (pp.273-288). Mahwah, NJ: Lawrence Erlbaum.

Hardin, B. & Hardin M. M. (2003). Conformity and conflict: Wheelchair athletes discuss sport media. *Adapted Physical Activity Quarterly*, 20, 246-259.

Macbeth, J.L. (2009). Restrictions of activity in partially sighted football: experiences of grassroots players. *Leisure Studies, 28* (4), 455-467.

Macbeth, J. & Magee, J. (2006). 'Captain England? Maybe one day I will': Career paths of elite partially sighted footballer. *Sport in Society, 9* (3), 444-462.

Macbeth, J. (2008). Equality issues within partially sighted football in England. In C. Hallinan & S. Jackson (Eds.), *Social and cultural diversity in a sporting world* (p.65-80). Bingley: Emerald.

Schantz, O.J. & Gilbert, K. (2001). An ideal misconstrued: Newspaper coverage of the Atlanta Paralympic Games in France and Germany. *Sociology of Sport Journal,* 18, 69-94.

Schell, L.A. & Duncan, M.C. (1999). A content analysis of CBS's coverage of the 1996 Paralympic Games. *Adapted Physical Activity Quarterly,* 16, 27-47.

Sherrill, C. (1997). Paralympic Games 1996: Feminist and other concerns: What's your excuse? *Palaestra, 13* (1), 32-38.

Smith, B. & Sparkes, A.C. (2008). Narrative and its potential contribution to disability studies. *Disability & Society, 23* (1), 17-28.

Thomas, N. & Smith, A. (2003). Preoccupied with able-bodiedness? An analysis of the British Media Coverage of the 2000 Paralympic Games. *Adapted Physical Activity Quarterly,* 20, 166-181.

Chapter 18
Paralympic Sport, British Media and the Absence of Black Faces

Brenda-Kammel Atuona

Introduction

From the inception of rehabilitative sports competitions for ex-service men and women with spinal injuries the Paralympic Games have experienced an astounding growth. Statistics provided by the International Paralympic Committee (IPC) demonstrate the extent to which the Games have grown from a small gathering of 130 athletes from two countries in 1952 to an international festival of almost 4000 athletes from 146 countries in 2008 (IPC, 2009). Considered as the summit of disability sport (Gold & Gold, 2007; Schantz & Gilbert, 2001) it has been suggested that the Paralympic Games have played a crucial role in changing attitudes by emphasising and elevating the status of disability sport where participants earn esteem as athletes in their own right, thereby challenging prevailing assumptions and stereotypes about 'disability' (De Pauw & Gavron, 1995; Gold & Gold, 2007; Krahe & Altwasser, 2006). Indeed, the growing importance of the Paralympic Games has been accompanied by an ever-increasing media presence and interest (Schantz & Gilbert, 2001; Brittain, 2009). The number of accredited media representations has more than doubled over the last four Games with the IPC (2009) reporting record attendance at the 2004 Athens Games of

2,600 representatives of the mass media. Whilst this provides evidence of a dramatic progression in the spheres of disability and disability sport, the nature of coverage afforded to the Paralympic Games has been the subject of critical debate amongst numerous writers (Stein, 1989; Schell & Duncan, 1999; Schantz & Gilbert, 2001; Thomas & Smith, 2003; Sherrill, 1993, 1997). Generally, criticisms have centred around the fact that media coverage of these Games has been: significantly less than that allocated to the Olympic Games (Stein, 1989; Schell & Duncan, 1999), of a pejorative and prejudicial nature (Thomas & Smith, 2003, 2009; Schantz and Gilbert, 2003) and an extension of the inequalities faced by women in society (Sherrill, 1993; Thomas & Smith, 2003, 2009). There has, however, been virtually no research looking into the treatment of Black disabled athletes and how they feature in relation to media coverage of the Paralympic Games. As such, this chapter seeks to give voice to some of these experiences and highlight the lack of vision of the 'black face' in Paralympic Games reporting. To this end it is based on a content analysis of four leading U.K. national newspapers coverage of the Beijing Paralympic Games which indicated an overall result of minimal coverage afforded to black and minority ethnic disabled people (2.9%). This chapter will also detail the Games experiences of disabled black and minority ethnic groups and go on to explain their absence in the media representation of Paralympic athletes and how this ultimately reflects on their position as a marginalised people in wider society. Furthermore, the chapter will include an analysis of the presence of Black athletes in the media to view the specific ways in which they are discriminated against and portrayed to wider populations. Finally, there is an analysis of how disabled people are portrayed in the media generally and the specific ways in which they are affected by these portrayals. In essence, this chapter will look at how these two unique forms of discrimination create a simultaneous oppression (Stuart, 1992) or multiple oppression (Vernon, 1997), by specifically emphasising the mal-treatment and more importantly the absence of Black disabled people from the media's sporting spotlight.

Black athletes in the media

Although the latter part of the twentieth century saw a marked growth of interest in the study of sport, race and ethnicity (Jarvie, 1991), racial stereotypes in sport remain among the least challenged stereotypes in today's society. However, the characterisation of black athletes should be a constant subject of discussion when considering their large representation in some high profile sports (Rasmussen et al., 2005). For example, the dominance of Kenyan long distance runners (Entine, 2000), and the high percentage of black athletes in the NBA and the NFL, and of relevance to this chapter, in Britain where Black people represent 8% of the total population they correspond to at least 50% of First Division Basketball players, boxing champions, the British athletic squad and one in five professional football players (Jarvie, 1991; Cashmore, 1998).

In many ways, the large concentration of black athletes has had a negative impact on their characterisation with the bulk of research findings displaying evidence of racism in sports coverage (Davis & Harris, 1998). These negative racial stereotypical ideals are considered to be produced and constantly promoted by the media with sports reporters and editors being the main protagonists (Rada, 1996; Childs, 1998). For example, it is often assumed that black individuals of African ancestry are inherently superior in physical ability (Rasmussen et al., 2005). While this may appear to be an appealing stereotype, Hoberman (1997) argues that the way we think about black athletic aptitude has been conditioned by a traditional way of thinking about black people. It could be argued that the mounting triumphs of black athletes serve up imagery and metaphors that reinforce racism.

The presentation of black individuals as 'natural athletes' with superior physical skills (Dufur, 1997; Murrell & Curtis, 1994, Rada, 1996; Wonsek, 1992) when commonly juxtaposed with the accomplishments of white athletes whose feats are attributed to their superior intelligence, hard work (Murrell & Curtis; Wonsek, 1992) superior leadership skills (Wonsek, 1992; Dave & Harris) and mental astuteness (Hoose, 1989: Buffington, 2005) ultimately feeds societal perceptions of black people as 'inferior' and 'unevolved' (Pious & Williams, 1995). This form of societal discrimination, as a matter of course, has repercussions for the perceptions of black people in disabled sports and in particular Paralympic Games representation.

However, Eastman and Billings (2001) found that common stereotypes of black and white athletes were not exclusive in the coverage of male athletes. They concluded that media coverage of women's basketball also demonstrated the tendency to use the 'natural athlete' versus measures of superior intelligence and work ethic framework in reporting. Similarly, Sabo et al., (1996) studied ethnicity within seven international athletic events and found very little bias against black athletes but many in the depiction of Asian and Latino-Hispanic athletes.

To this end, many of the studies looking at race and sport have focussed solely on propagated imagery of the black male athlete. Often overlooked is the way black females figure in media discourses. Indeed, as identified by Douglas (2002), is the fact that black women are absent as subjects of study, in an environment where the dominant theoretical frameworks in sports studies have not adequately taken into account the intersection of race and gender. When exploring the sociological perceptions of the black sporting body, a fundamental image emerges. It is of a woman of inordinate strength, with an ability to tolerate unusual amounts of misery. Succinctly, a woman who does not appear to have the same fears, weaknesses and insecurities as other women (Douglas, 2002) Descriptions of their physicality reveals a 'racialised construction of gender' and sexuality framing as the 'other' to reinforce white women as the hegemonic standard (Young, 1996).

An example, of this 'racialised construction of gender' in the sports arena have seen studies focussing on the World class Tennis players Venus and Serena Williams (Douglas, 2002). While McKay and Johnson, (2008) noted that:

"While Serena and Venus have been described as the 'Sisters Sledgehammer' (Bierley, 2004) and as having an 'Amazonian physique and piranha mentality' (Mott, 2000), Daniela Hantuchova, in contrast, was portrayed as playing tennis 'with grace and artistry, words that appeared to have been all but crushed by the blitzkrieg that was Venus and Serena Williams'" (Viner, 2007).

(Cited by McKay & Johnson, 2008)

It is to this extent that the construction of black women as primitive, transgressive and 'wild' ensures the black women's bodies remain the focus of white analyses of black capacities. Furthermore, as described by McKay and Johnson (2008), it is the ongoing pathologising of black women's' bodies as 'sexually grotesque' in tandem with the air of 'pornographic eroticism' in reportage which continues to portray them as racialised and sexualised spectacles. Indeed, both are considered to be bound by the corporeal negativity often present in media representation. Whereas both black men and women continue their struggle to articulate progressive ways by which they can escape the formidable 'prisons' of racism, black women, in particular, are faced with the additional task of breaking through the mist of sexism that shrouds them.

Furthermore, it has been suggested that there has been a reduction in the most overt expressions of racial difference in sports media (Buffington, 2005). As such, McCarthy et al., (1997) analysed news coverage of Black British football players over a two week period and found no overtly negative commentary in relation to physical appearance, athletic performance or athlete's race. However, there were many reporters who suggested black athletes had more brawn and less brains than white athletes. Similarly, Harrison et al. (2010) in their study of online articles of black male athletes, support the claim that that the media of today no longer produced reports explicitly laced with racial stereotypes. While the articles used in the study made no mention of race, it can be considered that the articles were framed in a way to persuade audiences towards negative stereotyping such as violent, irresponsible, guilty of crimes and unable to resist temptation. Their study supports suggested prevailing stereotypes of black athletes in the media outside of the sporting context (Hoberman, 1997; Bell-Jordan, 2008; Czopp & Monteith, 2006; Lapchick, 2000; Cose, 2002).

Disability, society and the media

Disability in Britain has traditionally been understood from an individualised and medicalised perspective (Thomas & Smith, 2003; Barnes, 1999; Swain et al., 2005). Developed during the period of industrialisation (Finkelstein, 1980; Barnes, 1999) this perspective, commonly known as the Medical model of disability, is a systematic approach to defining people with impairment(s) according to the character of their deficits and medical condition (Pledger, 2003). As a result of the emphasis placed on 'inability' resulting from impairment writers such as Thomas and Smith (2003) and Collins and Kay (2003) conclude that this model promotes the view of a 'disabled' person as dependent, passive recipients of charity in need of care and a cure.

As a direct result of the experience of people with impairments themselves (Barnes, 1999) and a growing dissatisfaction of the medicalised explanation of disability, a social explanation of disability emerged (Oliver, 1990; 1992). In contrast to the medical model, focus has shifted from impairment and inability to disability where this term is used to refer to a disabling society steeped in environmental and attitudinal barriers (Crow, 1996; Oliver 1992; Barnes, 1999). It is argued that disability is a construction of the society in which we live and not the 'fault' of the individual with an impairment or even an inevitable consequence of their limitations. It is therefore suggested that the eradication of negative societal disability can be achieved through the removal of physical, institutional and attitudinal barriers. However, criticisms have arisen from the absence of individual experience of impairment in this explanation. For example, whilst Shakespeare and Watson (2002) oppose defining disability solely on the basis of impairments, they suggest that it should not be reduced to an outcome of social barriers alone. Of great importance to them is the role impairment plays in the lives of people with impairment(s) which should give way to a new conceptualisation embracing all aspects of the lives of disabled people. Despite efforts made by those at the helm of the social model movement, the medical approach still pervades and is constantly extant in people's understanding of disability. The impact of stereotypes and imagery on the representation of disabled people by the media is a widely discussed issue (Barnes, 1992; Auslander & Gold, 1999; Thomas & Smith, 2003) because of the long held belief of the potential the media has to influence public perceptions. Experimental evidence has indicated that while the mass media has little power in changing people's opinion on issues that they have already formed a strong judgment, it has a profound affect when it comes to setting the agenda and priming people on new issues (Fog, 1999). This insight is crucial when considering the role media plays in informing members of the public who have no or limited personal experience of disability. Barnes in 1992 noted a growing awareness among disabled people of the resulting role media distortion of their experiences has played in their experience of institutional discrimination. He contends that negative stereotypical assumptions about disabled people are inherent to our culture and persist partly because they are constantly reproduced through the communications media. It is also important to note that as well as the tendency of the press to portray and reproduce particular stereotypical views of disabled people and their life experiences, the press is also believed to reinforce other social divisions particularly in relation to gender (Gill, 2006; Hermes, 1997; Gauntlett, 2002) and race (Lull, 2003; Hall, 1974; Hartmann & Husband, 1974; Rhodes, 1993). Yet while the gendered nature of media treatment of disabled people has increasingly been the focus of academic discourse (Thomas & Smith, 2003; Maas & Hasbrook, 2001), the specific ways in which black and ethnic minority disabled people figure in these discourses has remained largely unanalysed and untheorised.

Disability Sport and Media

The relationship between sport and the media in Western societies has been characterised as a 'symbiotic' one (Coakley, 2003; Trujillo, 2001) in which sports and media organisations have provided mutual resources and experienced complementary growth. Indeed, the global popularity of sport is due largely to the vast attention provided by the media. On the other hand, circulation and advertising of sport has enabled the media to achieve enormous sales as a result of this extensive treatment (Coakley, 2003). Interestingly, when interpreted from a critical perspective, sport media and disability intersect in captivating ways, as it has often been argued that sport and the media function hegemonically to reproduce and reinforce dominant ideologies of social order (Trujillo, 2001; Yiannakis & Melnick, 2001). In this manner the media coverage of sport reflects and perpetuates the dominance of leadership of nondisabled people over disabled people through pervasive expressions of held beliefs. Exclusive of media, the very concept and construct of sport can reinforce the status of disabled people in wider society. Sport is a creation of and for non-disabled people giving priority to certain types of human movement, with a prescribed set of standards by which athletes are measured (Devine, 1997). These standards are designed, according to Brittain (2004), to highlight and revere extremes of bodily physical perfection through associations with fitness, health, dynamism, youth and sex appeal which sharply contrasts with images of sport for disabled individuals' as 'ill', 'lame', 'crippled', 'mutilated' individuals (Schantz & Gilbert, 2001, pp. 47). Further to this point, Brittain (2004) contends that "disability sport [therefore] does not, apparently, provide images that fit within the norms that delineate sporting images within society" (p. 448) So, within this context, the idea of elite sport for people with disabilities - who fall short of societies standards of an ideal body- is paradoxical or in Brittain's opinion, (2004, p. 438) 'an anathema'. Mastro et al. (1988) lend support to this argument as in their opinion, part of the reason for this is that there is no culturally recognised need for competition and sports for disabled people beyond therapeutic programs. This is seen as further extending the schism between the social construction of sport and traditional perceptions of disability rooted in the medical model. Of import to this chapter is that a clear indicator of societal attitudes towards disability sport may be seen in the differences in media time spent covering the Olympic and Paralympic Games (Schantz & Gilbert, 2001; Brittain, 2009).

The reduced coverage of the Paralympic Games is supported by findings from a study conducted by Schantz and Gilbert (2001) who found that popular French and German newspapers reflected a generally low opinion with regards to the value of sport for disabled people. They concluded that disability sport is marginalised and trivialised in most newspapers. Barnes (1992) has previously noted the ways in which disabled peoples' experiences of disability are shaped by the media. In relation to coverage of disability sport studies, the use of language and terminology by newspaper journalists reaffirms traditional medicalised and individualised views of disabled people

(Thomas & Smith, 2003; Schantz & Gilbert, 2001) without acknowledging the socio-genetic dimensions of disability (Barnes, 1992; Barton, 1993). For instance, Thomas and Smith (2001) highlight how Calvin (2000) describes disability as releasing "Runners....from the solitary confinement of autism... [and]....swimmers....from the chrysalis of a broken body" (p. 114). They argue that in this way, disability is conceived of as an experience beyond the normal world and may be reflective of what some people across a range of societies perceive disability to be. This use of language, therefore, has the desired effect of evoking the emotion of pity, underscoring the perception of disabled peoples' lives being full of constant pain, requiring medical interventions to ameliorate their 'abnormalities' (Swain & French 2005; Thomas & Smith, 2003). A key observation in the work of Thomas and Smith (2003) was the tendency for newspaper coverage to draw comparisons between Paralympic and Olympic athletes in a way which appeared to depict Paralympians as emulating 'able-bodiedness'. In this sense, it is believed that Paralympic athletes may have been portrayed as responding to the perception held by some non-disabled people that their bodies are defective, and through sport a reformed body is created to legitimate their acceptance as people in the social world (Hargreaves, 2000; Thomas & Smith, 2003).

In many ways, participation in sport and physical activity for people with disabilities, is indeed, a way of managing the stigma of disability (Taub et al., 1999). As such, Nixon (1984) and Asken (1991) explain that participation aides the perception of disabled people as not being significantly different from their non-disabled counterpart. However, it should not be dismissed lightly as to how this idea can further undermine the attempts of disabled people to form an identity of their own and depart from one based on the ideals of non-disabled people.

Of great concern to disability sport writers is the nature of photographic coverage and the ways in which it can reinforce previously held perceptions of disability sport and disability in general. For example, it has been clearly shown that images of Paralympic athletes are often framed in a way to hide the disability (Pappous, 2008; Thomas & Smith, 2003; Schantz & Gilbert, 2001) and mostly feature wheelchair athletes (Thomas & Smith, 2003; Schell & Duncan, 1999; Schantz & Gilbert, 2001; Pappous, 2008). In relation to the extensive photographic coverage of wheelchair athletes, it appears to be a reflection of stereotypical perceptions of disability being synonymous with physical immobility and wheelchair use, which according to Barnes (1992) reinforces widespread ignorance about the realities of impairment. By focusing on wheelchair athletes and constructing media photographs that appeared to hide an athlete's impairment, Thomas and Smith (2003) suggest, that much of the coverage denies the athlete's identity as a person with an impairment which could ultimately disenfranchise those readers with disabilities, through focus placed on those who appear to be more physically capable of competing in sport.

Black disabled athletes' absence in the media

Whilst notably flawed, the social explanation of disability has enabled people with disabilities to assume a collective identity that has facilitated a challenge to their sub-ordination in wider society (Oliver, 1990, 1992) and has served as guidance for practices to include disabled people. It cannot be assumed, however, that all people with disabilities face a similar form of subordination. According to Vernon (1997), while things appear to be marginally improving for disabled people in general, the same cannot be said for disabled Black and Minority Ethnic people (BAME). As disabled people they experience disabling barriers, the effects of which are to exclude them from full participation in economic and social life (Barnes, 1991), and as members of a minority ethnic group, they are subjected to racism which excludes them from participating as full citizens in a predominantly white country (Brown, 1984; Donald and Rattansi, 1992; Jones, 1993). As mentioned previously, it has been suggested that disabled black people experience a 'double disadvantage'; that of being black in a racist and disabled in a disablist society (Confederation of Indian Organisations, 1984; McDonald, 1991). Considered as a rather simplistic equation, (Stuart, 1993; Begum, 1994), an alternative concept of 'simultaneous oppression' has been used to describe experiences of BAME disabled people (Stuart, 1992). 'Simultaneous oppression' in this instance refers to the fact that the realities of BAME disabled people are shaped by racist and disablist structures at the same time (Stuart, 1992). However, the experience of 'simultaneous oppression' is not unique to BAME disabled people. Disabled women have to contend with the simultaneity of disability and gender stereotypes (Fine & Asch, 1988; Lloyd, 1992; Lonsdale 1990; Morris, 1990, 1993; Deegan & Brooks, 1985; Hargreaves, 2000). Similarly, disabled gay men and lesbians, older people and those from the working class all experience the simultaneity of disablism and heterosexualism and/or ageism and/or classism (Vernon, 2001). On this basis, Vernon argues that the concept of 'simultaneous oppression' is inadequate in explaining the day-to-day reality of BAME disabled people on the grounds that racism (and/or heterosexualism and/or ageism and/or classism) is neither more nor less prominent than disablism and simply overlooks the complex and often variable interaction between different forms of social oppression (Vernon, 1997, 2001). In recent years there have been a number of writings expressing a general dissatisfaction that the differing experiences of black and ethnic minority people with disabilities are overlooked by social model theorists (Hill, 1994). It is believed that the disability movement, although economically and politically marginalised, as consisting in the main of white people, has power and advantage over BAME people. In Vernon's (1997) opinion, the disability movement and the white people taking part in it are a microcosm of white society who are equally subjected to stereotypes of BAME people portrayed in the media as their non-disabled counterparts.

Roberts (1994) acknowledged that while programming in the UK of disabled people experienced an increase, there is still an absence of black disabled people. A pilot study carried out found that out of 8,600 images located, 104 were of disabled people and out of the 104, only 9 of those were of black disabled people (8.7%). The study was also carried out on Black press and disability press which also showed an underrepresentation in both areas. The representation in the Black press and the disability press is therefore seen to be no more progressive than the white mainstream press.

While studies around gender difference in disability sport have often argued about the ill treatment of women in media coverage, very little has been done to look at the position of black disabled women in sport. Hardin et al., (2006) provide a unique analysis through their examination of the relationship between images of sport, disability, gender and race in four U.S. women's sport/fitness magazines. As was expected, non-white women with a disability were completely invisible which in their opinion emphasised an ableist emphasis on sexual difference. Similarly to Douglas, Hardin et al., (2006) argue that black disabled women in sport are guaranteed the bottom spot of the hegemonic hierarchy because they do not conform to 'white' standards of femininity but are also marginalised because of their 'lack of able-bodiedness'.

Although the media has the potential to produce distorted images of reality which in turn influence people's perceptions of disability, race and gender, the absence of visual images and coverage as experienced by disabled black people can lead to a dangerous invisibility (Roberts, 1994). The lack of attention from the media feeds a spiral of marginalisation and exclusion for black disabled people, emphasising their already low social status and 'keeping them in their place' from a traditional perspective. Furthermore, the marginalisation of athletic black disabled people robs young black disabled people of positive role models. As such, at the elite level, UK Sport estimates that 10.3% of its funded athletes are from BAME groups, which compares favourably with the 7.9% of the 2001 UK population from such communities (Long et al., 2009). However, upon analysis of representation in the GB squad for the 2008 Beijing Paralympic Games 3.6% of athletes were from BAME a group which does not reflect favourably on UK sport. While this may be only one reason why there is an absence of black faces in the coverage of disability sport, it is important to question the absence of black disabled people in elite Paralympic sport altogether.

Conclusions

The press coverage of the Paralympic Games provides a rich contextual environment for communicative analysis. This is because of the coming together of multiple nations of an array of creeds and colours. With the advent of the 2012 London Paralympic Games, there will be a change in the media perspectives because of the exclusive coverage of the Games by the

Channel 4 television network. Future studies should seek to look at the coverage afforded to black disabled athletes by network providers as well as the print media. Channel 4 provides us a great opportunity to do so.

The discussion within this chapter can prove useful in challenging existing perceptions in many ways and of these two are particularly important:

1. Media producers can learn and change the nature of coverage in respect to disabled people and more specifically widen their coverage of black disabled athletes as this can help to bring them out of obscurity.
2. Viewers of these sporting events and readers of these newspapers should become more conscious of such bias and become conscientious consumers of the media.

From a researcher's perspective it is important to consider the unique experiences of black disabled (male or female) athletes as race cannot simply be added to existing theoretical frameworks. The oppression of black disabled athletes is qualitatively different in kind to that of their white counterparts. However, since it is believed that sport both reinforces and reproduces persistent, resurgent and veiled forms of power struggles that permeate society, the targeting and removal of racist, disablist (and sexist) narratives in coverage of sport has the potential to enable Black disabled male and female athletes to envision and achieve equality within wider society.

References

Asken, M.J. (1991). The challenge to the physically challenged: Delivering sport psychology services to physically disabled athletes. *The Sport Psychologists*, 5, 370-381.

Auslander, G.K. & Gold, N. (1999). Disability terminology in the media: a comparison of newspaper reports in Canada and Israel. *Social Science and Medicine*, 48, 1395-1405.

Barnes, C. (1991). *A case for anti-discrimination legislation for disabled people*. London: BCODP.

Barnes, C. (1992). *Disabling imagery and the media: An exploration of the principles for media representations of disabled people*. Halifax: BCODP.

Barnes, C. (1999). Theories of Disability and the Origins of the Oppression of Disabled People in Western Society. In L. Barton (Ed.), *Disability and Society: Emerging Issues and Insights* (pp. 43-60). New York: Pearson.

Barton, L. (1993). Disability, empowerment and physical education. In J.Evans (Ed.), *Equality, Education and Physical Education* (pp. 43–54). London: The Falmer Press.

Begum, N. (1994). Mirror on the Wall. In N. Begum, M. Hill, & A. Stevens *Reflections: the views of Black Disabled people on their lives and community care* (pp. 17-36). London: CCETSW.

Bell-Jordan, K., (2008). Black, White and a Survivor of the Real World: Construction of Race in Reality TV. *Critical Studies in Media Communication*, 25, 353-372.
Brittain, I. (2004). Perceptions of Disability and their Impact upon Involvement in Sport for People with Disabilities at All Levels. *Journal of Sport and Sport Issues*, 28, 429-452.
Brittain, I. (2009). *The Paralympic Games explained*. London: Routledge.
Brown, C. (1984). *Black and White Britain*. London: PSI.
Calvin, M. (2000, October 29). Great Games that carry a priceless legacy. *The Daily Mail*, 114.
Buffington, D. (2005). Contesting race on Sundays: Making meaning out of the rise in Black quarterbacks. *Sociology of Sport Journal*, 21, 19-37.
Cashmore, E. (1998). *Making sense of sports*. New York: Routledge.
Childs, K. (1998, August 10). NABJ speakers charge bias in sports coverage. *Editor & Publisher*, p. 10.
Coakley, J, 2003. *Sports in Society. Issues and controversies*. McGraw Hill: New York.
Collins, M. & Kay, T. (2003) *Sport and Social Exclusion*. London: Routledge.
Confederation of Indian Organisations (Ed.). (1984). *Double Blind to be Disabled and Asian*. London: CIO.
Cose. E., (2002). *The Envy of the World: On Being a Black Man in America*. New York: Washington Square Press.
Crow, L. (1996). Including All Our Lives: Renewing the Social Model of Disability. In C. Barnes, G. Mercer (Eds.), *Exploring the Divide* (pp. 55-72). Leeds: The Disability Press.
Czopp, A. & Monteith, M. (2006). Thinking Well of African Americans: Measuring Complementary Stereotypes and Negative Prejudices. *Basic and Applied Social Psychology*, 28, 223-250.
Davis, L. R., & Harris, O. (1998). Race and ethnicity in US sports media. In L. A. Wenner (Ed.), MediaSport (pp. 154-169). London: Routledge.
DePauw, K. & Gavron, S. (1995). *Disability and Sport*. Champaign: Human Kinetics.
Devine, M. A. (1997). Inclusive leisure services and research: A consideration of the use of social construction theory. *Journal of Leisurability*, 24, 3-11.
Deegan, M.J. & Brooks, N.A. (1985). Introduction. In M.J. Deegan & N.A. Brooks (Eds.), *Women and disability: The double handicap* (pp. 1-6). New Brunswick: Transaction Books.
Donald, J. & Rattansi, A. (1992). *Race, Culture and Difference*. Oxford: Sage.
Douglas, D.D. (2002). To be young, gifted, black and female: A meditation on the cultural politics at play in representations of Venus and Serena Williams. *Sociology of Sport Online*, 5. Retrieved October 27, 2011 from: http://physed.otago.ac.nz/sosol/v5i2/v5i2_3.html
Dufur, M. (1997). Race logic and being like mike: representations of athletes in Advertising, 1985-1994. *Sociological Focus*, 30, 345-355.

Eastman, S.T. & Billings, A.C. (2001). Biased voices of sports: racial and gender stereotyping in college basketball announcing. *The Howard Journal of Communications*, 12, 183-201.

Entine, J. (2000). *Taboo: Why Black Athletes Dominate Sports and Why We're Afraid to Talk About It*. New York: Public Affairs.

Fine, M. & Asch, A. (1988). *Women with disabilities: essays in psychology, culture, and politics*. Philadelphia: Temple University Press.

Finkelstein, V. (1980). *Attitudes and Disabled People*. Geneva: World Health Organisation.

Fog, A. (1999). *Cultural Selection*. Kluwer: Dordrecht.

Gauntlett, D. (2002). *Media, gender and identity: An introduction*. London: Routledge.

Gill, R. (2006). *Gender and the media*. Cambridge: Polity Press.

Gold, J.R., & Gold, M.M. (2007). Access for all: the rise of the Paralympic Games. *Journal of the Royal Society for the Promotion of Health*, 127, 133-141.

Hall, S. (1974). "Black men, white media." *Journal of the Caribbean Artists Movement*, 9/10, 18-21.

Hardin, M., Lynn, S., & Walsdorf, K. (2006). Depicting the Sporting Body: The Intersection of Gender, Race and Disability in Women's Sport/Fitness Magazines. *Journal of Magazine and New Media Research*, 8, 1-17.

Harrison, C.K., Tayman, K.R., Janson, N. & Connolly, M. (2010). Stereotypes of Black Male Athletes on the Internet. *Journal for the Study of Sports and Athletes in Education*, 4, 155-172.

Hargreaves (2000). *Heroines of sport: The politics of difference and identity*. London: Routledge.

Hartmann, P. & Husband, C. (1974). *Racism and the Mass Media*. London: Davis-Poynter.

Hermes, J. (1997). No woman, no cry. In J. Corner, P. Schlesinger, & R. Silverstone (Eds.), *International media research: A critical survey* (pp. 65-95). London: Routledge.

Hill, M. (1994). They are not our brothers. In N. Begum, M. Hill & A.Stevens (Eds.), *Reflections: the views of Black Disabled people on their lives and community care*. London: CCETSW.

Hoberman, J. (1997). *Darwin's Athletes: How Sport has Damaged Black America and Preserved the Myth of Race*. New York: Houghton Miffler.

Hoose, P. M. (1989). Necessities: Racial barriers in American sport. New York: Random House.

International Paralympic Committee (2009). *Paralympic Games: Fact and Figures*. Retrieved October 27, 2009 from: http://www.paralympic.org/export/sites/default/Media_Centre/Media_Information/2009_07_Paralympic_Games_Facts_and_Figures.pdf

Jarvie, G. (1991). *Sport, Racism, and Ethnicity*. London: Falmer.

Jones, T. (1993). *Britain's Ethnic Minorities*. London: PSI.

Krahe, B. & Altwasser, C. (2006). Changing negative attitudes towards persons with physical disabilities: an experimental intervention. *Journal of Community and Applied Social Psychology*, 16, 59-69.

Lapchick, R. (2000). *Race, Athletes and Crime*. Retrieved October 27, 2011 from: http://web.bus.ucf.edu/sportbusiness/articles.aspx?y=2000

Long, J. Hylton, K., Spracklen, K., Ratha, A. & Bailey, S. (2009). *Systematic Review of the Literature on Black and Minority Ethnic Communities in sport and physical recreation*. Leeds: Carnegie Research Institute.

Lloyd, M. (1992). Does she boil eggs? Towards a feminist model of disability. *Disability, Handicap and Society*, 7, 207-221.

Lonsdale, S. (1990). *Women and Disability*. London: Macmillan.

Lull, J. (2003) Hegemony. In G. Dines & J.M. Humez (Eds.), *Gender, race and class in media* (pp. 61-66). California: Sage Publications.

Maas, K.W. & Hasbrook, C. A. (2001). Media promotion of the paradigm citizen/ golfer: An analysis of golf magazines' representations of disability, gender, and age. *Sociology of Sport° Journal*, 18, 21-36.

Mastro, J.V., Hall, M.M. & Canabal, M.Y. (1988). Cultural and attitudinal similarities: Female and disabled individuals in sports and athletics. *Journal of Physical Education, Recreation and Dance*, 59, 80-83.

McCarthy, D. & Jones, R. (1997). Speed, Aggression, Strength and Tactical Naiveté. *Journal of Sport and Social Issues*, 21, 348-362.

McDonald, P. (1991, March). Double discrimination must be faced now. *Disability Now*.

McKay, J. & Johnson, H. (2008). Pornographic eroticism and sexual grotesquerie in representations of African American sportswomen. *Social Identities*, 14. 491-504.

Morris, J. (1990). *Pride Against Prejudice*. Women's Press: London.

Morris, J. (1993). Feminism and disability. *Feminist Review*, 43, 57-70.

Murrell, A.J., & Curtis, E. M. (1994). Causal attributions of performance for black and White quarterbacks in the NFL: A look at the sports pages. *Journal of Sport and Social Issues*, 18, 224-233.

Nixon, H.L. (1984). Handicapism and sport: New directions for sport sociology research. In N. Theberge & P. Donnelly (Eds.), *Sport and the sociological imagination*. Fort Worth: Texas Christian University Press.

Oliver, M. (1990). *The Politics of Disablement*. Basingstoke: Macmillan.

Oliver, M. (1992). Changing the Social Relations of Research Production? *Disability, Handicap and Society*, 7, 101-114.

Pappous, A. (2008). *The photographic coverage of the Paralympic Games*, Paper presented at the Third Annual International Forum on children with special needs "sport and ability" Shafallah Centre, Doha, Qatar, 20-22 April.

Pledger, C. (2003). Discourse on Disability and Rehabilitation Issues: Opportunities for Psychology. *American Psychologist*, 16, 238-250.

Pious, S. & Williams, T. (1995). Racial stereotypes from the days of American slavery: A continuing legacy. *Journal of Applied Social Psychology*, 25, 795-817.

Rada, J.A. (1996) Color Blind-sided: Racial Bias in Network Television's Coverage of Professional Football Games. *Howard Journal of Communications* 7, 231–239.

Rasmussen, R., Esgate, A., & Turner, D. (2005). On your marks. Get stereotyped. Go! Novice Coaches and Black Stereotypes in Sprinting. *Journal of Sport and Social Issues*, 29, 426-436.

Rhodes, J. (1993). The Visibility of *Race* and *Media* History. *Critical Studies in Mass Communication*, 10, 184-190.

Roberts, P. (1994). Images of Black Disabled People in the Media. In N. Begum, M. Hill, & A. Stevens (Eds.), *Reflections: the views of Black Disabled people on their lives and community care* (pp. 56-67). London: CCETSW.

Sabo, D., Jansen, S.C. Tate, D. Duncan, M.C. & Leggett S. (1996). Televising International Sport: Race, Ethnicity and Nationalistic Bias. *Journal of Sport and Social Issues*, 20, 7–21.

Schantz, O. & Gilbert, K. (2001). An ideal misconstrued: Newspaper coverage of the Atlanta Paralympic Games in France and Germany. *Sociology of Sport Journal*, 18, 69-94.

Schell, L.A. & Duncan, M.C. (1999). A content analysis of the CBS coverage of the 1996 Paralympic Games. *Adapted Physical Activity Quarterly*, 16, 27-47.

Shakespeare, T. & Watson, N. (2002). The Social Model of Disability: An Outdated Ideology. *Research in Social Science and Disability*, 2, 9-28.

Sherrill, C. (1993). Women with disabilities, Paralympics and reasoned action contact theory. *Women in Sport and Physical Activity Journal*, 2, 51-60.

Stein, J.U. (1989). U.S. media – where were you during the 1988 Paralympics? *Palaestra*, 5, 45-47.

Stuart, O.W. (1992). Race and disability: Just a double oppression? *Disability, Handicap and Society*, 7, 177-188.

Stuart, O. (1993). Double oppression: an appropriate starting point? In J. Swain, V. Finkelstein, S. French, & M.Oliver (Eds.), *Disabling Barriers - enabling environments*. London: Open University Press/ Sage.

Swain, J., French., S. & Cameron, C. (2005). Controversial *Issues in a Disabling Society*. Maidenhead: Open University Press.

Taub, D., Blinde, E. & Greer, K. (1999). Stigma Management through Participation in Sport and Physical Activity: Experiences of Male College Students Physical Disabilities. *Human Relations*, 52, 1469-1484.

Thomas, N. & Smith, A. (2003). Preoccupied with Able-Bodiedness? An Analysis of the British Media Coverage of the Paralympic Games. *Adapted Physical Activity Quarterly*, 20, 166-181.

Thomas, N. & Smith, A. (2009). *Disability sport and society*: An introduction. London: Routledge.

Trujillo, N. (2001). Machines, Missiles and Men: Images of the Male Body on ABC's Monday Night Football. In A. Yiannakis & M.J. Melnick (Eds.), *Contemporary issues in sociology of sport*. Champaign IL: Human Kinetics.

Vernon, A. (1997). Fighting Two Different Battles: Unity is Preferable to Enmity. In L. Barton & M. Oliver (Eds.), *Disability Studies: Past, Present and Future* (pp. 255-262). Leeds: The Disability Press.

Vernon, A. (2001). Multiple Oppressions and Disabled People's Movement. In V. Bacigalupo, J. Bornat, B. Bytheway, J. Johnson, & S. Sparr (Eds.), *Understanding Care, Welfare and Community: A Reader* (pp. 64-68). London: Routledge.

Wonsek, P. L. (1992). College basketball on television: A study of racism in the media. *Media, Culture, and Society*, 14, 449-461.

Yiannakis, A., & Melnick, M.J. (2001). The Body in Culture and Sport. In A. Yiannakis & M. J. Melnick (Eds.), *Contemporary Issues in sociology of sport*. Champaign IL: Human Kinetics.

Young, L. (1996). *Fear of the Dark: Race, Gender and Sexuality in the Cinema*. London: Routledge.

Chapter 19
Debunking Disability

Media Discourse and the Paralympic Games

Maxine Newlands

Introduction

Newspaper headlines about Paralympic athletes have previously depicted the Paralympic Games with an emphasis on disability over athleticism. Headlines such as 'Public is often blind to some athletes' (The Globe and Mail, Canada, 1993); 'Ready, Willing and Disabled' (Washington Post, 1995); or 'Landmines claim limbs but athletes stand united' (Sydney Morning Herald, Australia, 2000) are just a sample of previous story headlines about Paralympic athletes. The problem many scholars have found is with how language used by journalists to represent Paralympians is often couched in either medical terms or a 'disabled-hero' (Hardin & Hardin, 2008) discourse with a focus on disability over elite athleticism. Much of the literature has found journalist framed Paralympian stories as negative, passive, medicalised, disability oriented, individualised or focuses on the Paralympics as minority sports, despite them being organised in tandem with a the Olympic mega-event. This is exacerbated by a lack of understanding by journalists and the public about the complex classification system. The range of classification, the different disabilities competing at the same level looks to reporters as an uneven playing field, and while organised needs to be balanced. The result is that the Paralympic Games are viewed by some, as second best to the Olympic Games, despite being organised mostly by the same committees, and held concurrently. As mentioned previously the language used by journalists to represent Paralympians is often couched in negative terms and there is a tendency to focus on the medical matters of the disabled athlete rather than the athlete as a person or an athlete.

What emerges are three discourses that shape the representation of the Paralympic Games, 1) Medical 2) Nationalistic and 3) media discourses. Other factors that reinforce these discourses, are the placing of Paralympic sports as minority sports; a lack of clarity in the classification system, and limited or little television coverage in some countries which all contribute to the Paralympic discourse. Indeed, the limited television coverage of disabled sports reflects wider cultural narratives and as Hardin and Hardin (2008) argue this discourse keeps "people with disabilities at the bottom of the social hierarchy" (p. 25). These tactics combine to create challenges to the media and Paralympic movement and assist in developing the problem of how to address the issue of negative reporting, increase coverage, and how the media can change socio-cultural opinions?

This chapter will address these problems, by examining why journalists find difficulty in portraying disability over athleticism, how to unravel the classification system, and the use of technology to entice a wider audience. It will draw from earlier literature (McDonald, 2008; Brittian, 2009; Buckley, 2008; Hardin & Hardin, 2008, Schantz & Gilbert, 2001; Thomas & Smith, 2003) to examine how the media represent Paralympic athletes, and an interview with UK broadcasters Channel Four Commissioning Sports Editor, drawing on original empirical data. It will examine how broadcasters can overcome these issues, by echoing the IOC's decision to juxtapose the Paralympic games level with the Olympic Games. While examining how discourse shapes public perception of Paralympians, this chapter will indicate that there are many other sporting and cultural hurdles to overcome before the Paralympic Games are seen as equal within the media discourse.

Problems of a Complex Classification System

A key problem is a lack of understanding by journalists of how different disabilities can compete at the same level, which in turn impacts on understanding and public knowledge of the sport. In this regard the International Paralympic Committee (IPC) recognise six different disability groups, Wheelchair, Amputees, Cerebral Palsy, Les Autres (the others), Blind and Intellectual Disability. The classification system for athletes came into effect at the 1960 Rome Paralympic Games. The first system was "based on medical examination that grouped competitors on the level of their spinal cord lesion" (Buckley, 2008, p. 90). This technique remained the same until 1976 when amputees and the visual impaired disability groups were added to the classification system. By 1980 cerebral palsy added an "additional eight classes" (Buckley, 2008, p. 91) to the system. Two years later the wheelchair basketball teams introduced a 'functional' evaluation into the classification that ran alongside the medical examination. The system focused on how the trunk of a body functions, (developed by Horst Strohkendl, 1996). This approach meant that "individuals with spinal cord injuries and polio with lower limb amputees" (Buckley, 2008, p. 90) were awarded points.

By 2003 the IPC approved a classification code that would support best practice, a clear classification code and international standards.[1] To qualify for Paralympic status an athlete must "have an impairment that leads to a permanent and verifiable activity limitation" (p. 10), and an athlete can compete in Paralympic sports if they have any "difficulties an individual may have in executing activities" (p. 24). According to the IPC, athletes are assessed by three initial categories, ["Physical, Technical and Observational".] Physical assessment involves an examinations of a potential Paralympic athletes, muscle tone, coordination, range of movement, endurance, sensorial, or intellectual abilities (for example: vision, strength or balance; p. 41); Technical assessment looks at how an athlete performs under stimulated sporting activists i.e. wheelchair use, swimming ability, archery skills, and Observational Assessment takes place during an event.

Currently, there are 18 sports in the classification system. These are: Skiing (Alpine and Nordic), Archery, Athletics, Boccia Cerebral Palsy, Cycling, Equestrian, Football [five and seven a-side], Goal Ball [blind], Ice Sledge Hockey, Judo, Power lifting, Rowing , Sailing, Shooting, Swimming, Table Tennis, Volleyball and Wheelchair sports include Basketball, Curling, Dance, Fencing, Rugby and Tennis. However, the classifications cannot be applied uniformly to all Paralympic sports. For example, an athlete competing in football may not necessarily qualify in rowing as each sport has a different classification system.

The problem for the media and the viewing public is that although the "classification attempts to place individuals with disabilities into groups of comparable ability and function" (Buckley, 2008 p. 90) there remains a complex problem for the IPC in order to sell "classification to the general public when faced with the spotlight of the media. Not all of society is comfortable with the idea of disability on full display in the sporting arena and complicated systems are also harder to explain" (Buckley, 2008, p. 98). In a mediatised world, aesthetics and the visual plays a key role generating meaning. The Paralympics reliance on aesthetics creates confusion of the viewer when presented with a line of competitors with differing disabilities. Channel Four Televisions, Commissioning Sports Editor, Deborah Poulton believes this is a contributing factors as to why journalists have reported poorly on Paralympic Sports because "there's been a great deal of a lack of understanding of classification" (interview with, Deborah Poulton). For ex-

---

1. http://www.paralympic.org/export/sites/default/IPC/Reference_Documents/2008_2_Classification_Code6.pdf page 8.

ample when a Paralympic athlete is given the classification S9[2], the journalists and public "don't understand what an S9 means, and the level, the range, the disabilities increase in that race, and you [the viewer] don't understand if it's an even playing field or there's a fairness on the field" (ibid). Thus visual imagery creates confusion because it acts as reasoning or interpretative devices and how the media frame the Games is significant in influencing public opinion.

The Media Message

In addition to a complex classification system, how media images frame Paralympic Games works to act as a series of codes which direct and guide the reader/viewer to interpret the information, and thus build a knowledge base in a set way (Gamson & Modiglian, 1989). The problem is that previously television images have often hidden the "disability side of things that's swept under the carpet...and it's all been close head shots, or very wide angles, and you've never really seen, for example what the disabilities are when they are racing" (interview with Deborah Poulton). This framing which negates the disability of the athlete makes a public acceptance of a disability difficult, because it works as "a central organising principle that holds together and gives coherence and meaning to a diverse array of symbols" (Gamson, 1992, p. 384). In other words, the disability becomes blind to the viewer.

Therefore these two factors, classification and media framing signal a lack of understanding by journalists to convey the Paralympic Games succinctly. The confused classification system means journalists revert to medical or anatomical discourses and a language that emphasising disability over sporting achievement. The linguistic traits that shape a Paralympic media discourse also contributes to the wider socio-cultural knowledge of disability and sport. Research has shown journalists rely on either a medical, or disabled-hero discourse, contained within discourses of nationalism, media and heroisms.

Theoretical Approach: Discursive Representations

Discourse is the way language is constructed to produce a set of codes and rules in which to reason. The rules of any language provide meaning dependent on the relationship between things (Hall, 1997 p. 18) and codes provide a means to communicate through "broadly the same conceptual maps" (Hall, 1997, p. 18). How language is constructed, and consequently knowledge is formed, is central to the "concept of discourse [which] is not about wheth-

---

2. An S9 classification is for swimmers with severe weakness in one leg only, very slight coordination problems or swimmers with one limb loss. Unless there is an underlying medical condition usually all of these athletes will start out of the water (Buckely, 2011).

er things exist but about where meaning comes from" (Hall, 1997, p. 45). Yet, how meaning emerges is not simply a case of "translating reality into language", but "discourse should be seen as a system which structures the way we perceive reality" (Mills, 2004, p. 55) and about "the production of knowledge through language" (Hall, 1984, p. 291). Moreover, discourse is also a "specific ensemble of ideas, concepts, and categorisations that are produced, reproduces, and transformed in a particular set of practices and through which meaning is given to physical and social realities" (Hajer, 1995, p. 44).

Yet, discourse "never consists of one statement, one text, one action or one source" (Hall, 1992, p. 293) but acts as part of a set of statements that is "characteristic of the way of thinking or the state of knowledge at any time" (Hall, 1992, p. 293). Once language forms a set of codes and rules to understand a subject, it links together with "a group of statements which provides a language for talking about a way of thinking about – a way of representing – the knowledge about a particular topic at a particular historical moment" (Foucault, 1992, p. 291). Here, Foucault's interpretation of discourse goes beyond Hall's notion that language creates meaning, to contextualise language from an historical position. How words are given meaning, and how that meaning is interpreted as a truth, when language moves from translucent horizontal understanding, to an opaque, vertical use of language leads to meaning being blurred in favour of setting the rules of discourse. Foucault's discourse shows that without an understanding of the historical process that gives language meaning, then discourse could present a false truth in favour of the hegemonic position through strategies of normalisation.

Normative values are achieved in part through a media discourse to shape public opinion, both off the Paralympic Games and disability as a whole. Journalists' use of language shapes public opinion and social practice. When language shapes meaning either in negative, positive, critical, or celebratory ways, but always gives meaning to news reports. Journalists draw from a set lexicon to structure a news piece and produce patterns and styles. The 'articulation' (in a Laclau and Mouffe sense) - the placing of words next to each other to give meaning - by journalists reveals a discourse about a subject to shape the meaning and public opinion. Public opinion is understood through different and competing discourses. Combined with the increasingly fast pace of news journalists tend to rely on and repeat values which influence the readers' or viewers' "central value system" (Hall, 1978, p. 55). Thus, when journalists apply a set language to news stories, or editors reaffirm a set of cultural codes in news production, they reinforce cultural codes and knowledge. In other words, language shapes meaning and meaning is controlled by those in a hegemonic positions either broadcasters or institutions or both.

Reviewing the Media and Paralympics

Studies into media discourse around the Paralympics, (Schantz & Gilbert 2001; Thomas & Smith, 2003; Hardin & Hardin, 2008) found that in newspaper reports there was an emphasis on nationalism, the negating of disability and many Paralympic Athletes were seen as underdogs overcoming lifes adversities.

Thomas & Smith's (2003), study took 62 articles from four British newspapers to examine the terminology used to describe athletes' disability; and the language used to represent the athlete's performance. Their research aimed to establish if "disability has traditionally been explained from an individualised or medicalised conceptionalisation" (Barton cited in Thomas & Smith, 2003), and people with disabilities are frequently depicted as "super humans who overcome their adversity in acts of heroism that evoke pity from the intended audience" (Thomas & Smith, 2003, p. 168). Their empirical data was drawn from a study of newspaper reports of the Sydney Paralympic Games (2000) between October 17th and October 30th, 2000. Their research questions aimed to establish 1) if there was a use of medicalisation to describe Paralympians, 2) if there was a comparisons between Paralympic and Olympic athletes, 3) were there any portrayal of athletes impairments, and 4) the coverage of male and female Paralympians (Thomas & Smith, 2003). Thomas & Smith found that 'conservative' newspapers devoted a larger amount of coverage to the athletes compared to the 'liberal' press. Their work revealed that some media reports "reaffirmed traditional or dominant conceptualisations of disability and people with disabilities" (p. 172); The British press placed an emphasis on Paralympians being portrayed as aspiring to emulate able-bodies success. There was some evidence that photographic coverage negated or denied the athlete's disability. Coverage of male and female Paralympians found male Paralympians were more likely cast in active poses, unlike their female counterparts. Thomas and Smiths findings contrast with Schantz and Gilbert's (2001) study on the French and German newspaper coverage of the previous games.

Schantz & Gilbert (2001) examined newspaper coverage of the 1996 Atlanta Paralympic Games. They found many articles failed to frame the Paralympic Games as a seriously sporting event. Most, newspapers made a tokenistic attempt at coverage that focused on the 'spectacle' or image (Schantz & Gilbert, 2001, p.86). Moreover, unlike Thomas and Smiths findings, Schantz and Gilbert found that aside from the theme of nationalism framing what limited stories on the Games, the conservative newspapers dedicated less column inches than the more liberal press, and "reporters still focus primarily on the 'disabled' instead of the 'athlete'" (Schantz and Gilbert, 2001). The "consumer driven, capitalist economy" of the United States places "people with disabilities as invisible", because they contrast with the American ideal that the body is "environmental constructed for the majority; people with disabilities are a liability for their inability to navigate it" (Hardin and Hardin, 2008). Only when a hero discourse is created by journalists and society, or aptly a David versus Goliath discourse occurs does disability become acceptable. Hardin and Hardin term this the super-crip' model and is "the presentation of a person, affected by a disability of illness, as 'overcoming' to succeed as a meaningful member of society to live a 'normal life' (Hardin & Hardin, 2008, p. 25). This 'strategy of normalisation' (in Foucauldian terms), is reinforced by the hegemony to provide a "low societal expectations of people with disabilities" so that "people with disabilities should be able to accomplish at the level of disabled hero. Consequently, all people with disabilities are judged by the supercrip standard" (Smart, 2001). Athletes defined by the "supercrip model promote ableism...where a higher value is put on 'normal' bodies that are part of the working majority" (Smart, 2001 in Hardin & Hardin, 2008, p. 27). Thomas & Smith (2003) also found that when the media presents athletes as "overcoming their disabilities and exposing the audiences to what might be seen as medicalised conceptions of disability, the media may have trivialised the performance of athletes with disabilities" (p. 174). The placing of normative values reaffirms the hegemonic position that those with disability are of a lower social standing, through the juxtaposition of disabled and able-bodies athletes.

Yet, Hardin and Hardin found some Paralympians believed the supercrip model was "good for the able-bodies public because it shows disabled individuals in a 'positive' light. Stories with supercrip framing also show how 'human spirit can overcome" (Hardin & Hardin, 2008 p. 29). Their empirical research found Paralympians "expressed frustration with the supercrip emphasis on disability sport as a 'human interest' sport; more progressive models would illuminate their athletics as valid" (Hardin & Hardin, 2008, p. 30). Moreover, a supercrip model makes disability acceptable, but only as a "disabled –hero framework" which works as a hegemonic device to keep people with disabilities at the bottom of the social hierarchy and deflect the cultures responsibility for it's albeit infrastructure" (Hardin & Hardin, 2008, p. 25). The result increases the opportunities to iterate an American 'self-actualisation' whilst encouraging a nationalistic discourse.

A nationalistic discourse is not specific to the USA, and can be found in German, French and British newspaper reports. Schantz and Gilbert's (2001) comparative study between French and German newspaper reporting of the Paralympic, found that both countries tended to cover a wide spectrum of athletes from various countries, as "during the Olympics readers and spectators are informed about all records and a great number of foreign star athletes", and during the Paralympics "the analysed newspapers reported almost exclusively national athletes and performances" (2001, p. 84). When reporting on the Paralympics they focused only on the individual countries success, i.e. French journalists' reports on French Paralympians. Germany also placed a nationalistic emphasis on their reporting as the *Frankfurter Allgemeine* newspaper claimed "You can rely on German Athletes" (Olympia cited in Schantz and Gilbert, 2001 p. 81). British press coverage of the Sydney Paralympic games followed a nationalistic discourse, and indicates a shift towards the achievements of the athletes, and less of a focus on disability, as Tanni Grey-Thompson's gold medal win in the 800m T53 final was defined as "Grey puts Britain top of the world", as the British team were praised as "Britain's brilliant Paralympians" (Thomas & Smith, 2003 p. 174). Yet, a nationalistic discourse seems more Eurocentric than the rest of the World, partly as Hardin and Hardin notes, because disability jars with the American ideology, and wider socio-cultural acceptance of disability in societies. In addition American coverage of the Paralympic Games has been limited to one hour a day.

American broadcaster NBC hold the largest percentage of broadcasting rights for the Olympics, and their decision not to broadcast live or as live coverage of the Paralympic Games could have an impact on influencing public opinion about disability. The intentional withdrawal of NBC and the USA to televise the Paralympic Games at the same level of the Olympic Games is a contributing factor as to why there remains a lack of understanding of disabled athletes by the public and society as whole. Indeed, if there were to be a change from the supercrip model, possibly a "change of personnel somewhere, somebody who has a personal experience of disability, so they're more awakened to Paralympic sport... if they've got nobody amongst them that got any reference points to it. I really don't know the reasons are for America not being so open to it" (interview Poulton 2011) it could give greater prominence to disabled sports. Thus with America currently opting out of reporting the Paralympics then it negates disability in society regardless of sporting excellence.

Although America may be singled out for its lack of engagement with the Paralympic other countries have a similar approach. In comparison, countries such as Taiwan also had no live media coverage of the 2004 Athens Paralympic Games. The Canadian Broadcast Company, and TV New Zealand showed four one hour specials of the 2000 Sydney Paralympic Games, and NBS has no live coverage of the 2000 Paralympic Games (Brittain, 2009). In the UK, the British Broadcasting Corporation (BBC) showed nightly highlights programmes from Athens (2004), which attracted two million viewers, but its coverage of the 2010 Winter Paralympics was limited to one hour a night, "despite dedicating 160 broadcast hours to the Winter Olympics on BBC2" (Sweeney, 2010). As Brittain notes, "....if the BBC provides more airtime to Olympic sports then it appears that it perceives to have far greater 'value' than its Paralympic counterpart" (Brittain, 2009, p. 75), but this is still considerably better than for viewers in the USA who had to wait six hours to see a one hour highlight show (Brittain, 2009, p. 80). Post 2008 there is evidence that media coverage of the Paralympic Games is increasing, which will in turn contribute to future media discourse. The tables below set out the number of accredited media at the Paralympic Summer Games.

Fig 1: Approximate number of Accredited Media in Attendance at the Summer Paralympic Games

Barcelona 1992	1,200
Atlanta 1996	2,000
Sydney 2000	2700
Athens 2004	3,000
Beijing 2008	5,500

Fig 2: Approximate number of Accredited Media in Attendance at the Winter Paralympic Games

Tignes1992	300
Lillehammer 1994	570
Nagano 1998	1,400
Salt Lake City 2002	800
Torino 2006	1,000

Source: Brittain 2009, p.81

Although the media presence is much lower than the summer games, partly because "...at each Paralympics, media organisations will send a smaller team than for the Olympics – in some case just one reporter where they might have had a team or 10 to 15 for the Olympics" (McDonald, 2008, p. 7). There is evidence of a steady increase in the number of journalists attending the Paralympics. McDonald notes how the number of journalist has more than doubled since the Atlanta Games (1996) with 20 journalists to 50 at the Athens Games (2004) (McDonald, 2008, p. 76).

Since an agreement was signed between the IOC and the IPC to secure and protect the organisation of the Paralympic Games, which declares that from 2008, the Paralympic Games will always take place shortly after the Olympic Games, using the same facilities. From the 2012 bid process onwards, the city that wins the rights to host those Olympic Games will be required to stage the Paralympics as well. The IOC and IPC's decision to ensure "...the Paralympic Games will be held after the Olympic Games, and will use the same sites and infrastructure" from 2012 onwards means the "city chosen to welcome the Olympic Games will also be obligated to organise the Paralympic Games" (Reichhart, Dinel, & Schantz: 2008, p. 57) and this decision goes some way to overcoming the obstacles. British Paralympian Gold medallists, Dame Tanni Grey-Thompson notes "The athletes also know that due to the single organising committee involved in London 2012 – and the integration for these Games has been better than ever before – the Olympics and Paralympics will be truly equal" (Tanni Grey-Thompson, 2011). Yet, there also needs to be a wider media campaign, not just for the Games but to challenge how the Paralympics are seen as "....a shop window, a prism through which the relationship that society maintains with people with disabilities reveals itself" (Reichhart, Dinel, & Schantz: 2008, p. 57). The emergence of commercial television Channel Four as rights holder for the 2012 games goes some way to addressing the issue.

The impact of this on media representation means journalists will be using the same media facilities, and venues as the Olympic Games. Since the 2008 Beijing Games, when "ABC Australia were broadcasting more Paralympic Games coverage then there had ever been before, and received a great deal of plaudits doing so. SPS in Germany did more Paralympic coverage than before... but if you look back on the history of media coverage on the Paralympic games, there has been an upward trend, and it particularly spiked around Beijing. So if it continues on that upward trajectory, as we get to the next games, and particularly as we've got an organising committee, who are very much pushing both Games" (interview Poulton 2011)

This is interesting as the IPC have also attempted to overcome these problems with their online media channel, Paralympicsport.tv. First launched for the Torino Games, 110 countries took advantage of the service, watching approximately four hours of sport. In Beijing fans from "166 countries took advantage of the service [with] Paralympicsport.tv has been used to provide worldwide coverage of a large number of sporting events for athletes" (Brittain, 2009, p. 82). The free to air internet based channel provides live and as-live footage. However, in light of the digital divide argument – not everyone has access to the internet-although Paralympicsport.tv "allows IPC to satisfy additional demand where only limited coverage is available or to provide coverage where none exists" (Brittain, 2009, p. 82), only a certain part of society can access the channel. Although the internet based TV channel offers greater access, in the UK, the acquisition of broadcasting rights for the 2012 Paralympic Games by commercial television Channel Four, signals potentially new opportunities for wider coverage and a chance to address some of the problems.

Solutions and Signals of Change?

Echoing Tanni Grey-Thompsons belief that the Paralympics are seen as "just something that follows on afterwards" (Gibson, 2010, p. 3) from the Olympic Games, Channel Four "...felt the Paralympics are right for innovation, it felt like an event that takes second place to the Olympic Games, to us it felt like an event that never achieved the depth of coverage it deserved, and we felt probably, that's largely because of the classification systems that govern Paralympic sport are relatively confusing". Channel 4 then will attempt to create a discursive challenge through the following three key areas: 1) debunking the classification system, 2) utilising technology and 3) addressing wider socio-cultural issues around the representation of disability by drawing attention to creating a cultural and media narrative around disability.

Channel Four's aim is to "make household names of Britain's Paralympians" (Scott-Elliot, 2010, p. 42); and "use the power of a home games to inspire change in attitudes to [Paralympians] sport" (Channel 4 spokesperson in Gibson, 2010, p. 3). They will attempt to complete this task by building on their innovative test cricket coverage (1999-2005). An aim of their Test coverage was debunking and demystifying the sport and they hope to echo that approach by debunking the classification system. During their cricket coverage they relied heavily on innovative technology, bringing Hawkeye to the public attention. However, for the 2012 Games, they will use technology to explain the classification through simple on screen graphics, in order to:

> "demystify sport for people, to increase the fan base, or keep the fan base there, err, and I think we've seen it with the off-side rule in football, and we've seen great innovation in rugby, but I think you know, with Hawkeye, perhaps that was the foundation for taking sport, and just demystifying, debunking, your know jargon busting... to try to capture the sports lover on the periphery who likes sports, but doesn't quite get their toe in deep enough, because they're confused a lot of the time"

(Interview with Poulton, 2011).

Channel Four is embracing disability, bringing it "to the forefront, and at the same time not overriding the fact that you are watching an elite sport" (ibid). They hope to achieve this by working with the IPC and the British Paralympic Association (BPA) because "they know a lot more about their sports than we do, and we're taking on-board their comments. We're very much trying to avoid the medical approach to disability sport because nobody wants to go down the medical route" (ibid). Yet, Poulton accepts this sometimes detracts away from the athleticism with more emphasis on disability, especially print journalists who are "interested in Jon-Allen Butterworth[3] the ex-Afghanistan [A British soldier serving in Afghanistan] soldier who got injured there, oh that's a great story, oh and by the way he's now trying out for the team 2012, and they are going on that angle of something that's more interesting than the sport itself" (ibid), demonstrating the fine balance required to circumvent the current media discourse. For example, "I think if you don't at least reference, oh Nathan[4] had his legs amputated aged nine, when he got hit by a train, your left, you can't get to know that person. You don't understand what's different about them, or why they are, who they are" (ibid).

---

3. Jon lost his arm in Iraq in 2007 while serving with the RAF. He spent a year in physical rehab before being introduced to cycling at a Paralympics GB talent day at Loughborough University. Unable to return to his job in the RAF, Jon decided to pursue a career in competitive cycling and stepped up his training to compete at elite international level. Retrieved September 1st, 2011 from: http://www.telegraph.co.uk/sport/olympics/paralympic-sport/paralympics-gb/8725610/Jon-Allan-Butterworth-Paralympics-GB-London-2012-Olympics.html-

4. Paralympic field athlete, Nathan Stephens, had both legs amputated after he was run over by a train aged nine.

Brittain drawing on Haralamos and Holborn's study (2000) notes that Broadcasting Standards Committee, now OFCOM, found that "...people with disabilities appeared in 7% of their of sample of television programmes and accounted for 0.7% of those who spoke" (Brittain, 2009, p. 73). In attempting to widen the spectrum out from sport to include the cultural context of disability, Channel Four will broadcast more Paralympic Sporting events e.g. (World Championships in Manchester) a weekly show that explains the different Paralympic sports pitting able-bodied athletes against Paralympians and drawing on some of their earlier programmes to challenge media discourses around disability. Such as Cast-Off, a ground breaking six parts comedy series last year (2010) that featured six disabled actors they hope to widen public understanding of disability. Another example occurred in an episode of the fashion programme 'How to Look Good Naked' with a participant in a wheelchair and an able bodied contestant. Although by juxtaposing the contestant with an able-bodied could be read as re-affirming Hardin and Hardin, and Thomas and Smiths observations that people in wheelchairs "receive greater media coverage than other athletes possibly because their impairments is not perceived to deviate substantially from dominant concerns about able-bodiedness" (Thomas & Smith, 2003, p. 169). However, just as the aim of their cricket coverage when Channel four build in a cultural narrative around the games they hope to emulate this approach during the Paralympics Games. Indeed, their cricket coverage won plaudits by "revolutionising cricket coverage" (Gibson, 2010) through a wider cultural narrative and innovative technology to 'jargon bust' the sport.

Media Technology

Technology is increasingly playing a leading role in the communication of sporting events to wider audiences. In recent years communications provider ATOS, are the technology providers for the 2004 Olympics and Paralympics, having been the IOC IT Partner of the 2002, 2004, 2006, 2008 and 2010 Paralympic Game, and will continue at the 2012 in London. For the London 2012 Games, they predict that technology will play a bigger role in two areas. "Firstly, in improving access to information as audiences worldwide expect more detailed and colourful information to be delivered, as it happens, to an increasingly complex network of channels. Secondly, the technology infrastructure will also enable a sustainable Olympic Games"[5]. In adopting technology to produce "on screen graphics, insightful analysis and commentary", unlike advanced technology like 'Hawkeye', the use of technology in the 2012 Paralympics coverage will be simplified using "graphics, analysis and commentary to bring something alive" (Poulton, 2011),

---

5. For more information about ATOS see the following. retrieved August 12, 2011 from: http://uk.atos.net/en-uk/olympic_games/london2012/default.htm

Utilising technology in a simply way, Channel Four hope to use "this expertise and technology to help make the Paralympics a serious respected and viable international sporting event" (McDonald, 2008, p. 77). The key way they will use graphics is to simplify and explain the classification system - "We are looking at the moment at a system whereby the classification system is debunked" (Poulton, 2011). This innovative approach aims to address the earlier complexities around the Paralympics Games. As Poulton notes:

> "You know, I think also, a lot of criticism levelled at Paralympic sports relates to, you know I don't understand what S8 means, I look at the swimming blocks and I see one girls got one arm, and ones got two, and I don't see how that's an even race. I think what we're trying to do is to add a layer of depth that allows the viewer to understand what you are watching is as humanely possible a level playing field, without going all medical on them. I think you'll lose a few viewers that way"
>
> (Interview: Poulton, 2011).

By debunking and demystifying the classification system, they hope to address the issue of aesthetics, whilst avoiding the use of close-ups, head shots and wider angles, or medicalisation, and passive forms in representing Paralympic Athletes.

Other factors which could aid this transition are the commercial element. The Paralympic Games are not connected with the five Olympic Rings and as such are open to sponsorship outside of the International Olympic Committee TOP's system. Channel four has no relationship with the IOC, they have a relationship with LOCOG and the IPC, the only relationship we have with the IOC is that we have to use the Athena system, which governs the use of marks of London 2012 logo. This has meant financial backing from two large UK based corporations, the supermarket chain Sainsbury's and telecommunications company, British Telecom. Moreover, Poulton (Channel 4) genuinely believes that journalists are beginning to move away from the discourse of nationalism and negative media discourse. She argues that:

> "There's a fundamental shift happening within our newspapers at the moment, I think, Oscar Pistorius, the South African Blade runner, is becoming quiet high profile, and Elle Simmonds, the swimmer is becoming quite well known. Dame Tanni Gray-Thompson became, I would argue, a household name and still is. So I think it's proven there's definitely an appetite to it... and we are definitely seeing an increase in the media running those stories...There's a greater interest in Paralympic Games because they are coming to home soil and specifically I think it's an increase in coverage around the world"
>
> (Interview: Poulton, 2011)

By debunking disability through a simplification of the classification system, supported by wider cultural narratives, Channel Four have set themselves a challenge to change the discourse. As Poulton notes there are signs that media representation is changing, and utilising the nationalist discourse to emphasis the return of the Paralympic Games to their country of origin, juxtaposed with the inclusion of greater numbers of disabled servicemen, may go some way to challenge the earlier emphasis on medicalisation, and the 'supercrip' model. Moreover the deliberate exclusion by America and the embracing of the highest percentage of coverage during the Beijing Games poses the question of whether the Paralympic Games still need the media giants of NBC and the BBC to survive and spread their popularity.

Conclusion

In short, how the media reports on the Paralympic Games has developed from a negative framing with an emphasis on disability over athleticism. Paralympic athletes have been presented in the world's media as individuals who are overcoming adversity, or as disabled hero's. This supercrip model places Paralympians into lower social cultural structures, reflecting the national hegemonic position, particularly in the USA. Alternatively, instead of emphasising the heroics of a Paralympians, some media have hidden or ignored a person's disability through wide shots, head shots or photographs that removes or ignores any disability. This is reinforced through limited television coverage of often only an hour a day. To combat the lower level output the IPC has moved to placing much of the footage online. Although this act offers more coverage it is only to those with internet access or for those who already have a knowledge base of Paralympic sports, and therefore are more inclined to access the service. What the internet television does appear to do is draw in new or greater numbers of viewers. The solution could come from the commercial sector with Channel Four's acquisition of the broadcasting right? We don't as yet know the outcome of this experiment. However, Channel Four's plans are ambitious, and given the high praise they received from their cricket coverage, could possibly draw greater numbers to Paralympic sports. This combined with the 2012 Games returning to the UK, and a greater number of Paralympic athletes as a consequence of the recent wars in Afghanistan and Iraq, reiterates the nationalistic discourse found in much of the earlier reporting. However, the most innovative move is the debunking of disability by explaining the classification system, which if successful should go some way in shifting media discourse and societies perspectives from disability towards focusing on the Paralympic elite athletes.

References

Brittain, I. (2009). *The Paralympic Games Explained*, London: Routledge.
Buckley, J. (2008). Classification and the Games. In K. Gilbert & O. J. Schantz (Eds.), *The Paralympic Games: Empowerment or Sideshow?* (pp. 90-102). Maidenhead: Meyer & Meyer.

REFERENCES

Buckley, J. (2011). Understanding Classification: A guide to the classification systems used in Paralympic Sports. Retrieved January 10, 2012 from: www.sportingwheelies.org.au/doc.php?ID=38 and classification documents retrieved January 10 2012 from: at http://www.paralympics.org.uk/page.asp?section=0001000100050004003&sectionTitle=Classification

Carvalho, A. (2000). "Discourse Analysis and Media Texts: a Critical Reading of Analytical Tools", paper presented at the 'International Conference on Logic and Methodology', RC 33 meeting (International Sociology Association), Köln, 3-6 October, 2000. Retrieved August 10 2010 from: http://repositorium.sdum.uminho.pt/bitstream/1822/3137/3/acarvalho_Kolnpaper_2000.pdf

Foucault, M. (1992). *The History of Sexuality*. London: Penguin.

Gamson, W. & Modigliani, A. (1989). Media Discourse and Public Opinion on Nuclear Power: a Constructionist Approach. *American Journal of Sociology*, 95 (1), 1-37.

Gibson, O (2010, January 18). Channel 4 Dives back into sport: The Broadcaster's surprise outbidding of the BBC for the Paralympics has given it a chance to reconnect with its core remit and sporting past. *The Guardian newspaper*, p. 3.

Golden, M. (1992). Not on the Front Page. *Progressive*, 56 (3), 43.

Hall, S. (1978). *Policing the Crisis: Mugging, the State and Law and Order*. London: Macmillan Press.

Hall, S. (1997). *Representation: Cultural Representations and Signifying Practices*. London: Sage Publications.

Hardin, M, & Hardin, B. (2008). Elite Wheelchair Athletes relate to Sport Media. In K. Gilbert & O.J. Schantz (Eds). *The Paralympic Games: Empowerment or Sideshow?* (pp. 25-34). Maidenhead: Meyer & Meyer.

Hajer, M. A. (1995). *The Politics of Environmental Discourse: Ecological Modernization and the Policy Process*. Oxford: Oxford University Press.

Jollimore, M. (1993, January 11). Public is often blind to some athletes, *The Globe and Mail* (Canada).

Laclau, E. & Mouffe, C. (2001). *Hegemony and Social Strategy: Towards a Radical Democratic Politics* (2nd ed.). London: Verso.

McDonald, M. (2008). Media and the Paralympics, In K. Gilbert & O.J. Schantz (Eds.), *The Paralympic Games: Empowerment or Sideshow?* (pp. 68-79). Maidenhead: Meyer & Meyer.

Mills, S. (2004). *Michel Foucault*. London: Routledge.

Mitchell, K. (1994, July 10th). Ready, Willing and Disabled, *The Observer Newspaper*, UK, p. 20.

OP-ed (1995, March 20). Don't Underestimate the Disabled, *The Washington Post*, p. A16.

Poulton, D. (2011, May 10). Commissioning Sports Editor for Channel Four Television, Interviewed by author, Maxine Newlands.

Redden, R. (2000, Oct 21). Grey puts Britain top of the World, *Guardian Newspaper*, p. 6.

Reichhart, F., Dinel, A., & Schantz, O.J. (2008).Spectating at the Paralympic Games. In K. Gilbert& O.J. Schantz (Eds.), *The Paralympic Games: Empowerment or Sideshow?* (pp. 57-68). Maidenhead: Meyer & Meyer.

Scott-Elliot, R. (2010, August 10). Channel 4 to Raise Paralympic Profile: London 2012, *The Independent* newspaper, p. 42.

Schantz, O.J. & Gilbert, K. (2001). An Ideal Misconstrued: Newspaper Coverage of the Atlanta Paralympic Games in France and Germany, *Sociology of Sport Journal*, 18, 69-94.

Smart, J. (2001). *Disability, Society, and the Individual*, Gaithersburg: Aspen Publishers.

Stephen, T. (2000, October 18). Landmines claim limbs but athletes stand united, *Sydney Morning Herald* (Australia), p.2.

Strohkendl, H. (1996). *The 50th anniversary of Wheelchair Basketball*. Münster, New York: Waxmann.

Sweeney, M. (2010). BBC criticised for scant coverage of Winter Paralympics', *The Guardian Newspaper*. Retrieved September 2nd, 2011 from: http://www.guardian.co.uk/media/2010/mar/12/bbc-criticised-coverage-winter-paralympics/print

Thomas, N. & Smith, A. (2003). Preoccupied with Able-Bodiedness? An Analysis of the British Media Coverage of the 2000 Paralympic Games, *Adapted Physical Activity Quarterly*, 20, 166-181.

Taub, O. Blinde, O & J. Greer (1999). Stigma management through participation in sport and physical activity: experience of male college students with physical disabilities, *Human Relations*, 52(11), 1469-1484.

Thompson, G. T. (2011). Is there is a genuine interest in tickets for London 2012 Paralympics? *The Daily Telegraph newspaper*. Retrieved September 8, 2011 from: http://www.telegraph.co.uk/sport/olympics/paralympic-sport/8749427/Tanni-Grey-Thompson-there-is-a-genuine-interest-in-tickets-for-London-2012-Paralympics.html

Chapter 20
An Implosion of Discontent

Reconceptualising the Rapport between the Media and the Paralympic Movement

Keith Gilbert & Otto J. Schantz

Introduction

To better understand the complexity of the relationship between the worlds media and the Paralympic movement, the Paralympics and Paralympic athletes we must first appreciate the integration and the broader reflection regarding the universality of the medias perception of disability on the one hand and the cultural aspects specific to Paralympic sport within the overall constructs of society as a whole. Indeed, as global sensitivity and respect towards difference and otherness has accelerated over the past few decades we would naturally assume that the relationship of the media to Paralympic athlete and the Paralympic movement has also been fast tracked but in our research and writing over the past twelve years we have found no such developments. In fact on delving further into the relationship between the Paralympics and the media we have encountered an 'implosion of discontent' between the athletes, Paralympics and the media. This implosion has not taken into consideration the expansion and development of the challenges which both sides have encountered over the years but rather inhibited the promotion of disability and in particular Paralympic sports and in general the reporting as well as the standing and notability of the Paralympics themselves.

We are often asked what is the relationship between the media and the Paralympics? As we have seen no discernible improvement in writing or reporting on the Games over the years we always answer in the negative and add that the relationship has become mired in the universal plethora of media hype surrounding the Olympics and not the Paralympics. To add further to this argument in a general statement which is sure to upset certain aspects of our community we believe that very few people in the sports industry and sports media seem to care about the Paralympics. These are by the way not only our thoughts but words from research that can be backed up by comments from several leading sports administrators. Subsequently, in the sports industry we have a situation where many believe that disabled and Paralympic sport is by far not as important as 'able bodied' sport. This situation is mirrored in the media and our global societies. Accordingly we ask ourselves the question if there is such an occurrence as an implosion of discontent between the media and the Paralympics then is this not symptomatic of wider society's negative perspective on disabled and Paralympic sport and indeed disability in totality? More recently, we believe that societies are becoming customarily inward looking and becoming more materialistic but still have the resources and wherewithal to actually embrace a bold program of social improvement to highlight the person with disabilities in sport and this could be led by the media who report on the Paralympics. Will this happen? We very much doubt that it will. There are many reasons for the status quo or 'implosion' between the media and the Paralympic movement. In order to discover these reasons we need to reflect on the findings of the authors in this book and attempt to define this phenomenon. What follows is a synthesis of the main outcomes of this text.

Marginalisation

"Heroes or Zeros" provides examples of research into the Paralympics and the media by highlighting issues of race, gender, ethnicity, sexuality, disability and the body as viewed from the athlete and collective media's perspectives. Within this social framework we focussed on the positives and negatives of the media coverage of successive Paralympic Games and the overall effect of the media coverage on society and the sporting community. In the following we are not always complimentary or positive in our outlook but we are honest and recognise that we provide the reader with a book which is the first of its kind and which hopefully stands to be dissected and discussed in media and academic circles prior to the London 2012 Paralympic Games and beyond. Essentially then, it is a book which describes the social mores of Paralympic sport and its relationship to the media from its humble historical beginnings through to the present day and all the while providing relevance for the future.

Notionally, we position our work in this book around the various theories surrounding the area of marginalization and in particular the media's marginalisation of disabled and Paralympic athletes and to this end when researching and discussing the academic directions for this book, we were struck by the need to explain the concept of marginalization within the Paralympics and how the marginalizations are portrayed or not portrayed by the media. The outcome of the authors work supported this supposition and as such we believe that it is clear that although Paralympic athletes and indeed individuals with a disability are in general marginalised in the global society, they are generally even more discriminated against in the media. This marginalisation takes many forms and is directed to differing areas of the Paralympic athlete's world. For example there is a notable absence of disabled women, black faces and individuals who are homosexual in the press and TV coverage on the Paralympics. It is as if these people do not exist. In actuality it can be argued that there is a form of double discrimination by the media towards disabled women athletes, athletes who are black and athletes who are gay in the Paralympic community. This lack of acknowledgement and reporting of events and individuals is a clear form of discrimination which could be easily rectified. For example instead of just reporting on disability sport every two years when a Paralympics rolls around the press could be providing stories and reports on a daily basis across all forms of media outlets. Why are they not doing this? Perhaps, as we believe, there is still some form of stigmatization within society to individuals with a disability and comparatively there is also greater stigma towards disabled people who play sport.

There is also marginalisation by the lack of reporting of some events during the Paralympic Games and providing detailed accounts of athletes from the most popular events which are arguably, swimming, athletics, rugby, basketball and cycling. Thus less popular sports like boccia, seated volleyball, table tennis, archery, goal ball and rowing receive little or no attention unless there is a national gold or silver medal winner. Paralympic bronze medal winners are rarely highlighted in the press. Even then there is scant information and very few press reports emanating from the past three Paralympics regarding these clearly unpopular events and their competing athletes. Do the media think that they are not worth showing the public? Do they rate lower on the viewing scale due to a lack of commercial worth? For example it is obvious that there is a disproportionate coverage both in the print and televised media of wheelchair athletes. Indeed, as previously mentioned wheelchair athletes and amputees appear to get the most media coverage. Perhaps this is because the collective media feel that members of society can better cope with those individuals and are less confident with individual athletes with an intellectual disability for example? Nevertheless, we feel that all aspects of the Games should be covered and not just the so called blue ribbon sports. The notion of political correctness in society is perhaps a reason why some Paralympic sports have become more popular in the media than others. It is easier to comment about some disabilities which are more socially acceptable and also to photograph them in a manner which does not offend some members of society. The fear of being seen as politically incorrect when referring to athletes with a disability can thus be a limiting factor in some sports being shown on television or in actuality being reported in the media at all. The media, have an enormous responsibility in our societies, due to its power to influence public opinion, and cannot be viewed as openly discriminating and marginalising against individuals with a disability or athletes with a disability. Interestingly, the same Paralympian who is thrust to the media's attention and glorified for two weeks every two years is often essentially marginalized within sport and society in general. After the Paralympics the sporting heroes become almost non-existent for the journalists, and their media value returns to zero. Perhaps we have forgotten in our eagerness to write about the Paralympics to highlight the fact that this marginalization is an ongoing and life determining issue in many Paralympians lives. Indeed, when the international tracksuit comes off the Paralympic athletes effectively look and behave like any other disabled people in society and immortality and marginalization are interchangeable and transient concepts for Paralympians. In short disabled athletes tend to become accepted into society and our living rooms when competing but remain marginalized in life thereafter.

Indeed, what happens to those athletes from smaller countries who cannot compete at the same standard as many bigger and more affluent nations? Their lack of technology, training and practice makes them marginalized before they arrive at the Paralympic Games. This marginalization is further compounded by the lack of media attention afforded to these individuals as most of the coverage is of the bigger, richer and better sponsored teams and their athletes. In fact, many smaller disregarded teams arrive at the Paralympic Games and leave the Paralympic Games without a single word being written, without interviews or photographs taken about their presence or their achievements. Where's the press and media equality in that scenario? In this regard the media are guilty of pandering to a Westernised grandiose ideal of the Paralympics by ignoring 50% of the rest of the world and their sporting achievements.

Marginalization occurs simply because of the fact that the number of media who remain for the Paralympics after the Olympics are often below one third the number which graced the Olympic Games. There is thus a need for more coverage and more interest from various aspects of the press and other media so that equality in reporting is evident. The non-representation of disabled people in the social context of life is thus magnified by their non-representation in the sports media over time and in particular throughout the Paralympic Games. The media interest in the Paralympic Games and the Paralympic athlete is therefore fleeting and smacks of hypocrisy and elitism. Perhaps if there were more disabled reporters then there would be better coverage of the Paralympics? In actuality as previously hinted the amount of media coverage and media visibility of the Paralympics correlates to the number of medals won and the national identity of the reporter and the athlete. To be fair the same phenomena can be observed during the Olympics but to a much lesser extent. Indeed, as disabled sport per se seems to have 'no' great news value, the media focus mainly on the aspects of geographical proximity or national identity.

Revulsion

There is a theme running through the majority of chapters in this book which is a hidden but powerful feeling of revulsion towards the Paralympic athlete from the media and consequently from much of society. This is perhaps a spinoff from the major theory that if you are different from the norm in society then people want little to do with you or to be associated with you in any way. In this instance we feel that the media has a large role to play in broadening the public's opinion and discourse around individuals with a disability and rectifying the problem of revulsion. This form of revulsion is especially prevalent in the poor reporting of athletes with intellectual disabilities and probably provides a large impact on the general public. This is a matter for further research. Whereas, if carefully thought through then, the media could have a large influence on people's perceptions of all forms of disability within the Paralympic arena. This position would go a long way towards arresting people's perceptions and the visibility and invisibility of Paralympians. Indeed, we argue that everything which is not standard in terms of the body is often hidden by the sports media as they are responsible for the ideas and concepts which are selected for the consumer of sports. It is felt that some reporters even feel uncomfortable interviewing Paralympic athletes because they engender pangs of revulsion in some individuals as generally the sports media are especially used to the perfect bodily form and the perfect performance. This projected media model of masculinity, perfect form, physical strength and high performance is not evident in many Paralympic sports and thus the reporters use the medical model to describe the athletes overcoming of fate, loss of motion and disability and ineptitude. This again reinforces the public's perception of the Paralympic athlete and because of their own misgivings and uncertainty revulsion and pity become further ensconced in the minds of the public.

As part of our research work we have been asking managers, coaches, athletes and others in elite sport across the globe what they think of the relationship between the Paralympics and the Olympics and why the Paralympics is reported upon so badly. Bye far and away the answer which we got from the respondents was short and brief. Nobody cares! People only seem to care about athletes of either sex, who are good looking, have amazing bodies and beat world records by performing amazing physical feats which are to them legendary. However, as we keep arguing, we feel that the media have a responsibility to educate society and to attempt to turn around these unethical and misinformed attitudes. This is difficult as some people are consciously or unconsciously repulsed by the disabled body and the members of the media are no exception. Hence the need for more media representatives in sport who are themselves disabled. This leads us to the notion of hyper-reality concerning the media and the Paralympics.

Hyper-reality

Hyper-reality, in the sense of Baudrillard (1994), is a manner of embodying what our realization of the world defines as actually 'factual' in a sports culture where broadcasters from differing cultures can profoundly influence and dictate the way in which a sporting moment or occurrence is reported. Reporters and cameramen can thus influence the perceptions of the reader and viewer of the outcome of the particular event. Every sport broadcasting creates "néo-réalité" (Baudrillard, 1970, pp.194-196) or second degree realities. The temptation to alter or embellish the reality seems even to be higher in reporting about the Paralympics in order to adapt it to the aesthetic populism, to efface problems, and to avoid violations against the socially requested political correctness.

Indeed, it is argued that this form of constant viewing of the body as abnormal can create situations of 'visual disturbance' and consequent 'mental disturbance' where the individual and in this case reporter attempts to create hyper-real situations to hide the truth about what they really perceive. Bodily imperfection is not tolerated in general by people in society and is certainly not tolerated by the worlds sporting mass media which, as mentioned previously, idolises flawless movement and the picture perfect and sculptured body. Hyper-realisation of Paralympic events, Paralympic athletes and both are perhaps more prevalent in the media than previously imagined?

The issue of truth portrayal is an important concept which has not been mentioned before. If the media are constantly reporting in hyper-real mode then it is suggested that the truth becomes secondary to the story. This coupled with the fact that all members of the media bring with them preconceived ideas and past experiences regarding disability and Parlaympic sport adds to the implosive nature of the occurrence. Paralympic media are thus guilty of not portraying the truth about Paralympic athletes and disability sport. This is due to their trans-fixation with able bodied athletes who they encounter in their normal job, as there are few if any reporters, who are solely working on disability sport or Paralympic sport on a full time basis. Many reporters work for two weeks every two years with disability sport and as such are not concerned with the finer points of the sports reporting which they deliver periodically to an even less knowledgeable public. It's our experience that many sports reporters just want to get the Paralympics out of the way so that they can go back to their families who they have not seen for many weeks, due to their work on the Olympic Games, and to their reporting on football, cricket or some other major sport where their real interest lies. If you add the surreal and hyper-real world of the Paralympics and the sights and sounds which that engenders and the discomfort which some members of the media inherently possess then you have a very real and recurring problem. Indeed, this fact alone makes the world's press feel as though they are out of their comfort zone. It can be argued that the Paralympic sports media provide images and reports on individual and team events which lack emotive elements. i.e. they are emotionless. Unlike their synergies with able bodied sport where emotion is a key factor in the development of the story or photographic capability in Paralympic reporting they prefer to create hyper-real situations to produce fake perceptions in the consumers realization of real world situations which Paralympic athletes have to endure on a daily basis. These hyper-reality illusions are designed to detach individual members of the public from any tangible sensitive and emotive disabling encounters, and in its place selecting false replications, and seemingly limitless procreations of essentially unfulfilled emotions becomes the norm. In this way the sports media do not interact with Paralympic and disabled athlete realities but prefer to reproduce endless untruths and hyper-real banalities. Nowhere is this fact more prevalent that when the media suggest that a Paralympian is in their eyes a 'supercrip': Someone who although disabled can perform amazing feats of endurance, speed or skill which is outside of the ordinary feats of disabled people on a daily basis. This hyper-real hero conjured up media driven Paralympian' - as viewed through the eyes of the media - is constantly portrayed through a series of fake hyper-real scenarios which distorts the real world of the athlete and turns them into some kind of 'bionic superperson' in the eyes of the public and probably damages the public perception of the ordinary persons with disabilities as they are compared to these "super-crips".

The Language of New Media

Although developments in the media have seen a gradual increase in the use of new media over the past ten years; this upsurge in media content and method of delivery has not been as prevalent in the broadsheet and television reporting of Paralympic sport as in most able bodied sports. This is surprising as we argue that new media is related specifically to a globalised information age and if advanced carefully can be utilised to cultivate new cultural connections which have the ability to be utilised in order to globally change people's perceptions of disability and Paralympic sport. These alternative media sources such as Twitter, Facebook, You tube, the internet in general and other digitized sources can be used to share the cultural of disability and the Paralympics, educate individuals in all societies about the Paralympics, assist in the communication of the Paralympics to everyone and build on line communities to support the Paralympic athletes and athletes with disabilities. With this proliferation of new media comes a social responsibility to portray the athlete's lives in an ethical and serious manner. As yet this appears to be an almost untapped source of media coverage of the Paralympic Games and we feel must be utilised for the future media coverage at all levels.

We do agree that there are Paralympic websites but argue that there are few which relate specifically to disabled sport in general. If we take the idea of the Paralympic sportsperson and their brand then we have seen an increase on British television of Paralympic athletes due mainly to the upcoming Paralympic Games. However, as television is not classed as new media we find few sightings of Paralympians on digital media outlets such as blogs etc. We argue the term 'new media' is a constantly changing cultural phenomenon which embraces emerging technologies which are often driven and supported by the virtual World Wide Web and are communities which go beyond topographical margins and cut across class boundaries. However, why are there few media outlets which fully embrace disabled sport and the Paralympics in its new media offerings? Perhaps there is a need for more involvement in the new media by the International Paralympic Committee and also better marketing of the Paralympic brand by Paralympic Games time reporters.

Along with this shift of the world's media towards new media reporting there appears to be an advanced lack of understanding by both journalists and consumers of the language which the new media attempts to portray to society as a whole. Understanding the language of new technology takes time and this lack of awareness by the consumer of media messages causes further angst to individuals who are not 'up to speed' with new technologies. Therefore many messages go missing in the public domain. This causes a form of Paralympic digital knowledge divide between the Paralympic media and the public where neither fully understand the nature of the language and meaning of the text to be delivered. Classification terminology provides an example of this lack of understanding. The journalists don't fully understand the language of classification and are thus hard pressed to explain it to the public in a meaningful and accurate manner. This medical language is difficult to develop in the media as its particularly central to the understanding of concepts in health which most consumers are totally ignorant about. Classification thus remains misunderstood by the majority of consumers of new media and indeed, old media. There is thus a need for a change in the nature of the Paralympic discourse in order that everyone understands the concepts and traditions of the individual sports. This change could be media led and new media driven.

This language then we feel is medicalized, disability oriented and difficult to understand for most people. This fact coupled with the low directly perceptible quality of some of the sports, lack of visible excellence and performance by the athletes and consequently the lack of public interest in some sports lends us to believe that some sports do not have a future either in the media or in the Paralympics. There really is no commercial future for sports that do not lend themselves to exciting media coverage and we would not be surprised to see the media outlets putting pressure on the International Paralympic Committee to drop so called soft sports from their programme, and reduce the number of classes. However, this can not be in the interest of the sportsmen and women with disabilities, included those with severe disabilities, who should be offered the possibilities to practice a great variety of sports, in fair competition.

Imaging the Paralympics

It is clear long before disabled athletes become Paralympians that media images of disability sport offer nothing to dispel the perceptions which people in society have of the disabled person. In point of fact Paralympic athletes have no control over the images which are displayed by the press and this becomes a problem and a source of bad artistic judgement by the photographers that often undermines, disregards and further marginalizes athletes. Indeed, it could be argued that photographs of disability and Paralympic sports events, if not carefully handled, can become a source of oddity, novelty and representation which could provide a rich source of negative perception of disability sport in the community.

Photographs can also provide a source for morbid contemplation and position the Paralympic athlete as being someone or something differing from the norm in society. Perhaps this morbidity is something which society understands as an innate draw towards the unusual or freak element of society. If we argue that photographs provide an objective and historical record of the Paralympic Games then we need also add that from the most part the photographs taken of Paralympic athletes do not provide clear reference to the nature of the sport, person or team being photographed. In other words the media representatives go out of their way to show images of disabled athletes which are 'politically correct' and sure not to upset their readers. There is perhaps still an assumption in the media that a misshapen body also correlates to an abnormality of the intellect and this is also a given in society as a whole. Photographs of Paralympians then always show aspects of perceived beauty, grace, skill and facial expression. Very rarely do they show the disability, impairment or deficiency. Indeed, there are far fewer photographs shown of the Paralympics than the Olympics and such techniques as shadowing, air brushing and black and white photography are used indicating that they live in a world devoid of colour. Indeed, photographers do not know the Paralympians they are photographing but the photo is always used to define the person or represent a contradictory theme – photos should then be made that are relevant to the context of the people who are depicted in them and not random shots. Why then are Paralympic athlete's photographs not appearing in the media very often outside of the Paralympic Games time? This is perhaps because photographs of disabled people are generally not shown in the daily press as they are presumed like other disabled individuals to be 'socially dead'. Photographs of the Paralympians or disabled athletes rarely make the sports pages of the newspaper let alone the social pages as discrimination and marginalisation appears rife in the sports photography world. To illustrate this point, have you ever seen a photograph of a Paralympic athlete on the front page of a newspaper? Until the recent events in London we doubt that very much.

We argue that the photographic messages that are portrayed in the press are only of certain high profile sports and Paralympians. Different people react differently to having their photographs taken and generally people with a disability are less inclined to like having a photograph taken which depicts some aspect of their disability. We are fairly sure that there will be few team photographs of boccia or seated volleyball in the newspapers during the London 2012 Paralympics Games and the individuals suffer terribly by being ignored. The photographs will be of medal winners who come from popular sports and not of others which have already been written off as boring, uninteresting and physically less challenging by ratings hungry producers and editors. Photographs can be a window to an others world, provide a glimpse of their life, and allow us to experience slice of their reality. We owe it to all Paralympic sports to provide coverage which is indicative of Paralympic athletes' lives as disabled people and who also just happen to be elite sportspeople.

Paralympic Cyborgs and the Media

Throughout the development of this book we were struck by the media's interest in how technological advances have opened up the Paralympic body for unprecedented levels of visual display, knowledge and surveillance. This media interest has been led by the incredible interest in Oscar Pistorius who has set new guidelines for the study of the cyborg sportsman. This fascination with the post human condition of the Paralympic athlete has been capitalised upon by the media and used to offset and change the public's opinion of the disabled athlete. It begs us to ask the question as to how technological advances will be reported in the media in the future? Is it ok to show and write about below knee amputees, new forms of wheelchair development and arm prosthesis? However, will they be willing to show athletes who eat with their feet, and whose feet face backwards or who are disfigured in some way through accident or birth? We doubt that this will occur.

The deformed body provokes the above mentioned revulsion due to our fears about our fragile human condition, the cyborg instead evokes fascination. Since the movie "Terminator" popular culture has been captivated by the hybrid creatures of machines and organism. While the mutilated and disabled body reminds us of our fragility and mortality, the mechanically enhanced body promises empowerment and longevity.

However, the mechanically enhanced sportsman is also a dread as he muddles up the traditional hierarchy of able-bodied and disabled athletes and as he raises the question of the "natural" performance spoiled by prospects of techno-doping. Nowhere was the notion of techno-doping more pronounced and highlighted than by the tantrum thrown by Oscar Pistorious at the 2012 Paralympic Games where this so called defender of cyborg technology found himself well beaten by a faster cyborg. Being beaten was a shock for Pistorious as suddenly he became the second fastest one hundred metre runner 'on no legs'. Interestingly, the media reports following this Pistorious outburst answered our previous question regarding - how technological advances will be reported in the media in the future? The media were all over the Pistorious incident and discussions included comments made by the experts from technology companies, space engineers, prosthetic leg manufacturers and International Paralympic Committee rules experts. Suddenly everyone in the Paralympic sports media had an opinion and become a so called prosthetic limb specialist. Interestingly, this discussion lasted for a few days but it soon dwindled and expectations are that there 'will more than likely' be little interest in Oscars prosthetic legs or indeed any others until the next Paralympic Games. However, as technology advances 'cyborgism' is set to become the new classification problematic for the IPC at future Paralympic World Championships and Paralympic Games and of course a future novel concentration for the sports media covering the Games.

These controversial perspectives and discussions are of great news value and offer the media plenty of material to report about.

Conclusive statements

In the field of hyper-commercialized sports the Paralympics are becoming increasingly irrelevant and the media's fear of being irrelevant when reporting about it has given their irrelevance an air of self-prophecy. Paralympic sport is too different from Olympic sport and the media is still trying to report on the Paralympics in the same way as they do on the Olympics. However, this scenario can only lead to its relationship downfall and finish in a disaster for both, Paralympians and the media. At the moment we believe that the Paralympic Games are an impasse as they don't and will not have the impact on public opinion which they were supposed to have according to the thoughts of the IOC and the IPC. The media in their own way much know the difficulties which they have to deal with in promoting Paralympic sport to society. However, they must clearly spend more time and work closer with the International Paralympic Committee to portray images and write stories which are relevant, sensitive and true. At the moment we have a scenario where the International Paralympic Committee are receiving much more funding in relation to media dollars but still not controlling the direction in which they are perceived in the community and also how their athletes are developed. Indeed, it falls to individual Paralympic Committees across the globe to provide media training and media savvy lessons to their high profile athletes. We argue here that in part this should be the responsibility of the International Paralympic Committee who should take control of their own media destiny rather than rely on increased media money and still be forced to go into damage control when something goes wrong at a Paralympic Games. There needs to be a well thought through disability media strategy which is offered to the media rather than relying on the Paralympic Games Organising Committees documents and hand-outs prior to the Paralympic Games. The Paralympics is like no other event in the world and there are special requirements which range from the use of political correctness to the covering of individual athletes, disabilities and events. However, there are few resources which Paralympic Committees and indeed the IPC can access to learn how to best promote athletes with a disability, Paralympic sport and disability sport in general. We hope this book will go some way towards rectifying the implosion of discontent which is being experienced by all.

References

Baudrillard, J. (1970). *La société de consommation*. Paris: Denoël.
Baudrillard, J. (1994). *Simulacra and Simulation*. Ann Arbor: The University of Michigan Press.

Chapter 21
Researching the Future

Otto J. Schantz and Keith Gilbert

This final section of the book has been designed to offer ideas for further research into the phenomenon of the media and the Paralympics. Thus the ideas herein are supportive of new research in the area and also to encourage the opening up of new research directions to support the knowledge regarding the relationship between the media and the Paralympics.

In general the media tends to gear up every two years for the Olympics and the Paralympic industries but there is very little work produced by researchers which actually compares the two Games. This is true in for all forms of the media. We feel that there is a great need to research the relationship between the Olympics and the Paralympics in order to tease out all of the disparities and probelmatics which are clearly evident but rarely spoken or written about.

There is a lack of understanding of thoughts and ideas of the Olympic and Paralympic television, radio and internet producer's perspectives regarding the many ways in which the Paralympics are delivered to the public. It would be of great interest to interview these powerful people and try to understand their ideas regarding the delivery of Paralympic sport to the public and also to follow their work on a daily basis throughout one of the Games time periods.

Throughout the years leading up to the Paralympic Games there are also minor and major competitions for example, like world championships and national championships. It is important that these events are covered in their entirety by the media. However, we know nothing of the reporting of these satellite events and it would make sense for researchers to delve into the relationship between the media and the 'other' Paralympic events so that as researchers and sports developers we have an overall picture of this phenomenon.

Certainly one of the major points arising from this book is the fact that there is very little if any research produced which highlights the relationship between the media and the athletes themselves. This area really needs more research so that we are able to finally hear the athlete's voices and thoughts regarding their own relationship with the media and what they perceive as important in the currently one-sided relationship.

Along with the above we argue here that there are several unexplored sociological dimensions which need further probing by researchers. These include issues of the media and their interconnections with race, gender, health, disability, sexuality, culture, and the body which arise in 'able-bodied' sport but are less obvious in the research culture surrounding the Paralympics. The contributions on race and masculinity from Brenda-Kammel Atuona (chapter 21) and Cynthia Barounis (chapter 15) in the present book are first efforts to stimulate further research in these directions.

We are interested in the development of the athlete as a researcher and now that new media is available to all then we would like to see more research attempted which uses the Paralympic athlete as a developer of their own research. This could be achieved through daily tweets or e-mail accounts of their life in the village and competing in the Paralympic Games themselves. Indeed, we value their own accounts of their media experiences and action research into their sensations and thoughts would be a good method of researching this area. Another method of research might be in the production of life histories and biographies of the athletes and the problems which they face on a daily basis.

Continuing with the above theme of the athlete as researcher we would like to see daily diaries written regarding the athletes perspectives about what they are reading in the media surrounding the Paralympic Games. More particularly it would be important to observe the attitudes of less powerful and smaller countries at the Games and their relationship or non-relationship with the media.

We view legacy as very important and argue here that the legacy of the Paralympic Games is very much driven prior to and during the Paralympics by all aspects of the media coverage and reporters perspectives on stories. Indeed, we feel that the media can make or break the Paralympic Games. There reporting and commentary on Paralympic legacy would make a really interesting research study in the future.

As a group of researchers working with the media and the Paralympics we really need to be cognisant of the importance of the photograph and film in developing people's perceptions of Paralympians, the Paralympic Games and disability. This thought has not gone un-noticed in this book however, there is little work which has actually analysed photographs or film of Paralympic athletes and we feel that there needs to be more 'visual sociological research' undertaken in the future.

Over the years we have been affected by the poor media skills of Paralympic athletes. When interviewed or photographed most are naive and easily influenced by the reporters or photographers and there is a need to research this aspect of the Paralympians lives so that they can better understand the media processes and also better project their own characters and messages. How do the Paralympians cope under the media spotlight? How are they affected personally by the questions of the reporters? And what can they do to change the public's perceptions of themselves by utilising the media to their own advantage? These are questions which might be asked to initiate research in this area.

Importantly, there is a need to understand and a need to know about the media policies of the International Paralympic Committee as there lead can make big differences in the way in which Paralympic sport, Paralympic athletes and disabled sports-people are perceived by the general populous. We understand that they are working hard on this very task but if researchers knew more of their insider strategies' then we could perhaps develop stronger arguments to support the IPC in their endeavours. This would make an enlightening and interesting study.

Previously in the text we argued that the media, Paralympic athletes and the International Paralympic Committee were greatly influenced by the media strategies of the (OCOG) Organising Committee of the Olympic Games. Indeed, the OCOG media guidelines have been set by the IOC themselves. In many ways we feel that these guidelines are not specific to the Paralympic Games and research needs to be attempted which develops a (OCOG) media package specifically for the Paralympics and not just roll over the media documents with different titles for the IPC.

Furthermore, we are interested in the fact that there are few disabled people working at the Paralympic Games in the important positions within the media. It would be interesting to have some idea of the 'take' which the individuals with a disability have on their own work. Indeed, what are their perspectives? Why are there so few disabled people working in the Paralympic media during Games time? And also what can be done to bring ex-Paralympic athletes more into the media frame of reference?

Finally, we need more studies on the impact of the Paralympic media coverage. This is a field which, for obvious reasons, but mainly due to its complexity, is almost completely under-researched. Empirical studies for example like the one from Capucine Germain and Julie Grall (chapter 12) on the impact of Paralympic photos on the recipients are extremely rare. We know more and more about the contents, the quality and quantity, the intercultural or international differences of media reporting on Paralympic sports, but we know almost nothing about its impact on the audience. We urgently need to gather data about the recipients and explore the effects the

Paralympic coverage produces on them. Questions need to be asked for example: Do the media contribute to extending the knowledge on disabled sport and disability in general? Is Paralympic reporting capable of changing attitudes towards people with disabilities? Or does it for example hinder inclusive attitudes by reinforcing the binary and incompatible by categorizing able-bodied on the one side and disabled sportspersons on the other?

It is imperative that we have answers for these and other questions as we go forward with our research into the relationship between the media and the Paralympics. The ideas set out above are only a small sample of where we would like to see research on the media and the Paralympics proceeding in the future. The research on media and Paralympic sport is still in its infancy, and there is a need as well as the strong potential of its further development. We hope that the new field of studies on 'Media, Paralympics and disability' goes forward in 'leaps and bounds' so that we can, in the future, truly define the area and develop answers which support Paralympic athletes and individuals with a disability. We hope that our book will be a modest contribution to this development and stimulate further research and theory building on this exciting topic which is the relationship between media, Paralympic sports and society.

Index

A

ABC Australia 217
abilities 8, 9, 66, 90, 140, 187, 190, 211
able-bodiedness 21, 112, 134, 154 176, 191, 199, 201, 206, 220, 224
ableism 215
adapted physical activity 20, 103, 133
adapted physical activity 20, 21, 52, 112, 129, 130, 133, 134, 191, 206, 224
Adorno, Th. W. 6, 17
ADSF 77
advertising 17, 18, 37, 74, 92, 131, 133, 198, 203
Afghanistan 219, 222
Africa 30, 158, 159
ageism 200

aging 178
airtime 49, 50, 107, 216
Akihito, Crown Prince 30
Al Gore 30
Aladji Ba 33
Albert, P. 35
Alberto, C. 20
Albertville 97
Albright, A. C. 14
Alexander Spitz 46
Allison, J. A. 21
alternative masculinity 175, 177
Altheide, D.L. 128
Altwasser, C. 205
American Championships 183
amputation 168
André, Dominique 33
Andrews, D.L. 128
Ann Cody 161

Anne Cécile Lequien 34
apartheid 30
archery 28, 69, 106, 119, 211, 227
ARD 38, 42, 43, 46, 49, 50, 52, 88, 93
Arêche-Beaufort 150
Argentina 127, 131, 184
Arnhem 30, 106
Arnhem 30, 106
Arnie Bolt 32
Asch 128, 130, 200, 204
Asian Championships 183
Asken, M.J. 199, 202
Assey D. 134
Assia El Hannouni 33
Associated Press 163
Athens 12, 33, 34, 88, 91, 105, 110, 115, 118, 119, 120, 183, 193, 216, 217
Athléteam Handisport 33
athletics 11, 21, 45, 49, 78, 89, 90, 114, 163, 177, 181, 183, 185, 205, 215, 227
Atlanta 6, 7, 8, 16, 20, 30, 52, 75, 96, 99, 103, 105, 112, 114, 120, 132, 133, 191, 206, 214, 216, 217, 223
ATOS 220
Attali, M. 35
attitudes 1, 2, 4, 5, 7, 8, 27, 41, 99, 106, 107, 119, 184, 193, 198, 204, 205, 218, 229
Atuona, B.-K. viii, xi, 7, 13, 193
Augustin, D. 35, 64
Auslander, G.K. 128, 197, 202
Australia 16, 86, 155, 209, 217, 224
Austria xi 78, 81, 82, 83

B

Bach, M. 21
Bacigalupo, V. 207
Bailey, S. 205

Balle, F. 35
Banet-Weiser, S. 129
Barcelona 20, 30, 102, 216
Barnes, C. 65, 73, 129, 132, 196, 197, 198, 199, 200, 202, 203
Baroffio-Bota, D 129
Barounis, C. viii, xi 13, 171
Barr, C. 157, 164
barrier-free programming 42
barriers 8, 134, 197, 200, 204
Barton, L. 107, 111, 199, 202, 207, 214
Baudrillard, J 2, 14, 230, 235
BBC 3, 38, 40, 41, 42, 45, 46, 47, 48, 49, 50, 51, 52, 106, 107, 108, 109, 110, 111, 158, 161, 163, 186, 216, 221, 223, 224
BBC2 38, 216
Beat Bösch 66
beauty 7, 10, 19, 55, 114, 140, 151, 172, 233
Bec, Serge 31
Beck, D 67, 72, 73
Becker, H.S. 139, 145
Becker, P. 4, 14, 67, 73
Begum, N. 200, 202, 204, 206
Beijing vii, viii, 11, 12, 65, 66, 77, 78, 79, 85, 86, 87, 88, 90, 91, 92, 93, 98, 103, 110, 115, 118, 119, 120, 125, 133, 137, 138, 141, 142, 159, 160, 161, 188, 194, 201, 216, 217, 218, 221, 241, 242
Bell, A. 4, 14
Bell-Jordan, K. 196, 203
Bennett, R. 177
Bentle, Vera 92
Bentle, Verena 92
Berelson, B 2, 14, 18
Berger, P. 144, 145
Berghaus, M. 2, 14
Bert, Philippe 29
Bertling, C. vii, x, 10, 37, 51, 55, 56, 59, 60, 62, 63, 64, 67, 72, 75, 113, 114, 120,

Bertschy, S. vii, xi, 11, 65, 68, 72, 73
Bette, K.-H. 3, 15
Bild (Bildzeitung) 8, 63, 79, 81
Billings, A.C. 7, 16, 129, 195, 204
bionic 231
Birmingham 108
black disabled athletes vii, 13, 14, 30, 129, 193-197, 200-202, 203, 226, 206
Black, L. 190
blind *see* visually impaired
blind football 183, 184, 187, 188
Blinde, E.M. 15, 134,
Blinde, O. 224
blindness 89, 184
Blödorn, M. 62
boccia 221, 227
Bochet, Marie 148
body 12-26, 72, 89, 124, 132, 138-142, 158, 159, 160, 165-170, 174, 182, 185, 195, 199, 211, 214, 226, 230, 233; athletic body 57, 100, 140 Athlet's body 141, 143; beautiful body 58; body assignment paradox 31; cyborg body 13; deformed body 27, 234; disabled body 12, 33, 97, 100, 139, 141, 143, 151, 154, 169, 172, 229, 234; disabled sports body 98, 99; female body 3, 176, 177; hybrid body 169; ideal body 198; mutilated body 166, 167; normative body 162; perfect body 89, 138, 168; performing body 27; social body 26, 152, 167; sporting body..3; technological body 100; technotopic body 174;
Boetsch, G. 102, 132, 146

Bogdan, R. 129
boosting 41, 81
Borcherding, B. 182, 190
Borcila, A. 15
Bornat, J. 207
Bös, K. 5, 18, 56, 58, 67, 72, 74, 78, 79, 80, 83, 89, 92
Bosshart, L. 63
Bourdieu, P. 15
Bourdonnaye, Gilles de la 34
Bourseaux, Yannick 148, 151, 152
Braithwaite, D. 17, 191
Brand, J.S. 2, 17
Brandt, H. 67, 74
bravery 31, 142, 143
Braynt, J. 129
Brazil 184
British Broadcasting Corporation *see* BBC
British Paralympic Association 47, 51
Brittain, I. vii, xi, 11, 105, 106, 107, 108, 111, 157, 163, 184, 186, 190, 193, 198, 203, 216, 217, 218, 219, 222
broadcasting 10, 11, 38, 41, 42, 43, 44, 49, 78, 86, 87, 88, 89, 90, 91, 97, 108, 138, 140, 187, 216, 217, 218, 222, 230
Brooks, N.A. 200, 203
Brown, C. 200, 203
Brown, D. 63
Brummet, B. 129
Bryant, J. 17, 19, 63, 74, 130
Bryson, L. 18
Buckley, J. 210, 211, 222
Buffington, D. 195, 196, 203
Bühler, R. 66, 73
Bulgaria 31
Bull, M. 187, 190
Burger, R. 35
Buysse, J. A.M. 129, 182, 190
Bytheway, B. 207

C

Calvin, M. 199, 203
Cameron, C. 206
Campbell, K. K. 18
Canabal, M.Y. 205
Canada vii, xi, 12, 15, 110, 112, 113, 114, 115, 117, 118, 127, 163, 175, 177, 202, 209, 223
Carstarphen, M. 133
Carvalho, A. 222
CAS 159, 160, 161, 162, 164
Casert, R. 159, 160, 163
Cashman, R. 110, 111
Cashmore, E. 194, 203
Catalan nationalists 31
CBS 6, 20, 52, 110, 112, 133, 191, 206
celebrity 1, 186
cerebral palsy 77, 185, 211
cerebral paralysis 98, 100
Chaiyapum 125, 126
Chambre des Communes 15
Chance, J. 130
Channel Four 109-112, 190, 202, 218, 221, 223, 210, 217-219, 221-223
Chaplin, Charlie 187
Chapuis-Lucciani, N.G. 102, 132, 146
Charbonnier, L. viii, xi, 12, 147
Cheetah legs 158, 159, 160, 161, 162
Cheng, H. 130
Chevé, D. 102, 132, 146
Chiari 190
Childs, K. 195, 203
China 79, 80, 82, 85, 86, 88, 184
Christensen, K. 130
Christie, J. 119, 120
Christl, R. 52
Chu, D. 20
cinema 172, 178, 207

citizenship 40
classification 14, 81, 88, 90, 117, 209, 210, 211, 212, 218, 220, 221, 222, 232
classism 200
Cloerkes, G. 7, 15, 63
Clogston, J. S. 5, 15, 119, 120, 129
Coakley, J.J. 15, 198, 203
Coe, Sebastian 110
Cohen, G. 21
Cold War 30, 31, 173
Cole, C. 15
Collins, M. 134, 157, 163, 196, 203
Colombini Robert 31
Combeau-Mari, E. 27, 35, 95, 101
Combrouze, D. 98, 101, 131, 147, 155
Comisky, P.W. 63
commodity 3, 41, 185
compassion 12, 80, 141, 142, 143, 144, 147, 150
Connolly, M. 204
consumer 38, 214, 229, 232
content analysis 6, 8, 20, 65, 87, 112, 133, 191, 194, 206
Cooky, C. 132
coping 6, 31, 35, 90
Corner, J. 204
Corson, Y. 130
Cose, E. 196, 203
Coutant, E. viii, xi, 13, 165
Crolley, L. 129
Cronenberg, David 154
Crossman, J. 21, 129, 134
Crow, L. 197, 203
Crowley, E.P. 18, 138, 145
CRPD 162
CTNERHI 18, 145, 155
Cuba 30
cultural diversity 191
cultural pluralism 5
Curtis, E. M. 195, 205

cyborg 8, 13, 152, 154, 169, 174, 234
cycling 89, 183, 219, 227
Cyrulnik, B. 31, 35
Czopp, A. 196, 203

D

dance 14
Darcy, S. 111
Davis Megan V. 173
Davis, L. J. 172, 177
Davis, L. R. 195, 203, 203
Dearing, J. W. 2, 15
Debord, G. 155
Deegan, M.J. 200, 203
Deffontaines, N. 138, 145
Defrance, J. 138, 145, 166, 170
Delforce, B. 27, 35, 102
Dellinger, K. 129
Department for Culture, Media and Sport 40, 51
Department of Canadian Heritage 163
DePauw, K.P. 3, 6, 7, 15, 67, 74, 129, 185, 190, 203
Devenney, M. 148, 155
Devine, M. A. 198, 203
DGUV 91, 92
Die Welt 56
Dinel, A. 217, 223
Dines, G. 205
Dinold, M. vii, xi, 11, 77
disability 1-13, 15-17, 21, 22, 28, 31-34, 39, 40, 41, 43-50, 55-59, 61, 65-67, 70-73, 77-83, 86, 88-90, 95, 96, 98, 99, 101, 102, 105-113, 117, 119, 122, 123, 127, 129, 131, 132, 134, 137-139, 142, 144, 147-149, 151-154, 157, 163, 165, 167-170, 172, 173, 176, 177, 181-187, 190, 191, 193, 194, 196-201, 203, 205, 206, 209, 210-216, 218-220, 221, 222, 225, 226, 227-235
Disability Now 109, 205
disability sport 2, 5, 7, 10- 12, 15, 40, 41, 43- 50, 56, 67, 72, 77-81, 86, 105-110, 148, 149, 152, 182, 184-186, 190, 193, 194, 198, 199, 201, 215, 219, 227, 230, 233, 235
disability studies 123, 182, 191
disabled masculinity 172, 177
disabled sport 2, 10, 32, 56-62, 86, 97, 98, 100, 107, 108, 113, 139, 150, 165, 166, 184, 189, 195, 216, 229, 232
disablism 200
disadvantage 113, 200
discourse viii, 2, 5, 12, 14, 19, 95, 96-98, 101, 114, 121, 126, 129, 131, 134, 150-152, 154, 161, 163, 164, 170, 184, 189, 197, 205, 209, 210, 212-216, 219, 221-223, 229, 232,
discrimination 3, 7, 29, 30, 95, 97, 107, 122-124, 186, 194, 195, 197, 202, 205, 227, 233
discursive frame 12, 155
distorted images 201
documentary 40, 171-173, 176, 177, 187
Dodd, J. E. 128, 130
Doll-Tepper, G. 129
dominance 194, 198
Donald, J. 200, 203
Donges, P. 51
Donnelly, P. 205
Donsbach, W. 15
doping 32, 81, 82, 88, 158, 159, 234
Dörr, D. 39, 51
double discrimination 97, 205, 227
Douglas, D. 129, 195, 201, 203
drugs 4

Du Toit, Natalie 161
Dufur, M. 195, 203
Duhamel, A. 15
Dumermuth, M. 44, 51
Dumitrescu, A. 128, 129
Dummer, G. M 15
Duncan, M. C. 6, 7, 8, 15, 16, 20, 37, 52, 105, 112, 123, 124, 126, 128, 129, 130, 132, 133, 185, 191, 194, 199, 206
Dyrchs, S. 37, 51, 62

E

Eastman, S. T. 16, 19, 129, 195, 204
Eco, U. 16
Egypt 30
Ehrenberg, A. 140, 145
Eideliman, J.S. 141, 145
Eilders, C. 4, 16
Eitzen, S. D. 9, 16
Elias, N. 4, 16
Elliot, D. 130
embodiment 169, 174
Embser-Herbert, M. S. 129
Emmanuel Assam 34
Emmerich, A. 66, 74
empowerment 9, 202, 234
entertainment 2, 5, 26, 42, 43, 44, 45, 49, 55, 57, 58, 59, 60, 61, 67, 113
Entine, J. 194, 204
Enting, B. 7, 16
equality 29, 86, 92, 122, 140, 202, 228
equestrian 183
Erbring, L. 2, 16
eroticism 57, 113, 196, 205
Esgate, A. 206
ESPN 159
ethics 13, 166, 167, 168; ethical standards 45
ethnicity 41, 194, 195, 203, 204, 206 226
ethnocentrism 68
European integration 42
Evans, J. 111, 202

F

Facebook 231
failure 9, 66, 67, 68, 71, 73, 80, 82, 83, 128
fair play 39
Fairhall, Neroli 119
fame 1
Farnall, O. 2, 16, 130
fear 5, 39, 58, 79, 80, 110, 112, 160, 187, 228, 235
Fediuk, F. 52
femininity 132, 142, 175, 176, 201
Feminism 205
fencing 28, 34
Ferez, S. 102
Ferri, B. 130
FIFA World Cup 26
Figaro 26, 100
films 5, 172
Fine, M. 128, 130, 200, 204
Finkelstein, V. 196, 204, 206
Fiske, J. 16
Fog, A. 197, 204
Folkam S. 31, 35
Fong, A. vii, xi, 12, 113
Foucault, M. 5, 16, 213, 222, 223
France xi, 11, 18, 20, 26, 35, 52, 75, 95, 96, 97, 98, 100, 101, 102, 103, 112, 120, 133, 149, 184, 191, 206, 223
Frank, G. 130
Frankfurter Allgemeine Zeitung 56 82, 215
freak 233

freak show 28
French vii, x, 6, 7, 11, 20, 26, 27, 28, 29, 31, 75, 95, 96, 97, 98, 99, 100, 101, 103, 114, 133, 138, 147, 149, 190, 198, 199, 206, 214, 215
Friedman, D. L. 22
Frith, T. 130
Früh, W. 2, 16, 63, 68, 74, 130
Fullerton, R. 130

G

Galtung, J. 4, 16
Gamson, W. 212, 223
Gamson, W. 223
Garel, J-P. 140, 145
Garland-Thomson, R. 173, 174, 176, 177
Gatlin, Justin 160
Gaudet, H. 18
Gauthier-Manuel, Vincent 148, 149
Gavron, S. 7, 15, 193, 203
Gebauer, G. 16
Geierspichler, Thomas 78, 81
gender 11, 15, 97, 122, 123, 125, 132, 134, 172, 175-178, 190, 195, 197, 200, 204, 205, 207, 226; gender bias 7, 16, 129; gender difference 131, 174, 201
Genolini
Génolini, J.P. 5, 6, 16, 95, 99, 101, 130
Gerhards, M. 74
Germain, C. 12, 137, viii, xi
German Paralympic Media Award 91
Germany xi, 10, 11, 16, 20, 38, 39, 42, 43, 44, 46, 48, 52, 56, 75, 81, 82, 86, 96, 103, 112, 120, 133, 191, 206, 215, 217, 223

Geske, N. vii, xi 10, 37
Giami, A. 99, 101
Gibson, O. 218, 220, 223
Giddens, A. 147, 155
Giese, S. 37, 51, 62, 63
Gilbert, K. vii, viii, x, xi, 1, 5, 7, 8, 14, 20, 37, 52, 66, 67, 72, 75, 96, 103, 105, 106, 107, 112, 113, 114, 115, 120, 122, 133, 155, 182, 185, 187, 191, 193, 194, 198, 199, 206, 210, 213, 214, 215, 222, 223, 225, 240
Gill, C.J. 16
Gill, R. 204
Gleich, U. 63, 66, 74
Gleyse, J. 132
globalised market 45
goal ball 183, 227
Goffman, E. 139, 144, 145
Goggin, G. 8, 16, 155
Gojard, S. 145
Gold, J.R. 193, 204
Gold, M.M. 193, 204
Gold, N. 128, 197, 202
Golden, A. 8, 16, 17, 67, 72, 74, 182, !90, 223
Golden, M. 223
Goldenberg, E. 16
Golobic, T. S. 19
Gonser, N. 51
Gorin, V. 98, 101
Grall, J. viii, xi, 12, 137
Grand Prix event, Helsinki 160
Grannell, Colin 157
Great Britain 10, 38, 39, 40, 46, 47, 48, 86, 105, 106, 107, 108, 109, 110, 111, 189
Greenberg, B.S. 17
Greer, J. 224
Greer, K.R. 134, 206,
Gregg, N. 130

Grey-Thompson, T. 191
Grignon, C. 141, 145
Gumbrecht, H. U. 63
Gundlach, H. 53
Guttmann, A. 3, 17, 130
Guttmann, L. 17, 92, 106, 112
Guyot, Frédéric 34

H

Hackforth, J. 2, 3, 17, 67, 74
Hajer, M. A. 213, 223
Halbestam, J. 177
Hall, M.M. 205
Hall, S. 5, 17, 197, 204, 212, 213, 223
Hallahan, D. P. 18, 138, 145
Haller, B. 7, 17, 185, 191
Haller, M.D. 177
Hallinan 191
Hantuchova, Daniela 196
Haraway, D. 174, 177
Hardin, B. 5, 7, 17, 66, 67, 74, 130, 181-186, 188, 191, 209, 210, 213-215, 220, 223
Hardin, M 5, 7, 17, 66, 67, 72, 74, 130, 181-186, 188, 191, 201, 204, 209, 210, 213-215, 220, 223
Hargreaves, J. 130, 130, 199, 200, 204
Harris, O. 195, 203
Harrison, C.K. 196, 204
Hartmann, P. 197, 204
Hartmann-Tews, I. 130
Hasbrook, C. A 132, 197, 205
Haselbauer, T. 63
Haslam, A. 19
hegemony 17, 74, 122, 128, 215
Heidelberg 15, 63
Heilbrunn, B. 140, 145
Henning, A. 67, 74
Hermes, J. 197, 204
hero 2, 5, 8, 9, 12, 13, 17, 27, 33, 74, 97, 148, 149, 150, 151, 152, 153, 154, 168, 170, 209, 212, 214, 215, 222, 228, 231
heroism 33, 214
Hervé 102, 132, 146
Herwald-Schulz 51, 56, 62, 63
heteromasculinity 172, 175, 176
heteronormative masculinity 173, 174
heteronormativity 172, 175, 176
heterosexual 172, 174, 176
heterosexualism 200
hierarchy 17, 131, 185, 186, 191, 201, 210, 215, 234
Hiestand, M. 17
Higgs, C. T 130
Hill, M. 200, 202, 203, 204, 206
history 12, 13, 59, 62, 77, 95, 99, 114, 133, 217
Hoberman 204
Hoberman, J. 195, 196, 204
Hoc, J.M. 130
Hochepied, F. 33, 35
Hoffmann-Riem, W. 62
Holicki, S. 17
homophobic 175
Hooper, S. 131
Hoose, P. M. 195, 204
Hoover-Dempsey, K. V. 131
Horkheimer, M. 6, 17
Howe, D. P. 5, 6, 17, 21
Huang, C.J. 110, 112
Hug, M. 66, 74
Hughes, E.C. 139, 145
Humez 205
Hums, M. 157, 164
Hungary 30, 31
Husband, C. 197, 204
Hutchison 177, 178
hybridization 169
Hylton, K. 205
hyper-reality 230, 231

I

IAAF 159, 160, 161, 163, 164
IBSA 183
identification 9, 39, 43, 138, 145, 149, 150, 168, 175
identity 14, 18, 29, 33, 39, 128, 130, 139, 148, 166, 167, 168, 199, 200, 204, 228, 229
image 6, 17, 48, 56, 74, 97, 100, 101, 113, 124-126, 129, 138, 145, 152-154, 166, 167, 168, 170, 173, 174, 185, 195, 214
impairment 27, 77, 98, 99, 100, 148, 173, 186, 196, 197, 199, 211, 233
imperfection 55, 230
Imwold, C. 128, 134
INAS-FID 99
inclusion 21, 26, 28, 29, 91, 99, 129, 133, 157, 221
India 30
infantilisation 124, 125, 126
Ingstad, B. 7, 18
Institut de l'Enfance et de la Famille 18
integration 10, 26, 29, 31, 32, 38, 39, 40, 41, 42, 43, 44, 45, 46, 49, 50, 91, 92, 123, 144, 169, 217, 225
intellectual disability 88, 227
intellectual disability/mental disability 6, 77
International Olympic Committee see IOC
International Paralympic Committee see IPC
internet 110, 122, 123, 165, 218, 222, 231
Interstate Broadcasting Treaty 42
IOC 18, 92, 114, 160, 162-163, 210, 217, 220, 221, 235
IPC 12, 14, 18, 48, 51, 85, 91, 92, 99, 111, 112, 114, 120, 160, 162, 183, 193, 204, 210, 211, 217, 218, 219, 221, 222, 232, 235
IPC Swimming World Championships 47
Iraq 30, 177, 219, 222
Israel 30, 202

J

Jackson, J. 18, 131, 132, 191
Jahnke, B. 81, 83
Jamaica 30
Jamieson, K. H. 18
Janda, S. vii, xi, 11, 85
Jansen, S.C. 206
Janson, N. 204
Jarvie, G. 194, 204
Jeannot Joël 33
Jensen, K. 132
Joffe, H. 145
Johnson T. J. 134
Johnson, H. 195, 196, 205, 207
Jollimore, M. 223
Jones, R. 7, 18, 131, 132, 205
Jones, T. 200, 204
Jordan 30
Jørgensen, P.E. 20, 103, 133
journalism 60, 74, 131, 190
journalist 32, 80, 110, 149, 150, 153, 209, 217
judo 89, 183

K

Kafer A. 131
Kagelmann, H.J. 20
Kane, M. 131
Karmasin, M. 38, 41, 51, 53
Katz, S. vii, xi, 12, 113
Kauer, O. 5, 18, 67, 72, 74, 78-80, 83, 89, 92
Kauer-Berk, O. 56, 58, 63
Kaumanns, R. 51
Kay, T. 157, 163, 196, 203

Keenan, Sandra 120
Keller, C.E. 4, 18, 66, 138, 145
Keller, Patricia 66
Kellner, D. 2, 18
Kemper, R. 37, 51
Kenya 30
Kepplinger, M. H. 18
Kerlan, A. 99, 101
Keuther, D. 39, 52
Kew, F. 157, 164
Kientz, A. 138, 145
Kilbourne, J. 131
Kimmel, M. 175, 178
King Juan Carlos 31
King, K. 131
Klapper, J.T. 18
Klein, M.-L. 131
Klein, S. 86, 93
Kleine Zeitung 79, 81, 82, 83
Klemm, T. 78, 83
Klingler, W. 74
Knoll, E. 51
Kolb, S. 67, 73
Korf-Sage, K. 63
Krahe, B. 193, 205
Kroeber-Riel, W. 63
Kronen Zeitung 78, 79, 83
Krüger, A. 4, 18
Kuhn, R. 18
Kurier 79, 83

L

La Croix 147, 148, 151, 152, 154
Lachal, R.-C. 4, 6, 18, 96, 98, 101, 131, 147, 155
Lachheb, M. 139, 140, 145
Laclau, E. 213, 223
Lahmy, Eric 32
Lambiase, J. 133
Lämmer, M. 64
Langenbucher, W. 53
language 14, 44, 45, 58, 107, 118, 119, 132, 162, 198, 199, 209, 210, 212-214, 232

Lapchick, R. 196, 205
Latzl, D. 40, 52
Lazarsfeld, P.F. 2, 18
Lazarus, R.S. 31, 35
Le Cameroun catholique 25
Le Goff, J. 102
Le Meur, Jean-Yves 148
Le Monde 100, 131, 145
Lebel, E. 98, 101, 141, 142, 145
Lebersorg, J. vii, xi, 11, 77
Lee, J. 131
Lefèvre, Y. 103
Leggett S. 206
Lenzen, L. 91, 93
les autres 102
Les Echos 100
Léséleuc, E. de viii, xi, 12, 19, 27, 35, 96, 97, 99, 102, 103, 121, 124, 131, 132, 133, 138, 145
Levine, S. 18
Leyland, M. 172, 178
LFK 42, 52
Libération 14, 100
Lillehammer 217
Lipovetsky, G. 153, 155
Lits, M. 148, 149, 155
Lloyd, M. 108, 200, 205
LOCOG 109, 110, 221
Loew, G.-L. 27, 35
Loisean, Ludivine 34
Lomo Myazhiom, A. vii, xi, 10, 25
London 2012 12, 73, 91, 109, 110, 112, 160, 217, 220, 221, 223, 226, 234
London Marathon 41, 186
Long, J. 201, 205
Longman, J. 132, 164
Longmore, P. K. 4, 18
Lonsdale, S. 200, 205
Los Angeles 16, 31
Löscher, K. 91, 93
Louveau, C. 131
Lucht, J. 42, 43, 52
Luckmann, T. 144, 145
Luebke, B. 19

Luhmann, N. 2, 19
Lull, J. 197, 205
Lynn, S. 130, 204
Lyotard, J.-F. 5, 19

M

Maas, K.W. 132, 197, 205
Macbeth, J.L. 184, 191
Mad Max 173
Maffesoli, M. 167, 170
Magee, J 184, 191
Maguire, J. 3, 19
Malec, M.A. 132
Mandel, J. 178
Marcellini, A. vii, xi, 11, 19, 27, 35, 95, 96, 98, 100, 101, 102, 103, 131, 132, 133, 137, 138, 139, 141, 143, 144, 145, 146
Margaret, Princess 30
marginalisation 29, 124, 201, 227, 228, 233
marketing 232
Marti, W. 66, 74
Martin, P. 130
Martin, S. B. 132
Marty, C. 5, 6, 20, 103, 133
masculinity 3, 142, 171, 172, 173, 174, 175, 176, 177, 178, 229
masculinization 172
Masemann, V- 134
Masteralexis, P. 157, 164
Mastro, J.V. 198, 205
Mayring, P. 68, 74
McCallister, S. G. 15
McCarthy, D. 196, 205
McCombs, M. 2, 19, 66, 74
McDonald, M. 210, 217, 220, 223
McDonald, P. 200, 205
McGeorge K.K. 21
McHugh. J. 158, 164
McKay. J. 195, 196, 205
McLuhan, M. 26, 35

McQuail, D. 1, 19
McShane, E.A. 18, 138, 145
meaning 1, 10, 27, 41, 48, 57, 99, 101, 139, 148, 152, 153, 154, 166, 187, 203, 211, 212, 213, 232
media 1, 3-19, 22, 25-29, 32, 37-41, 49, 52, 53, 55-59, 61, 62, 65-69, 72-74, 78-81, 83, 86, 87, 89, 90, 91, 93, 95, 97-100, 103, 105, 112, 118, 120-125, 129-134, 137, 138, 140-144, 147, 148, 150-154, 157-162, 165-170, 181-191, 193, 194, 196-207, 211-218, 220, 224-235, x; media discourse 2, 14, 96, 101, 114, 195, 210, 213, 219, 221, 222; media effects 2; media offerings 39, 232
medical model 6, 197, 198, 229
Melnick, M.J. 198, 207
mental disability *see* intellectual disability
Mercer, G. 65, 73, 129, 203
Merten, K. 19
Merton, R. K. 2, 18
Messner, M. 16, 123, 129, 132
Metz, S. 27, 29, 35
Meyer, F. 93
Meynaud, F. 138, 146
Michiko, Princess 30
Midi Libre 100
Mikosza, J. M. 132
Miller, A. 16
Mills, S. 213, 223
mimesis 98, 99, 100, 143, 151
Ministry of Propaganda 42
minorities !7, 39, 41, 43, 45, 49, 130, 204
Mitchell, K. 223
modernity 166, 169
Modigliani, A. 223
Möller, J. 67, 74
monstrosities 139
Montaignac, C. 28, 29

Monteith, M. 196, 203
Montpellier xi, 96
Mor, Cyril 34
Moragas, Spa M. de 132
Morgan, Cliff 107
Morgan, S. 107, 133
Morin, Nathalie 148
Morisbak, I. 20, 103, 133
Morning, Emeric 34
Morris, J. 200, 205
Moualla, N. 139, 140, 145
Mouffe, C. 213, 223
movies 172, 178
Müller, N. 35
multimedia 4, 44
Mulvey, L. 176, 178
Münch, R. 19
Murderball 13, 171, 172, 173, 174, 175, 176, 178, viii
Mürner, C. 37, 52
Murphy 139, 146
Murphy, R.F. 146
Murrell, A.J. 18, 131, 132, 195, 205

N

Nagano 217
narrative 4, 13, 31, 148, 152, 154, 155, 172-178, 182, 188, 189, 191, 218, 220
National Collegiate Athletic Association 123
National Union of Journalists *see* NUJ
nationalism 212, 214, 221
NBA 194
NBC 7, 15, 110, 184, 216, 221
Nebelung, T. 64
Nelson, J. 4, 5, 15, 19, 115, 120, 132
Netherlands xi, 30
new media 231, 232
New Zealand 119, 216
Newell, C. 8, 16, 155

Newlands, M. viii, xi, 14, 209, 223
news 2, 4, 11, 14, 16, 21, 26, 28, 30, 31, 40, 45, 46, 48, 49, 56, 57, 59, 66-69, 72, 73, 88, 90, 93, 97, 106, 110-112, 118, 131, 132, 163, 164, 182, 196, 213, 229, 234
news agency 56
news factor 4, 182
news value 4, 66, 68, 229, 234
newspaper 4, 5, 6, 7, 11, 19, 21, 22, 25, 28, 33, 58, 60, 65, 68, 69, 75, 78, 80, 81, 83, 105, 106, 108, 109, 113, 115, 125, 131, 133, 134, 147, 148, 150, 151, 185, 198, 199, 202, 214, 215, 223, 224, 233, 234
newsworthy 4, 109
NFL 194, 205
Nixon II, H. L. 157, 164
Nixon, H.L. 132, 199, 205
Noelle-Neumann, E. 1, 2, 19, 21
Norden, M. F. 178
norm 149, 170, 182, 229, 231, 233
normalisation 27, 39, 213, 214
normality 29, 149, 154, 155
NUJ 109, 112

O

Oakes, P. J. 2, 19
ÖBSV 77, 78, 83
Oehmichen, E. 19
Oelrichs, I. vii, xi, 10, 37
OFCOM 219
Oliver, M. 132, 197, 200, 205, 206, 207
Olympic charter 18, 114
Olympic Games 7, 8, 10, 15, 20, 21, 56, 57, 61, 67-69, 71-73, 78, 86, 90, 92, 110,

129, 130, 131, 134, 138, 140, 141, 210, 217, 218, 220, 228, 230
Olympics 7, 8, 11, 15, 16, 17, 19, 21, 31, 44, 46, 56, 65, 68-74, 99, 106, 107, 110, 114, 141, 158, 159, 160-162, 170, 184, 190, 215-17, 219, 220, 226, 228, 229, 233, 235
oppression 14, 21, 182, 194, 200, 202, 206
ORF 52, 78, 83
Ossur 158, 164
Österreichischer Behindertensportverband 83
Österreichisches Paralympisches Komitee 78, 84
otherness 5, 168, 172, 225
Ottway, H. 19
over-representation 98
ÖVSV 77, 84
Owen, A. 7, 21

P

Paillette, S. 27, 35, 96, 97, 102, 103
Pappous, A. 7, 19, 27, 35, 97, 98, 101, 102, 103, 105, 112, 124, 131, 133, 138, 141, 145, 199, 205
Paralympic Movement 14, 47, 85, 225
Paralympics/Paralympic Games vii, viii, x, 4, 9, 13, 14, 17, 21, 26, 27, 29, 31, 39, 41, 44, 45, 46, 47, 48, 49, 50, 57, 59, 60, 61, 68, 69, 70, 71, 72, 73, 74, 80, 82, 83, 87, 92, 95, 97, 100, 101, 109, 121, 131, 150, 157, 158, 162, 163, 166, 167, 169, 170, 171, 177, 185, 190, 211, 213, 219, 220, 223, 225, 226, 227, 228, 229, 230, 231, 232, 233, 234, 235; Arnhem 30, 106; Athens 12, 33, 34, 88, 91, 105, 110, 115, 118, 119, 120, 183, 193, 216, 217; Atlanta 6, 7, 8, 16, 20, 30, 52, 75, 96, 99, 103, 105, 112, 114, 120, 132, 133, 191, 206, 214, 216, 217, 223; Barcelona 20, 30, 102, 216; Beijing vii; vii, 11, 12, 65, 66, 77, 78, 79, 85, 86, 87, 88, 90, 91, 92, 93, 98, 103, 110, 115, 118, 119, 120, 125, 133, 137, 138, 141, 142, 159, 160, 161, 188, 194, 201, 216, 217, 218, 221; Heidelberg 15, 63; Rome 28, 210; Seoul 86, 105, 107; Sydney 16, 32, 33, 51, 56, 58, 62, 86, 88, 96, 98, 99, 102, 103, 107, 108, 110, 114, 131, 133, 214, 215, 216,; Tokyo 28, 29, 30; Toronto 30, 106, 112, 133;
ParalympicsGB 110, 112
Parks, J.B. 131
Passeron, J.C. 141, 145
pathetic 5, 115, 118
patronising 4, 8, 107
Paveau, M.-A. 154, 155
Pedersen, P. M. 134
Peltu, M. 19
perception 6, 12, 18, 57, 58, 61, 82, 150, 153, 154, 158, 166, 167, 168, 169, 185, 199, 210, 225, 229, 231, 233
perfection 58, 77, 152, 198
Pfister, G. 3, 7, 19, 130
Phillips, M. G. 132
philosophy 13
photo 33, 60, 151, 233, 228, 234
photography 12, 99, 100, 151, 233, 234
Pinard, Pascal 34
Pious, S. 195, 206

Pistorius, Oscar viii, 13, 89, 100, 102, 120, 142, 157, 158, 159, 160, 161, 162, 163, 164, 169, 170, 221, 234
pitiable 5, 115, 147
pity 6, 9, 20, 80, 107, 109, 114, 147, 199, 214, 229
Planchon, Aimé 31
Plas, J. M. 131
Pledger, C. 196, 205
Pleßmann, R. 88, 93
Poland 30, 31
political correctness 227, 230
politics 10, 18, 19, 44, 58, 80, 130, 132, 133, 182, 203, 204
Popescu, C. viii, xi, 12, 147
portrayal 13, 41, 107, 172, 214, 230
post-human 152, 154, 169
postmodern 18, 152
postmodernism 166
post-modernity 166, 169
Poulton Deborah 211, 212
Poulton, D. 211, 212, 216, 218, 219, 220, 221, 223
power 2, 16, 86, 108, 129, 130, 141, 153, 170, 172, 177, 182, 185, 197, 200, 202, 218, 228
prejudice 108
print media 3, 4, 6, 7, 8, 56, 58, 78, 79, 80, 83, 134, 147, 185, 186, 202
programming mandate 10, 38, 39, 40, 41, 43, 45, 46, 48, 49, 50
prosthesis 142, 153, 165, 167, 169, 177, 234
PSB 10, 38, 39, 40, 41, 42, 45, 46, 47, 48, 49, 50, 87
psychology 26, 202, 204
public opinion 2, 14, 26, 74, 169, 212, 213, 216, 228, 235
public service 10, 38, 41, 42, 43, 45, 50, 87, 90
public service broadcasting see PSB
public service mandate 45
public value 41
Puppis, M. 51
Purpose Remit 41, 50

Q

queer 177
Queval, I. 140, 146
Quinn, N. 105, 110, 112

R

Raab, N. vii, xi, 11, 85, 93
race 7, 13, 89, 163, 194, 195, 196, 197, 201, 202, 203, 205, 212, 220, 226, 233
racism 195, 196, 200, 204, 207
Rada, J.A. 195, 206
radio 26, 41, 44, 106, 109, 111, 122, 190
Radtke, P. 62, 63
RAF 219
Rasmussen, R. 194, 195, 206
Ratha, A. 205
Rattansi, A. 200, 203
Raufast, A. 138, 139, 146
Raufast, L. 138, 139, 146
recipients 4, 56, 60, 61, 72, 87, 90, 196
Redden, R. 223
rehabilitation xi, 21, 31, 32, 106, 172, 173, 205
Reichert, T. 133
Reichhart, F. vii, xi, 10, 25, 217, 223
Reinhardt, J.D. xii, 11, 65
representation 31, 37, 39, 46, 73, 97, 98, 100, 101, 124, 129, 138, 140, 147, 151, 153, 154, 166, 167, 175, 185, 194, 195, 196, 197, 201, 210, 217, 218, 221, 228, 233
Revelle, R. 134
Rhein-Zeitung 8

Rhodes, J. 197, 206
Riboud, Romain 148
Ridder, C. 53
Rieder, H. 52
Riggs, K. E. 19
Riley II, C. A. 4, 7, 19
Rioux, H. 21
Roberts, P. 201, 206
Robertson, R. 19
Robinson, J. 133, 161, 164
Rodriguez, L. 130
Rodriguez, S. 133
Rogers, E. M. 2, 15
role model 108, 186, 188, 201
Romania 31
Rome 28, 210
Rose, G. 133
Ross, D. 130
Rössler, P. 68, 74, 87, 93
Roters, G. 74
Rother, N. vii, xi, 10, 37
Rowe, D. 3, 19, 133
rowing 45, 85, 89, 183, 211, 227
Royal Charter 40, 41, 51
Rozenberg, J. 102, 132, 146
Rubin, H.A. 172, 178
rugby 33, 158, 171, 172, 173, 174, 219, 227
Ruge, H. 4, 16
Ruiz, J. 133
Rulofs, B. 130
Rundfunkstaatsvertrag 42, 50, 52
Russell, Scott 120

S

Sabo, D. 195, 206
Sage, G. H. 19
sailing 183
Salmon, C. 148, 155
Salt Lake City 47, 48, 51, 56, 62, 114, 217
Salwen, M. B 133
Sandfort, L. 5, 20

Saxer, U. 53
Schäfermeier, A. 84
Schantz vii, viii, x, xi, 1, 5, 6, 7, 8, 14, 20, 28, 35, 37, 52, 66, 67, 72, 75, 92, 93, 95, 96, 103, 105, 106, 107, 112, 113, 114, 115, 120, 122, 133, 155, 182, 185, 187, 191, 193, 194, 198, 199, 206, 210, 213, 214, 215, 217, 222, 223, 225, 240,
Scharenberg, A. 18
Schauerte, T. 63, 78, 84
Scheid, V. 52
Schell, B. 133
Schell, L. A. 6, 7, 8, 20, 37, 52, 105, 112, 185, 191, 194, 199, 206
Schierl, T. 37, 39, 51, 52, 56, 59, 60, 62, 63, 64, 67, 72, 75, 83, 113, 114, 120
Schimanski, M. 5, 6, 20, 72, 75
Schinzel, H. 86, 93
Schlesinger, P. 204
Schmitt, J. C. 99, 100, 103
Scholz, M. 4, 20, 37, 52
Schönau, C. 67, 75
Schönbach, K. 2, 20
Schrader, M. P. 21
Schüle, K. 81, 83
Schulz, W. 15, 19, 20, 21, 66, 75
Schwartz, A. 118, 161, 164
Schweer, M. 52
Schweizer Fernsehen *see* SF
Schwier, J. 63
Scott-Elliot, R. 218, 223
seated volleyball 227, 234
Segrave, J. O. 20
sensorial disabilities 6, 98
Seoul 86, 105, 107
Sepulche, S. 149, 155
sex 113, 171, 172, 174, 176, 198, 229
sexual 3, 15, 21, 58, 113, 114, 124, 129, 133, 172, 174, 175, 176, 201, 205

sexualisation 124
sexuality 3, 13, 41, 133, 172, 174, 175, 176, 195, 226
Seymour, W. 21, 176, 178
SF 38, 44, 45, 46, 48, 49 52
Shakespeare, T 65, 73, 129, 197, 206
Shakespeare. 129
Shapiro, D.A. 178
Shapiro, J. P. 4, 5, 8, 20, 20
Shaw, B. 16, 21
Shaw, D. 66, 74
Shaw, P. 130
Sherrill, C. 7, 21, 134, 191, 206
Shifflett, B 134
Shildrick, M. 133
Shugart, H. 134
Siegenheim, V. 51
Silva, C. F 5, 21
Silverstone, R. 204
Simmel, G. 166, 167
Simon, J.L 144, 146
skiing 77, 78, 150, 153
Smart, J. 7, 215, 223
Smith 2, 6, 7, 16, 21, 105, 112, 133, 134, 177, 178, 182, 185, 194, 196, 197, 199, 206, 207, 210, 213, 214, 215, 220, 224
Smith , B.G. 177, 178
Smith, B. 191
Smith, K. A. 16, 130
Snooker World Championships 41
social model 111, 197, 200
psychology 26, 202, 204
societal attitudes 184, 198
society 2, 3, 5, 11, 14, 15, 26, 27, 37, 38-40, 42,-45, 50, 55, 58, 62, 67, 80, 107, 111, 114, 119, 144, 148, 151-153, 166-168, 194, 196-198, 200, 202, 207, 211, 214, 216, 217, 218, 225, 226-230, 232, 233, 235
sociology 95, 127, 166, 170, 205, 207
Somkuan 125, 126

South Africa 30, 89, 90, 158, 159, 160, 161, 221
Spain 31, 96, 99, 127, 129, 184
Spanny, B. 67, 72, 75
Sparkes, A.C. 182, 191
Sparr, S. 207
spectacularization 3
Speed, H. 129, 205
sponsors 3, 68, 107
sponsorship 58, 221
sport specific coverage 4
sportivisation 124
Sports Illustrated 123, 131, 133
Sports Illustrated for Kids 123
sportswomen 1, 9, 122, 125, 205
Spracklen, K. 205
SRG 38, 44, 45, 49, 52, 53
Staab, J. F. 66, 75
Stallman, Jason 119
Stange, T. 88, 93
Stautner, B. K. 2, 21
Stein, J.U. 105, 112, 194, 206
Steininger, C. 53
Steinmann, W. 35
Stephen, T. 224
stereotype 8, 68, 116, 117, 118, 119, 124, 195
Stevens, A. 202, 204, 206
stigma 99, 134, 140, 143, 152, 199, 206, 227, 224
stigmatization 124, 139, 140, 141, 143, 144, 227
Stiker, H.J. 98, 101, 103, 139
Stoke Mandeville Games 17, 106
storytelling 148, 150, 151, 154
Strohkendl, H. 211, 224
Stuart, O.W. 194, 200, 206
subcultural 177
success 9, 31, 32, 49, 66, 67, 70, 71, 73, 80, 81, 82, 83, 86, 131, 153, 172, 214, 215
Sudan 30
Süddeutsche Zeitung 57, 79, 82
Süssenbacher, D. 41, 51, 52, 53

Sutcliffe, M. 160, 164
Sutton, J. 21
Swain, J. 196, 199, 206
Sweeney, M. 216, 224
swimming 11, 34, 72, 89, 90, 99, 183, 211, 220, 227
Swiss Television *see* SF
Switzerland 10, 38, 39, 44, 45, 46, 48, 72, 73, xi
Sydney 16, 32, 33, 51, 56, 58, 62, 86, 88, 96, 98, 99, 102, 103, 105, 107, 108, 110, 111, 114, 131, 133, 155, 209, 214, 215, 216, 224
Syria 30

T

table tennis 34, 89, 227
taboo 58, 172
Taiwan 110, 112, 216
Tarde, G. 25, 26, 35
Tate, D. 206
Taub, D. 134, 199, 206
Taub, O. 224
Taylor S. 129
Tayman, K.R. 204
techno-doping 234
technology 13, 86, 100, 154, 158, 174, 177, 210, 218, 220, 228, 232
technotopic body 174
Teipel, D. 37, 51
television 3, 8, 19, 26, 38, 40, 44, 78, 86, 87, 91, 92, 96, 97, 98, 106, 107, 109, 122, 123, 138, 149, 185, 202, 207, 210, 212, 217, 218, 219, 222, 228, 231, 232
tennis 11, 32, 34, 78, 89, 90, 131, 134, 196, 227
Terminator 234
Teso, E. 129

The Archrival 160, 164
The Bucks Herald 106
The Courts of Arbitration for Sport 159, 164
The Daily Telegraph 109, 111, 224
The Globe and Mail 21, 116, 117, 118, 134
The Guardian 224
The New York Times 115, 116, 117, 118, 119
The Sunday Telegraph 111
The Times 106
The Washington Post 115
Theberge, N. 205
Thomas, N. 6, 7, 21, 78, 81, 105, 112, 133, 134, 182, 185, 191, 194, 196, 197, 199, 206, 207, 210, 213, 214, 215, 220, 224
Thompson 17, 191
Thompson, G. T. 224
Tokyo 28, 29, 30
Torino 217, 218
Toronto 30, 106, 112, 133
Tour de France 26
transgender 177
Tremblay 110, 111
trivialized 66, 124, 125
trivializing 4
Trowler, P. 134
Troxler, R. 41, 53
Trujillo, N. 198, 207
Truong, N. 100, 102
Tuggle, C. A. 7, 21
Turner, B. S. 19, 21
Turner, D. 206
TV coverage 3, 6, 101, 182, 227
Twitter 231

U

Uganda 30
Ukraine 86

UN Convention on the rights of persons with disabilities..75, 162, 164
universalism 30
University of Mainz 58
Urquhart, J. 7, 21, 134
USA vii, xi 86, 113, 114, 116, 118, 120, 122, 129, 163, 215, 216, 222
USSR 31

V

value 3, 4, 12, 29, 41, 43, 45, 51, 58, 60, 66, 67, 68, 107, 110, 140, 142, 144, 170, 185, 198, 213, 215, 216, 228, 229, 234
Van Dijk, T. A. 134
Vancouver Sun 115, 116, 117, 118
Vattimo, G. 63
Venus de Milo 168, 172
Vernon, A. 194, 200, 207
VI football 184, 187, 189
Vidal, M. 102
Vincent 129, 134
Vincent, J. 124, 129, 134,
visibility viii, 10, 12, 15, 28, 74, 97, 108, 129, 135, 138-141, 151, 166, 190, 206, 228, 229
visually impaired/blind 7, 77, 87, 119, 154, 183-184, 186-188, 190, 209, 211, 212, 223,

W

Wallston, B. S. 131
Walsdorf, K. 130, 204
Wann, D. L. 7, 21
Washington Post 115, 116, 117, 118, 209
Wasilewski, L. 22
Watson, N. 197, 206

Waxman, B. F. 21
Weigl, M. 78, 84
Weiller, K. H. 130
Weinberg, P. 63
Welsch, W. 63
WeMedia 4, 177
Wenner, L. A. 129, 134, 203
Wermke, J. 63
Wernecken, J. 66, 75
wheelchair 6, 11, 32, 33, 74, 77, 89, 90, 108, 110, 119, 171-174, 177, 185, 186, 188, 199, 211, 220, 227, 234
wheelchair basketball 34
Whisenant, W. A. 134
White, D., M. 21
Whyte, S. R 7, 18
Wieviorka, M 140, 146
Wikus, Christoph 78
Wilke, J. 19, 21
Wille, F. 27, 35, 102
Williams, C. L. 129
Williams, L. 16
Williams, Serena 195, 196, 203
Williams, T. 195, 206
Wilson, D.J. 173, 78
Wilson, Daniel 173
Wilson, W. 16
Winter Paralympic Games 97, 151, 217
Winter Paralympic Games/Winter Paralympics 47-50, 216, 224 151; Albertville 97; Lillehammer 217; Nagano 217; Torino 217, 218;
Wired Magazine 164
Wittstock, S. 87, 93
Wittstock, Swantje 93
Wolbring, G. viii, xi, 13, 157, 158, 162, 163, 164
Woldt, R. 42, 53
women 7, 11, 15, 16, 19, 21, 32, 44, 85, 90, 91, 97, 99, 113,

122-124, 128-131, 134, 169, 171, 172, 174, 176, 177, 185, 193-196, 200, 201, 204, 227, 233
women and disability 203
Wonsek, P. L. 195, 207
Woodill, G. 5, 21
Woods, N. 133
World Championships 41, 47, 108, 183, 219
World Championships, Manchester 219
World Cup 26, 44, 92, 106, 109, 110, 112
World Disabled Games 56, 59, 60
World War II 31, 77
World Wide Web 18, 232

Y

Yiannakis, A. 198, 207
Yoshida, R. K. 4, 22
You tube 231
Young 207
Young, L. 195, 207
Yugoslavia 30

Z

Zavoina, S. 133
ZDF 38, 42, 43, 44, 46, 47, 49, 53, 88, 93
Zillmann, D 17, 19, 63
Zimmermann, R. 20
Zola, I.K. 5, 22, 134